Between Crown and Commerce

THE JOHNS HOPKINS UNIVERSITY STUDIES IN
HISTORICAL AND POLITICAL SCIENCE
129th Series (2011)

1. Junko Thérèse Takeda, *Between Crown and Commerce: Marseille and the Early Modern Mediterranean*

Between Crown and Commerce

Marseille and the Early Modern Mediterranean

JUNKO THÉRÈSE TAKEDA

The Johns Hopkins University Press
Baltimore

Printed in the United States of America on acid-free paper
2 4 6 8 9 7 5 3 1

The Johns Hopkins University Press
2715 North Charles Street
Baltimore, Maryland 21218-4363
www.press.jhu.edu

Library of Congress Cataloging-in-Publication Data

Takeda, Junko Thérèse, 1976–
Between crown and commerce : Marseille and the early modern Mediterranean / Junko Thérèse Takeda.
p. cm.
ISBN-13: 978-0-8018-9982-9 (hardcover : alk. paper)
ISBN-10: 0-8018-9982-6 (hardcover : alk. paper)
1. Marseille (France)—Commerce—History—18th century.
2. Marseille (France)—Commerce—Mediterranean Region.
3. Mediterranean Region—Commerce—France—Marseille.
4. Merchants—France—Marseille—History—18th century.
5. Marseille (France)—Social conditions—18th century.
6. Marseille (France)—Politics and government—18th century.
7. Citizenship—France—Marseille—History—18th century.
8. Plague—France—Marseille—History—18th century.
9. France—History—Louis XV, 1715–1774. I. Title.
HF3560.M3T35 2011
382'.094491201822—dc22 2010026158

A catalog record for this book is available from the British Library.

Special discounts are available for bulk purchases of this book. For more information, please contact Special Sales at 410-516-6936 or specialsales@press.jhu.edu.

The Johns Hopkins University Press uses environmentally friendly book materials, including recycled text paper that is composed of at least 30 percent post-consumer waste, whenever possible. All of our book papers are acid-free, and our jackets and covers are printed on paper with recycled content.

IN MEMORIAM

Kinuko Takeda
Efu Takeda
Iwao Takeda
Edward Randall
Odetta Gordon
Henry Y. K. Tom

Contents

Acknowledgments

I owe the completion of this book to the generous support of mentors, colleagues, family, friends and institutions. First, I would like to express my deep gratitude to my advisors and teachers in the History Department and Interdisciplinary Graduate Program in the Humanities at Stanford University. The idea for a research project on Marseille began in conversations between me and my mentor, Keith Michael Baker. I would like to thank him for his intellectual guidance and friendship. Jessica Riskin helped shape and clarify my ideas at every stage of the project, from its inception, through its completion as a dissertation, to its transformation into a monograph. Paul Robinson instilled in me an appreciation for clear writing and tried to teach me perfect punctuation. Carolyn Lougee Chappell's knowledge of archival work provided the basis for my own journey into the archives in France. Helen Brooks, Bob Gregg, Brad Gregory, Mary Lou Roberts, and James Sheehan expanded my understanding of early modern and modern European history in profound ways. I am fortunate to have such teachers.

My graduate training also benefited from the assistance of several colleagues and friends who provided me with advice and encouragement. I am grateful to Sebastian Barreveld, John Broich, Malgorzata Fidelis, Suzanne Mariko Miller, Yair Mintzker, Kaneez Munjee, Libby Murphy, Mary Jane Parrine, Maria Riasanovsky, Alvaro Santana, Cecilia Tsu, and Marie-Pierre Ulloa at Stanford University for making life on The Farm and in the San Francisco Bay Area such a memorable experience. I thank the members of my dissertation-writing group, Alex Bay, Abosede George, Jehangir Malegam, and Erika Monahan, for their critiques and suggestions. Linda Huynh, Lynn Kaiser, Monica Moore, Debra Pounds, Margo Richardson, Monica Wheeler, and the late Gertrud Pacheco took care of all my administrative needs. The Stanford Bay Area French Culture Workshop, the Seminar on Enlightenment and Revolution, and the Modern European Seminar provided venues for an inexperienced graduate student to present her ideas to the academic community.

Several professors, archivists, librarians, and friends offered hospitality and supported my research in Provence. I owe a great debt to Arnaud Decroix, Pierre Echinard, Jacques Guilhaumou, and Frédéric Proal for their welcome and assistance. I would like to thank the Académie de Marseille and the wonderful staff at the Bibliothèque Méjanes in Aix-en-Provence, including Michèle Allard, Chantal Barrièlle, Jacqueline Benueviste, Philippe Ferrand, Michel de Laburthe, Florence Nielsen, and Marcel Roqueplan. Thank you to Henri Baldinger, Stéphanie Jabbour, and François Jonniaux at the Archives de la Chambre de commerce de Marseille for their kindness. My gratitude also goes to Audrey Rio at the Musée national de la marine.

As the book matured into its current form, I have benefited from the generosity and support of colleagues both near and far. John Ackerman, Andrew Aisenberg, Rafe Blaufarb, Gail Bossenga, Michael Breen, Sara Chapman, Henry Clark, Eric Dursteler, Colin Jones, Richard Keller, Amalia Kessler, Richard Maber, Natalie Rothman, David Kammerling Smith, Jay Smith, and Kent Wright provided invaluable advice at conferences, workshops, and dinners. The Medieval Renaissance Seminar and the Workshop on Empires, Nations and Culture, both at Syracuse University, allowed me the opportunity to present chapters and work in progress. A special thank you to the Department of History at Syracuse University, whose members have shown more support and encouragement than any assistant professor could hope for. Thank you to the administrative assistants in my department for their patience and help shipping off articles and book printouts to their intended destinations. My gratitude to students who read parts of my work and offered suggestions and comments.

Henry Tom, Suzanne Flinchbaugh, and Deborah Bors at the Johns Hopkins University Press provided me with much guidance and support, helping me fine-tune my arguments and writing, and my anonymous readers offered invaluable suggestions and criticism. Peter Dreyer provided careful copyediting, and Tom Broughton-Willett created the index. I thank them all.

The initial stage of my project was financially assisted by the Stanford History Department Graduate Fellowship, Graduate Research Opportunity Grants from the Stanford School of Humanities and Sciences, the Lurcy Fellowship, and the Mellon Foundation. My gratitude to Roni Holeton in the Stanford University Dean's Office and John Bender at the Stanford Humanities Center. In the book's latter stages, I have been fortunate to receive support from the Society for French Historical Studies and the Western Society for French Historical Studies. From Syracuse University, the Appleby-Moser Faculty Research Grant for the Maxwell School of Citizenship, the Pigott Faculty Research Fund, the Laura J. and

L. Douglas Meredith Award and the Meredith Professorship Program, and the Department of History have provided assistance for my research and writing. I would like to thank Bronwyn Adam, Mitch Wallerstein, and Michael Wasylenko for their generosity.

An earlier version of Chapter 1 was published by Cambridge University Press as "French Absolutism, Marseillais Civic Humanism, and the Languages of Public Good" in *The Historical Journal*, 49(3), September 2006, pp. 707–734. An earlier version of sections in Chapter 3 was published by Maney Publishing (Leeds, UK) as "Levantines and Marseille: The Politics of Naturalization and Neutralization in Early Modern France, 1660–1820" in *Seventeenth-Century French Studies*, 30(2), 2008, pp. 170–181. Both are reprinted with permission.

I should not forget to acknowledge those who shaped my intellectual development much prior to my discovery of Marseille and early modern history. Andrew Campbell, John Leistler, and Andrew Wittekind at Charlotte Latin School encouraged my love of books and strange thoughts. Frank Borchardt, Malachi Hacohen, Catherine Peyroux, James Rolleston, and Ron Witt at Duke University introduced a very green undergraduate to the history of ideas.

My family has been an unending source of support and laughs through my intellectual journey. The final phase of my dissertation writing was darkened by the deaths of my grandparents, Iwao and Efu Takeda, and of my mother, Kinuko Takeda. The last stage of my book preparation was clouded by the passing of family friends, Odetta Gordon and Edward Randall. Yet, their devotion is contained in every sentence of this work. Thank you to Kenichi Takeda, my father and partner in survival, for his optimism. And, finally, Mark Schmeller, my partner in love and in history, appeared in my life at just the right time to fill each page of this book with his insight and every part of my being with joy.

Between Crown and Commerce

Introduction

Commerce, State-Building, and Republicanism in Old Regime France

The early modern period saw two major transformations reshaping Europe: the gradual expansion of commercial society and the rise of the modern state. Historians often view these two developments as complementary and call them "mercantilism." This book tells a different story. By exploring these processes in France from a local angle, it argues that absolute statecraft and commercial aggrandizement did not involve the mere imposition of policies unilaterally decided upon by the Crown. Rather, they were bolstered through the complicated participation of two significant political entities: French municipalities and the Ottoman Empire. Moreover, this book demonstrates that these two developments—which accelerated during the reign of Louis XIV—did not necessarily march in lockstep. In fact, individuals involved in commerce and debates about market society altered social relationships and triggered political developments in ways that often interrupted the Crown's authority and its state-building initiatives. In other words, commerce did not automatically empower the monarchy; rather, it also stimulated and strengthened local organizations, practices, and languages that competed with royal power and ideology.

This is a book about state-building and civic politics in the context of a globalizing economy. It explores the relationship between French commercial expansion into the Mediterranean market and Bourbon statecraft under Louis XIV and his successor, the regent duc d'Orléans, through the lens of a particular port city, Marseille. Situated on the southern margins of the French kingdom, and culturally and politically peripheral from the Crown's perspective, Marseille nonetheless became strategically essential for France's commercial contacts with the

Ottoman Empire. Marseille had a two-millennia-long tradition of Mediterranean trade, and it was the only French port privileged to trade directly with the Levant. The Crown saw in it opportunities for royal aggrandizement, commercial growth, and personal gain, and thus the city became central to efforts to strengthen and enrich the French state.

Marseille's municipal traditions, however, strengthened and interrupted royal commercial and statist expansion. A close study of this city, which became France's most important Mediterranean port after Louis XIV conclusively asserted royal authority there in 1660, aptly illustrates the challenges municipalities faced in negotiating between the Crown's centralizing impulse and their own local political practices. A city ruled by commercial elites who saw themselves as inheritors of a long heritage of autonomous self-rule, Marseille was a crucible where civic, French, and various Mediterranean identities converged, collided, put pressure on one another, and reformulated the political culture of the city and beyond.

The study of broad developments in French statist politics through a focus on Marseille offers a valuable new perspective into understanding the dynamics of how traditional local institutions, practices, languages, and rituals interacted with new circumstances and sociopolitical realities in early modern Europe. The expansion of commercial society and the innovations in political centralization championed by the monarchy may suggest that the transformations occurring in western Europe thrust the continent into the "modern age." This book however, demonstrates that the state-building tactics of the Sun King were much more a piecemeal mixture of old and new methods of rule, and constant renegotiations between local and royal approaches to governance, rather than the replacement of "premodern" by "modern" systems.

As a former republic whose institutional networks, legal traditions and political practices traced to Greek and Roman antiquity, Marseille had deeply rooted structures that resisted change at the same time that they provided foundations for commercial expansion and state-building. The city's established contacts with the Levant and its chamber of commerce, which predated French monarchical interventions served as a springboard for Louis XIV's commercial initiatives, while simultaneously generating impediments to royal centralization. Most important, the city's political tradition of classical republicanism—conventionally averse to royal kingship, absolute authority, and commerce—became integral to the development of a new understanding of virtuous French citizenship. The city's commercial elite mobilized this republicanism to imagine themselves as exemplary citizens charged by the king with the unique responsibility of strengthening France's Mediterranean presence, while simultaneously using it to resist French royal presence in their own city. Such persistence and malleability of classical republicanism held lasting implications for Marseille and France more generally. Practiced in civic contexts and adapted to absolutist aggrandizement, it ultimately became the political language of revolution at the end of the eighteenth century.

This book argues that Marseillais elites—aldermen, members of the chamber of commerce, local go-betweens who served as the city's representatives at court, merchants, religious leaders and new nobility—mobilized classical republicanism to support and criticize the expansion of Mediterranean commerce and royal authority as they materialized in their city between 1660 and 1720. In other words, classical republicanism heavily informed conflicting ideas regarding international commerce in absolutist France. In its original form, this political language that had emerged in ancient Greece and Rome did not provide a generous reading of commerce. According to this tradition, the stability of the body politic rested on virtue, practiced through the alignment of personal interests with the public good, and the active participation of citizens in public affairs. Ancient republican political theorists understood political virtue as the political community's sole impediment to social, cultural, and moral decline. Commerce could only distract citizens from the *res publica*; luxury cultivated in commercial society would lead them to prefer personal interests over the general good. According to John Shovlin, ancient Roman moralists had described how "luxury enervated and feminized men, sapping their capacity for military virtue; it was a tool of despots who used it to weaken the commitment of their subjects to liberty; it made both rulers and their subjects self-serving, vitiating their capacity to place the public welfare before private interest."[1]

Seventeenth- and eighteenth-century writers drew on this tradition for various purposes: moralists to condemn luxury, royal critics to denounce the Crown's despotic extensions of power, members of the second estate to protest against the growing tide of arriviste financiers, venal officeholders, and merchants who threatened to wrest power away from the sword nobility (*noblesse d'epée*). While these elites by no means formed a united group, their arguments overlapped. Though reluctant to condemn commerce altogether, they warned how luxury was fundamentally irreconcilable with virtue. Bent out of political shape by luxury, weakened states, they argued, could be destroyed by imminent catastrophic events, be they wars or natural or medical crises.

This republican vocabulary that was fundamentally critical of commerce proved useful to many French elites who were uncomfortable with the privileged role that Louis XIV and his controller-general, Jean-Baptiste Colbert, assigned to commercial expansion. It should be pointed out, however, that one did not necessarily need to borrow from the classical republican handbook to articulate misgivings about the market. The late seventeenth century saw both royal and local elites expressing concern regarding the corrosive forces of the market; the republican vocabulary was one of several that individuals could adopt in order to convey their ambivalence about commerce. This unease was particularly pronounced in Marseille, given the climate of suspicion that clouded the relationship between the monarchy, merchants, and local administrative bodies that ran commercial enterprises in the city. Led by Colbert, royal administrators remained mistrustful of Marseillais in general, whom they considered recalcitrant and incapable of recognizing what was in the interests of their own city and the kingdom at large.

Furthermore, while advocates of commercial expansion, the controller-general and his intendants duplicated the traditional view that saw merchants as fundamentally untrustworthy, morally vacuous creatures.[2] Although a promoter of commercial expansion, Colbert was nonetheless aware of the dangers involved in a growing marketplace. While both Colbert and Colbertism were targets of the republican anti-luxury argument, the controller-general tempered his expansion of international trade and manufacturing with calls for rigorous reform and merchant supervision.[3] As Amalia Kessler has recently shown, "the growing legitimacy of commerce . . . derived from the fact that it operated directly under—and on behalf of—royal power."[4] Even as Colbert announced in 1669 that "commerce is the most proper means to reconcile different nations and entertain the most opposed spirits in great and mutual correspondence,"[5] he and subsequent royal administrators maintained that commercial expansion required royally determined regulations that would deter merchants from corrupt practices. Royal elites in support of Colbertism believed that commerce was beneficial for state and society, but they doubted the political commitment and moral fortitude of merchants. Commerce was potentially good, but merchants were bad. Royal and municipal elites came together to strengthen French commerce without shaking off entirely the Christian worldview that condemned the pursuit of worldly goods as sinful and the classical republican idiom that denounced merchants as morally and politically decrepit.

Over the last decades of the seventeenth century, however, a new positive assessment of commerce began to emerge among French administrative elites. While many voiced concern about merchant self-interest, they began to concede that mercantilist expansion and administrative centralization seemed to render obsolete the darker age of aristocratic rebellions, religious and civil wars, and domestic political chaos. Indeed, supporters of commercial expansion would help solidify what would become the dominant Enlightenment reading of historical progress; leading eighteenth-century men of letters would optimistically suggest that political strife and natural disasters would ultimately be eradicated as new rational forms of communication and sociability led humanity toward progress and perfection.[6] The marquis de Condorcet would offer one of the most emblematic visions in this vein in the latter half of the eighteenth century; "with progress in industry and welfare, which establishes a happier proportion between men's talents and their needs, each successive generation will have larger possessions," he wrote, "the improvement of medical practice, which will become more efficacious with the progress of reason and of the social order, will mean the end of infectious and hereditary diseases and illnesses brought on by climate, food, or working conditions."[7] According to the historical equation to which disciples of modernity and *doux commerce* subscribed, commercial exchange was the motor for progress; new networks of exchange and communication would weave together a strengthened social fabric that would enhance human knowledge, wealth, health, and "civilized" behavior.

Such formulations that defended commerce as the foundation of society began emerging in the late seventeenth century, and specifically, at the commencement of Louis XIV's personal reign in 1661. This book considers in particular, how classical republican traditions were unpacked and combined with new ideas to formulate positive assessments of certain kinds of merchants and commercial activity. During the late seventeenth century, royal elites, merchants, moralists, and even nobles began advocating a new commercial civic spirit that challenged the traditional anti-merchant and anti-luxury argument. With Henry Clark's definition of "commercial humanism" in mind, I interpret commercial civic spirit as the set of attitudes that reconciled an enthusiasm for commercial prosperity with the classical republican sensibility that defined virtue as the aligning of personal and public interests.[8] Promoters of commercial civic spirit rescued commerce—previously devalued as detrimental to civic virtue—and recast it as the ultimate mark of good citizenship. They disputed the classical tradition by elevating commerce as a useful public activity and by reserving for certain merchants the ability to be politically and morally virtuous.[9] They particularly extended their positive visions toward elite wholesale traders, or *négociants*, whom they considered to be honorable, noble, and exemplary leaders of commercial society. The market world substituted for the political *res publica*; elite merchants functioned as its best citizens. Meanwhile, these authors retained their prejudices against retail traders, financiers, and speculators, whom they continued to categorize as small-minded, fraudulent delinquents.

The late seventeenth century also witnessed the development of a new kind of "republican historicism" that provided a positive reading of commerce. The classical historical discourse on republics held a rather pessimistic view. It saw civic virtue as the republic's only lifeline through time. It projected that self-interest and fluctuations of human passions would corrode civic virtue, corrupt the body politic, and destroy liberty. This traditional republican vision of history was formulated on the distrust of human will and on the nightmarish assumption that republics reeled toward a crisis, a moment, as Keith Baker describes, "in which the very existence of the body politic hangs in the balance, in which it will either recover its health and vigor or fall into an irreversible, fatal sickness."[10] Archbishop François de la Mothe-Fénelon revived and adapted this historical vision most famously in *Télémaque*, the "most read literary work of eighteenth-century France."[11] In his epic, Fénelon insisted that ostentatious shows of prosperity projected by commercial states were harbingers of a dark future characterized by depopulation, "idleness and effeminacy" and the extinction of virtue.[12] He used the classical tradition to discredit financiers, venal officeholders, and merchants who were gaining access to political power; he called upon the old nobility to help the king banish "pomp and luxury" and rebuild a politically and morally sounder state.[13] Meanwhile, in a different setting, Jansenist ecclesiastics and parlementary magistrates also revitalized this dark historical worldview, drawing on the metaphor of a republic in crisis to condemn sybaritic depravity and despotic papal and royal authorities.

In contrast to this somber historical view, the modified republican historicism developed by apologists for international commerce maintained that monarchs and commercial activity could rescue republics from downward spiraling trajectories. Kings, it held, liberated republics and set them back on a positive historical track, while commercial activity provided a new public space where merchants could cultivate their virtues. Such a revisionist view of history proved particularly attractive to Marseillais elites. It could be applied to provide a positive spin to increased royal presence and interference in civic governance, while also legitimating the city's flourishing trade with the Levant.

REPUBLICANISM AND ABSOLUTISM

How and why could republican ideologies and vocabularies find increasing use and relevance in an absolutist regime like Bourbon France? How did the process of state-building—a process that on the surface strengthened and centralized power in the royal person at the expense of local political authority—allow for intensified use of republican idioms? This study presents two answers to this question. First, municipalities could serve as repositories of classical republican traditions in an absolutist polity. The French kingdom was comprised of cities and towns whose administrators often used classical republican vocabulary to maintain the municipal body politic. Classical republicanism was particularly well practiced in Marseille; the city's governing body of aristocratic consuls and councilmen drew on classical language that underscored the former republic's historical connections to Athens, Rome, and Carthage. The royal conquest of Marseille in 1660 did not erase this tradition. The new merchant-administrators who replaced the former government continued to employ classical republican vocabulary: administratively, to discern the public good for the community, and historically, to imagine the commercial and moral regeneration of Massilia, classical Marseille.

Second, the relationship of accommodation fostered between municipal elites and the Crown from the reign of Louis XIV created a space where civic vocabulary and traditions could be co-opted and spread by the state. A common attitude toward the market enabled local elites who privileged political and commercial autonomy to share common patterns of speech with a developing centralized state that sought to restrict that autonomy. Marseille was not the only municipality where increasing encounters with the Crown energized historical republican traditions and rhetoric. The relationship between royal and civic political culture could be characterized as an ever-changing series of Venn diagrams; royal and civic languages were deployed by individuals who existed in spheres that were both distinct and overlapping with one another. In particular, Marseillais elites' and the Crown's common enthusiasm for commercial expansion allowed the classical republican concept of virtue and civic excellence to become compatible and interchangeable with the Crown's language of utility to the state.

This study, therefore, suggests a contradiction in the policies of the Bourbon monarchy: the Crown that sought to expand its power and limit local autonomy adapted political concepts stemming from the city to sustain absolutist claims. The monarchy helped intensify civic and republican sensibilities throughout France while gutting France of actual republics. Classical republican traditions potentially damaging to the Crown were co-opted in service of the monarchy. They became one of the most prominent political traditions that fractured the Old Regime and energized the French Revolution.

My central argument, therefore, is that the classical republican tradition served the interests of elites who both embraced and rejected royal commercial expansion. More important, local and royal elites working commonly, but not together, on commercial expansion, simultaneously helped develop a positive understanding of commerce while reinvigorating an anti-absolutist political tradition. Such an argument takes the current historiographies of classical republicanism and French absolutism in new directions. First, it adds a civic dimension to historiography on French republicanism.[14] Building on the historical analysis of civic humanism in Italian Renaissance and early modern Anglo-Atlantic studies, historians of France have recently demonstrated how the monarchy's critics increasingly gave republican idioms a prominent role in eighteenth-century French political discourse.[15] This research has shown how the classical republican tradition was a key element of political contestation in eighteenth-century France; it has debunked the assumption that classical republicanism drew on antique political models that vanished under French absolutism.[16] While my work extends this new historiography, it introduces a unique argument: classical republicanism was not only configured in opposition to the monarchy. It was adopted by the Crown. Republican virtues of civic participation, "disinterestedness," simplicity, Spartan discipline, and frugality were upheld as models for good behavior both in local and state contexts.

The interaction between republican traditions and state-building is a topic of increasing interest to historians of Europe, who have recently discovered that regional and state political traditions are not consistently at odds.[17] Meanwhile, this study offers an alternative to approaches historians have taken in regards to absolutism. Research exploring the relationship between the monarchy of Louis XIV and provincial elites has fallen into two principal categories. Scholars following the Tocquevillian tradition have held that the Crown broke the power of provincial elites by widening the orbit of a depersonalized, bureaucratic state that overrode corporate privileges. Meanwhile, competing scholarship has offered that absolute monarchy was not quite absolute, maintaining that Louis XIV's government was founded on compromise and "social collaboration" between the Crown and provincial elites.[18] These have studied the contradictory ways in which the Crown empowered local institutions and individuals: the state augmented its domestic and international standing by encouraging a commercial society that ate at the foundations of Old Regime structures.[19]

This study modifies both of these claims. First, I move beyond the question of whether the state smothered or strengthened local political bodies and traditions. Mine is a dynamic story of mutual transformation: the Crown transformed cities, but civic traditions transformed the Crown and state. Second, emphasizing the distrust between royal and local elites, this book characterizes the relationship fostered between Crown and locality as one of accommodation rather than of collaboration. It focuses on the correspondences between royal administrators, intendants, the Marseille *échevinage* (municipal magistracy) and commercial institutions to argue that these bodies and individuals made accommodations, which I take to mean varying degrees of adaptation in their views, behaviors, and speech patterns. Through such modifications, they tailored the new situation of commercial expansion to benefit themselves without entirely becoming willing collaborators.[20]

Over the past decades, the subject of the rise of commercial society has increasingly interested French historians as a result of major transformations in the historiography of the Old Regime and the Revolution. The 1970s revisionist turn that drew historians away from Marxist interpretations of the French Revolution and initiated research in political culture has, curiously, opened up opportunities to examine social questions from new directions. Initially, the break from Marxist social history led revisionist historians to concentrate on the ways political discourses and contestations led to the crisis of the monarchy and made the French Revolution thinkable and possible. Postrevisionist historians have begun to bridge these two earlier historiographical trends by demonstrating that political discourses were used to address and evaluate certain social, material, and cultural changes occurring in the Old Regime. The rise of commercial society was one such change. Royal and civic elites in the late seventeenth and eighteenth centuries mobilized idioms of classical republicanism and commercial civic spirit to make sense of the multilayered transformations wrought by economic expansionism: the generation of wealth and luxury; the disappearance of boundaries between estates; the proliferation of tax farmers, speculators, and financiers; the refining or debasing of taste and manners; commerce's effect on arts and sciences.

But what historians have labeled as a rise of commercial society was not always understood as a rise to contemporaries, who recognized that theirs was a new age of commercial change and economic growth. Certainly, many Enlightenment philosophers who advocated this change understood it as the necessary kind of progress that drew humanity toward perfection. But as Michael Sonenscher has recently shown, from the vantage point of the darker "other side of the Enlightenment," the changes in commercial society and economic practices were leading France toward decay, catastrophe, and crisis; "the eighteenth century focused largely on [the] menace" produced by wealth and a credit-driven state.[21]

This book builds on this emphasis on the more sinister obsessions in the Century of Light. Anxieties over merchant virtue, mistrust between royal and civic elites, the worries that luxury would produce despotism, and debates over how economic crises would prompt political and moral decay all suggest that the late early modern period was as much conceivable as a period of decline as one of advancement. The distrustful and pessimistic musings of the eighteenth century most often associated with Jean-Jacques Rousseau or with Jean-Paul Marat and the Jacobins more generally were more commonplace among French elites of the Old Regime than previously assumed. And this pessimism emerged, in large part, due to the vertiginous sociopolitical transformations energized by Louis XIV and his impulse to expand his monarchical regime.

CRISES AND HISTORICAL CHANGE

Two cataclysmic events, the conquest of 1660 and the plague of 1720, serve as the bookends to this study of the revisions in rooted civic structures, rituals, and discourses in the context of absolutist state-building: the first where Marseille was subdued by Louis XIV, the second where the city, remodeled as a French commercial hub, nearly collapsed as a result of a southern invasion by "Oriental plague." The first of these involved a military invasion from the north. The monarch who would eventually earn the title of Sun King ordered six thousand troops to march on Marseille, a "republican" stronghold, and to construct the citadel of Saint Nicolas with cannon facing the city. Accompanied by Anne d'Autriche, the duc d'Anjou, the prince de Conti, and his chief minister, Cardinal Mazarin, Louis XIV entered Marseille through a breach in the wall of Porte Réale, the symbol of the city's republican past. Letters patent of 5 March 1660 ordered an overhaul of the municipal government. This was a strategy on the part of the French monarchy both to disable the Marseillais nobility's attempts at maintaining their city as an autonomous aristocratic republic, and to establish a commercial center designed to expand international trade under royal guidance. Marseille's chief *viguier* would henceforth be chosen by the king and operate under the eye of a royal intendant in Aix. The king abolished the consulate and Council of Three Hundred. He forbade Marseillais nobility from participating in municipal politics. Subject to royal approval, four *échevins* (municipal magistrates or assessors) elected from among the city's *négociants* would administer it, aided by a Council of Sixty also consisting of merchants.[22] The king left behind 3,500 Swiss and French troops to prevent further rebellion.

The conquest was an ostentatious show of Bourbon state-building, and it jump-started its drive to extend French commerce into the Mediterranean. Marseille's days as an aristocratic republic were over. It was repackaged as a politically compliant commercial trading center.[23] The Crown projected that merchant elites newly promoted to power would effectively collaborate with the monarchy to extend French commerce in the Mediterranean market. Over the next decades, Marseille became the only French city with the privilege of conducting duty-free trade with the Levant. The city more than doubled in size and population. Revenues soared, and the French out-traded the British and Dutch in the Mediterranean.

The same commercial activity that generated local prosperity and provided the French Crown with an opportunity to harness a provincial city to its statist ambitions could also introduce potentials for disaster. While the Mediterranean market offered possibilities for royal expansionism and commercial growth, increased contacts with the Ottoman Empire introduced Marseille to demographic instabilities and the specter of medical catastrophe. Calamity came to pass sixty years after the conquest, in May 1720, when the merchant vessel *Grand Saint-Antoine* returned to Marseille from the Levant, carrying among its 400,000 *livres* worth of cargo the most dreaded disease of the early modern period: plague. Health intendants of Marseille's Bureau de la santé had received news of renewed pestilential outbreaks in Palestine and Syria that year and had toughened restrictions on ships from eastern Mediterranean ports.[24] The *Grand Saint-Antoine*, however, sped into Marseille.[25] The ship's merchandise was clandestinely unloaded, allegedly upon orders by the *premier échevin*, Jean-Baptiste Estelle, who was incidentally part-owner of the vessel.[26]

In a matter of weeks, the plague spread through Marseille. In the outbreak's worst months, mortality rose to a thousand daily fatalities. The epidemic was equally lethal to commercial activity. Austria, England, the Netherlands, and Spain, as well as administrators of Calais, Bern, Luxembourg, and Italian city-states suspended trade with France's southern port.[27] A state already crippled by the collapse of John Law's economic system found itself paralyzed by simultaneous medical and financial crises. The epidemic continued its ravages for over two years, claiming the lives of approximately 50,000 inhabitants in the city. Over half of Marseille's population, in addition to countless more in the Provençal countryside, passed away before the Crown announced the end of the plague with a Te Deum of Deliverance on 15 January 1723.[28]

Organized as a narrative set between conquest and plague, this study makes three major contributions beyond enhancing our understanding of absolutism and republicanism. First, it reconsiders the meanings of "center" and "periphery" in this context. Generally speaking, historians have inherited the traditional divide in France between Langues d'Oïl and Langues d'Oc that located political and cultural supremacy in Paris and the north over the southern half of France. The center is still understood as Paris; the farther from Paris, the more peripheral. *Between Crown and Commerce* argues that in the early modern world, Paris, Fontainebleau, and Versailles could be seen as the hinterland that lay beyond the commercially and politically dynamic Mediterranean universe. This study considers two still-ignored major events on France's Mediterranean coast: the first where Marseille was conquered by Louis XIV, the second where it was stricken with "Oriental plague." Both events brought Mediterranean France into focus as the heart of French commercial activity, but more important, as the center where French subjects and their non-French trading partners came together in an international marketplace to construct new political concepts and alternative political traditions to absolutism, circulating them statewide.

Second, an analysis of these catastrophic events contributes to recent research on crisis studies. Traditionally, social and economic historians led the study of early modern catastrophe, "crisis mortality," and subsistence crises. The research of historians of Britain and France focused primarily on how economic factors contributed to demographic change; taking into account variables ranging from nutrition, prices, ecological differences, sociological fluctuations, class and gender inequalities, and administrative practices, these attempted to trace what caused catastrophe and death in early modern society.[29] Such studies provided an impressive collection of quantitative data and demonstrated how interactions among fields in the social sciences—economics, geography, sociology and history—further our historical understanding of catastrophic crises; however, they have disregarded the connections between events, language, and culture.[30] As Daniel Gordon observed in regards to plague studies, the dominant social approaches maintained that catastrophes do not "modify society but merely highlight its stable structures, such as class antagonisms and professional boundaries."[31] Rather than approaching catastrophes as dynamic events in and of themselves, these studies privileged an ahistorical structuralist reading over one of contingency and change.

A new approach to crisis studies developed in the past decades, particularly in regards to medical catastrophe, following the pioneering works of Susan Sontag and Colin Jones, who called attention to the metaphorical and mythical dimensions of disease.[32] This present work meshes with their cultural approach to the study of crisis. By "crisis," I mean a moment where relatively stable meanings and representations are overthrown or reformulated. Understanding conquest and plague as ruptures from the everyday, seventeenth- and eighteenth-century municipal leaders deployed different sets of languages and practices to make sense of and manage catastrophic events, while sidestepping other idioms. The traditional classical republican language was one of the many vocabularies that became a useful tool for elite administrators, ecclesiastics, and commentators to understand these events, to maintain a sense of social and political order, and to assess the advantages and damages related to commercial activity.

Finally, combining the history of commercial expansion and state-building with a study of catastrophe (particularly of the medical sort) is valuable because it allows for a consideration of French political traditions in a transnational Mediterranean context. Bubonic plague, once endemic to the European continent, had retreated to Asian, sub-Saharan, and eastern-European territories by the seventeenth century. According to many French writers, the plague belonged to non-Western states that they described as founded on perverted forms of politics, sociability, and culture.[33] The frequency with which French and Marseillais *négociants* entered into the Mediterranean commercial universe sharpened discussions regarding the contagious effect of "oriental" physical and moral diseases and the dangers they posed to French politics and society. The *négociants* who formed Marseille's municipal administration were as much cosmopolitan inhabitants of French trade colonies in the Mediterranean as they were citizens of Marseille. Could virtue, patriotism, and fidelity to the French Crown be sustained beyond the shores of France? Could *négociants* who spent considerable time away from Marseille and France demonstrate exemplary civic behavior upon their return? Or would these *négociants* who associated with Turkish traders become political, cultural, and religious traitors and pollute France by spreading "Asiatic" customs and behaviors? Debates over whether commerce and merchants were the stable foundations for state and society were rendered more complex given this transnational commercial environment.

The Great Plague of Marseille that appeared in the context of these discussions over politics, commerce, and sociability presented French elites with a unique set of questions: Was the outbreak of a medical crisis within French commercial society an anomaly or the unsurprising consequence of commercial expansion and royal aggrandizement? Was plague indicative of fundamental problems in French politics, commerce, and morality? Did commerce benefit or poison society? Could commerce be regulated to avoid catastrophe and corruption? If not, what alternative foundation for society was there? Competing versions of classical republican thought—one antagonistic to commerce, the other supportive of it—came to a head during and after the Great Plague of 1720. Positive assessments of commerce that redeemed certain merchants as beneficial to state, society, and history became difficult to sustain during medical catastrophe. Nonetheless, the Crown and municipal elites' commitment to international trade and exchange was too great for such claims to totally wither away. The years immediately following the catastrophe saw intensified use of the idioms of classical republicanism and commercial civic spirit, as elites now keenly aware of the physical threats posed by commercial activity sought new ways of cultivating the virtues and patriotism they agreed were requisite for a well-functioning state.

Ultimately, the eighteenth century did not see French elites definitively choosing between traditional classical republicanism and its modified pro-commercial variant; rather, both persisted through the Enlightenment, one focusing on the promises of commercial expansion, the other directing attention to its dangers. The ways in which they coexisted through the end of the Old Regime allowed French elites to become well-versed and well-practiced in concepts of republican "civic excellence"[34] and patriotism before the French Revolution. This concept of *civisme*, so integral to the Revolution of 1789, developed not only in Paris, traditionally seen as the "center" of the kingdom, but often in cities far from the capital, where local elites juggled their identities as royal subjects, municipal citizens, and cosmopolitan merchants.

THE STRUCTURE OF THE BOOK

In its first three chapters, this book examines how particular groups of royal, municipal, and intellectual elites appropriated classical republican traditions while participating in commerce from 1660 to 1720. They discuss the different forms of accommodation they negotiated as they tried to skirt the real and imagined threats that could undermine commercial activity and political stability. Chapter 1 focuses on discussions among controllers-general, royal intendants, Marseillais *échevins*, and the Chamber of Commerce. Once the Crown instituted a new municipal administration, it began introducing regulations to control Franco-Levantine commerce. These royal initiatives were premised on the idea that unsupervised commercial activity threatened the public good. The Marseillais merchant elite resisted these developments. The Crown and the merchant-administrators commonly believed that commercial expansion could benefit the general good. They disagreed, however, over how to derive this public good. Would commercial expansion be successfully realized through the sovereign gaze and regulatory policing of an absolute king, or would it materialize through the political participation of citizens interested in the public well-being? Controllers-general, royal intendants, *échevins* and the Chamber of Commerce haggled over whether absolutist ideology or the city's civic traditions legitimately determined the public good.

Municipal merchant deputies and royal councilors of state, however, gradually found ways to synchronize civic and absolutist concepts of deriving the public good. The Crown's desire to maximize the productivity of its subjects created an opportunity where utility to the state could be articulated in terms of civic excellence, and vice versa. This was particularly the case in discussions held by the Conseil du Commerce (1700), an advisory board comprised of royal councilors of state and merchant deputies from France's major cities that deliberated commercial regulations. Merchant deputies strengthened the new commercial civic spirit by suggesting that elite merchants were exemplary citizens who dedicated themselves to the common good.

Chapter 2 explores aristocratic responses to commercial expansion in Marseille. As the Crown began considering *négoce* an honorable activity, and *négociants* as an "aristocracy of commerce,"[35] some ennobled aristocracy supported the market. Though the Crown had banned the traditional Marseillais nobility from municipal power in 1660, a number of nobles of the robe—mostly local antiquarians and historians—praised commercial expansion, arguing that kings liberated republics. This republican reading of history, similar to narratives developed in Renaissance Florence or Venice, was a cyclical story leading from ancient perfection via ruin to future regeneration. Local chroniclers began their narratives with the myth of classical Marseille, lamented how the republic had been corrupted, and celebrated its long-awaited resurrection. These historians obscured the memory of the conquest and cultivated a culture of historical amnesia, by imagining the French monarch rescuing the ancient republic out of its moral and economic doldrums. Such evaluations diverged from the discomfort that nobility of the sword around the kingdom expressed about commercial expansion. Commerce, these argued, destabilized ancient social hierarchies and weakened the state. Combining classical republican suspicions of luxury with the religious ideal of "disinterestedness," the sword nobility advocated an agricultural society governed by a virtuous aristocracy. The Crown's support for commercial expansion drove a wedge between the sword and robe nobility, and this division became apparent in historical discussions.

Chapter 3 studies how the presence of non-French merchants in Marseille affected conversations between royal and municipal administrators. Following the conquest, the Crown threw open the city gates to greater numbers of foreign traders and immigrants, while great numbers of Marseillais and French traders departed for non-French ports. Such demographic shifts put pressure on the partnership between city elites and royal administrators, as well as their common commercial engagement. One major issue—Colbert's recruitment of foreign professionals to Marseille—exacerbated tensions between royal and civic elites. The controller-general invited Levantine Armenians and Jews in particular to become French and trade for their adopted king. Royal and Marseillais elites employed different languages of public good, usefulness to the state, and civic virtue to debate over the flow of Jews, Armenians, and Protestants into Marseille and France. Royal intendants and Marseille's chamber of commerce discussed whether naturalized subjects could interest themselves in the public good of a country originally foreign to them. The chamber and controllers-general did not come to an agreement until the latter half of Louis XIV's reign, when renewed warfare and religious intolerance amplified xenophobic rhetoric against non-Christian trading partners across France.

The chapter places these Marseillais discussions about foreign and naturalized traders in the larger context of French Orientalisms in seventeenth and eighteenth-century France. Early modern French utterances regarding the Mediterranean East and the Ottoman Empire in particular were fraught with tensions. Historically an ally of the sultan, the French king oscillated back and forth between fostering positive views of his non-Christian trading partner and his people, and reactivating derogatory stereotypes of non-Christian barbarians. Under royal supervision and patronage, authors—doctors, merchants, ambassadors, nobles, and travel writers—who penned publications on the Ottoman Empire encouraged *négociants* to conduct missions abroad, while warning of the dangers present in Ottoman territories. The challenge for the Crown was to alert merchants to dangers connected to international trade without extinguishing enthusiasm for commerce. Meanwhile, outside the royal court, Protestant expatriates, sword nobility, amateur observers, and specialists in "Oriental languages" added to the number of Frenchmen collecting information on the Levant. All of these different writings provided a collection of Orientalist vocabularies that royal and local administrators, merchants, and intellectuals could employ to craft both inclusive and exclusionary arguments regarding non-French and naturalized French populations involved in international commerce.

The specter of catastrophe, most notably plague, however, always threatened to annihilate the commercial activities that rested on the precarious cooperation among royal and local administrators, and French, naturalized French, and non-

French merchants. Chapters 4, 5, and 6 turn to this dark cloud that hovered over the international market. Chapter 4 examines how the Crown and Marseillais administrators developed regulatory systems to protect commerce and avert medical catastrophe. Members of Marseille's Bureau de la Santé ran quarantines and collaborated with other European health bureaus to keep informed of the latest epidemics. The Crown increasingly intervened in the bureau's affairs as it did in commerce, calling for new regulations and demanding clearer communication with royal authorities.

Strategies developed to avert medical catastrophe brought centuries-old medical ideas together with newer scientific and political ideas of health and disease. Ancient Hippocratic traditions and emergent Orientalist stereotypes of the Ottoman Empire converged to contrast a healthy Western civilization—ruled by public-minded rulers, officials, and citizens—with a decadent Ottoman Empire, founded on despotism, self-interest, and caprice. Meanwhile, scientific, geographic and moral arguments overlapped as plague writers stressed the need for citizens to prioritize public health over particular wants. Plague discussions drew on civic republican traditions, religious sensibilities against self-interest, and absolutist visions of a utopian sanitary order. Justified in the name of the public good, systems of surveillance became increasingly severe all over Europe as municipal leaders worked to eliminate disease.

Nonetheless, the Great Plague of Marseille, the subject of Chapter 5, appeared in 1720. Plague suspended commercial activity between France and its neighbors. It strained relationships between the French monarchy and Marseillais administrators. The Crown had extended its powers by exploiting the ambiguities of Marseillais republicanism. Downplaying the political freedoms that once characterized the republic, it had focused on the commerce that had also formed the city's republican identity. The plague's arrival on board a merchant ship and the subsequent mortality seemed to demonstrate that Marseille's administrators had chosen wrongly by opting for the Crown's strategy of commercial expansion and state-building. Levantine commerce and a corrupt merchant-run quarantine system had brought plague to Marseille. Plague thus stimulated a critique of commercial society and strengthened classical republican traditions antagonistic to commerce.

Civic leaders did not, however, relinquish their ties with the monarchy. Instead, the Crown played a critical role in establishing a municipal order that reactivated severe classical republican traditions. City administrators and royal commandants emphasized communal mobilization and polarized political virtue against individual interest and commercial and moral corruption. The royal military and civic leaders implicated the market as a breeding ground of immorality. They gathered suspects—defined as those who put the population in medical and moral danger—and quarantined and summarily executed them. The plague years constituted a moment imagined as an ultimate crisis for a city whose citizens redefined civic engagement without commerce.

Marseillais elites therefore depended on old civic traditions, republican vocabularies, and new forms of royal aid to formulate responses to commercial and medical catastrophe. Chapter 6 demonstrates how this mélange of civic republicanism and monarchical bureaucracy converged with the religious reaction to plague, by examining Jansenist and Orthodox reactions to commercial crisis. Throughout France, Jansenist discussions predating the epidemic had applied the rhetoric of republican civic participation to ecclesiastical rule; these debates kindled criticisms of commercial luxury and royal and papal absolutism that became immediately pertinent in the context of the political and social chaos generated by plague. The Catholic establishment, meanwhile, located the causes of plague in immorality, particularly of the kind they believed was spawned by commercial excess and religious heterodoxy. Supported by pope and Crown, they cultivated a civic devotion—the Cult and Festival of the Sacred Heart of Jesus—to rid the community of such decadence. Meanwhile, ecclesiastics stressed the importance of civic aid and charity during medical crisis, and likened Catholics' struggle to choose between redemption and damnation to citizens' conflicts between political virtue and corruption.

Chapter 7 discusses how Marseille and France recovered from the medical and economic crises of 1720. Ultimately, the critique of commerce during the epidemic did not decimate France's international market; commercial expansion reached new heights as France and Marseille turned again toward the Mediterranean to rebuild the French economy and centralized state. The mid eighteenth century was, in many ways, the crowning point of the optimistic philosophy of *doux commerce*. But as the claims of commercial apologists reached a crescendo, powerful arguments against commerce continued to resound, from calls for more vigilance in patriotic civic education to claims in favor of agricultural pursuits. Plague reactivated a language of opposition that would check and counterbalance blind enthusiasm for commerce. Remembering the epidemic, French authors would express their ambivalence about market luxury, royal aggrandizement, and their tendencies to corrupt moral and political virtues. Eighteenth-century elites faced the challenge of reconciling their hopes in an upward-moving historical trajectory toward civilization, progress, and perfectibility with their darker republican musings about a cyclical history of decline and human fallibility. Such was the problem both for commentators in the Enlightenment and for revolutionaries during the Terror. This study of eighteenth-century nightmares—both real and imagined—of a commercial society and expanding state at the crossroads of progress and crisis might serve to renew a sense of the Enlightenment's relevance for the postmodern society of today, for which, regrettably, the political and economic impact of a catastrophic event resonates all too well.

CHAPTER ONE

Louis XIV, Marseillais Merchants, and the Problem of Discerning the Public Good

Louis XIV's conquest of their city in 1660 visually and politically introduced Marseillais to the French Crown's methods of expanding its domestic and international power. Bourbon statecraft became synonymous with commercial expansion under Jean-Baptiste Colbert, who decided that France needed to extend its commerce as early as 1651. "Providence has placed France in a situation where its own fertility is useless, expensive, and inconvenient without the benefits of commerce," he had written as a go-between for Cardinal Mazarin and the king, "Through [commerce], all the things one needs are carried from one province to another and to foreign lands."[1]

The Crown recognized Marseille as a city well suited to serve as a focal point for French international commerce. The city's trading networks with the Italian city-states and Levant spanned centuries. As early as the Middle Ages, civic leaders had established consulates in Levantine and other Mediterranean ports to stimulate trade. Marseille's Chamber of Commerce, founded in 1599, was the first French institution of its kind. Colbert, therefore, decided to build on the city's centuries-long strengths in Levantine commerce, bestowing on it the royal privileges needed "to render this port the most famous in the entire Mediterranean Sea" and "the most important city in the kingdom." "Marseille," he wrote to the royal intendant in Aix-en-Provence, "is *the* city necessary for us to wage continuous economic warfare against all foreign commercial cities, and especially against the English and the Dutch, who have long encroached on all Levantine commerce."[2]

By conquering Marseille and creating a merchant *échevinage* there to manage a royally regulated marketplace, the Crown built on the city's commercial strengths for purposes of royal aggrandizement. The Crown went along with Marseille's heritage of relative independence on the condition that the city's new leaders renounced separatism and identified themselves more closely with the French monarchy. From the royal perspective, the monarchy's political presence in Marseille offered nothing but benefits for the city, its administrators and merchants: an invigorated market, a monopoly in the Levant trade, and improved defenses against piracy, smuggling, and contagious epidemics arising from foreign trade and travel.

The new Marseillais merchant elites, however, were neither overt royalists nor acquiescent collaborators. The *échevins* and *négociants* played a double role: they were instruments of centralization and advocates for municipal interests. The Crown and the merchant-administrators commonly accepted that commerce might benefit the public good, but their assumptions over how to achieve this public good fundamentally conflicted. Moreover, while the Crown hoped the *négociants* promoted to positions of administrative power would facilitate its expansionist plans, royal ministers and intendants doubted the Marseillais administrators' capacity to align their own interests with those of the state.

Royal and civic elites agreed that proper governance required the alignment of private with public interests. Two different traditions, however, fed this preoccupation over how to reconcile such interests. As mouthpieces of absolutist ideology, Colbert and his intendants in Provence argued that only the monarchy could recognize the public good and channel diverse interests to serve this good. Applying this logic to the market, they insisted that centralized administration and the monarch's sovereign gaze were essential to police self-interested merchants. Marseille's *échevins* and members of the Chamber of Commerce questioned this. Suspicious of the Crown's claims to be the sole purveyor of the public good, they deployed their civic vocabulary and argued that the public interest could only be realized if virtuous citizens articulated the will of the community and that Frenchmen who were "foreign" to Marseille had little knowledge of what might be good for the city. They claimed that methods for commercial expansion and regulation developed outside of Marseille's walls—even by the Crown—threatened to bring financial disaster, moral ruin, and political turmoil.

This chapter elaborates on the deep mistrust between royal administrators—Colbert and his intendants—and Marseille's *échevins* and Chamber of Commerce from 1660 to 1683. While they jointly took major strides to expand French trade in the Mediterranean region, their steps toward developing a positive vision of commerce, and of each other, were rather unsteady. The Crown remained skeptical of merchants' moral and political strength. However, after Colbert's death, new administrators obscured the tensions between absolutist and civic ideologies. Between 1683 and 1708, the Crown began fostering a more inclusive political atmosphere that allowed local representatives to articulate how their regions' commercial interests aligned with the good of the state. In the Council of Commerce in Paris, royal and local delegates combined absolutist and civic traditions to deliberate over how to realize the public good. In the end, Louis XIV's conquest of Marseille did little to stamp out traditional civic formulations of virtuous political and social conduct.

TOWARD THE CONQUEST: A BRIEF BACKGROUND

The city chosen by Louis XIV and Colbert to serve as the center of operations for royally supervised Franco-Levantine commerce was an oligarchy that enjoyed a long tradition of autonomous rule and anti-royalist activity. Founded by Greek seafarers from Phocaea around 600 BCE, Marseille—originally Massilia—accumulated considerable commercial and cultural power in the ancient Mediterranean until Julius Caesar sacked it in punishment for supporting Pompey in the Roman civil wars.[3] Its consuls' attempts to keep Marseille independent of Catalan counts and French kings through the Middle Ages ultimately failed; the city fell to Charles d'Anjou, brother of Saint Louis (King Louis IX of France), upon his seizure of Provence in the thirteenth century.[4] Though Provence united with France in 1486 during the reign of Louis XI, the primary organizer of the union, the Marseillais Palamède de Forbin did his utmost to preserve the territory's autonomy, dictating that Provence join "not as an accessory to a principal, but as principal to another principal."[5] Louis XI assured Provence "administrative and political autonomy . . . under the authority of a lieutenant general under the service of the king."[6] The French Crown installed a royal governor, lieutenant-general, and intendant in the regional capital, Aix-en-Provence, but it brought the province into its orbit as a *pays d'état*, distinguished from *pays d'élections* by its greater independence.[7] With its heritage of Roman law and administrative and fiscal liberties, Marseille's status as an aristocratic city-state was virtually unchanged.[8]

From 1486 to 1660, Marseille's administrative and legal structures remained intact despite modifications necessitated by conflicts among ruling aristocratic and merchant families.[9] Most notable among the city's constitutions were the

Rules of Cossa (1475) and Saint-Vallier (1492), and the *Règlement du sort* (1652). The first placed the city in the hands of a *chapitre*, composed of several magistrates and two councils. Conflicts between the nobles and merchants led to the creation of the Rule of Saint-Vallier, which instituted a municipal council of seventy-two members, who annually rotated in by thirds. Three consuls, a noble, a squire, and a merchant presided as leaders of the city. The Rule was replaced by the *Règlement du sort*, which established a 300-person council and instituted the ancient tradition of election by lots.

By the mid seventeenth century, however, the monarchy's interference in Marseillais politics began creating a volatile environment that polarized those loyal to the Crown against those who mounted the political platform brandishing the rhetoric of civic independence. In 1638, Cardinal Richelieu, disregarding decisions made by the royal governor of Provence, appointed to first consulship Antoine de Valbelle, the lieutenant general of Marseille. Years later, in 1657, the governor's son took his revenge by elevating Valbelle's opponents to the first and second consulships. Valbelle's supporters, led by Gaspard de Glandevès-Niozelles, allied against the new consuls under the banner of Marseillais independence. Amid escalating violence, the Crown charged Niozelles with attempting to assassinate the royal *viguier.* Accused of lèse-majesté, he lost his noble title and privileges. The Crown hoped that Marseille's elections of 1659 would restore order, but the city council, emboldened by a tide of anti-royalism, elected Niozelles' friends to consulships. The new consuls defied the royal order to turn in Niozelles, who mysteriously disappeared.

These disturbances prompted Louis XIV to take control of Marseille. Fresh from his military triumphs on France's northern frontier, the monarch, who had just engineered the Treaty of the Pyrenees and was preparing to marry María Teresa of Spain, decided to take a detour on the way to his bride.[10] As the royal entourage wove toward the Bidasoa River, where the future queen awaited, they headed southward toward Provence.[11] In January 1660, Louis celebrated the rededication of the famed ancient Roman obelisk in Arles, and by March, he had installed himself in the provincial capital of Aix-en-Provence, within striking distance of Marseille. Meanwhile, he sent the royal governor of Provence, the duc de Vendôme, ahead of him with six thousand troops. The wedding procession would march over Marseille's ruins before proceeding toward the bride.

This conquest, among other events that transpired in 1660, ushered in a new era for Louis XIV. The king was married by June of the same year. Within a few months, Mazarin was dead, and Louis announced that he would assume complete personal control of the French Crown. And in place of a prime minister, a new controller-general, Jean-Baptiste Colbert, worked to fulfill the monarch's ambitions of royal aggrandizement, commercial expansion, and personal glorification.

COLBERTISM IN MARSEILLE (1660–1683)

Between Louis XIV's conquest of the city and Colbert's death in 1683, the controller-general introduced several projects to realize the vision of a Marseille qua "center of Mediterranean commerce," operating under royal direction. First, Colbert ordered urban expansion. The *agrandissement de Marseille* in June 1666 transformed the medieval port into a city capable of supporting amplified commercial activity and increased populations of royal naval personnel, galley slaves, and foreign merchants. This expansion was intended to visually impart the message that Marseille was a French city equipped to lead international commerce. On the heels of urban expansion, the Edit sur la franchise du port de Marseille of April 1669 made the city a duty-free port. In order to attract international business and boost domestic sales, Colbert abolished the taxes previously required of foreign merchants entering the city. His five subsequent initiatives were intended to curb corrupt practices in the market and to rein in Marseille's commercial activity under royal management. These included the creation of mandatory escorts to protect French merchant ships from Barbary corsairs, the regulation of currency exchange, consulate reform, and the negotiation of new *capitulations* (treaties privileging French subjects) with the Ottoman Empire, and the expansion of Marseille's Bureau de la santé to protect against merchandise-borne diseases originating in the Levant.

COLBERTISM AND THE CITY: THE *AGRANDISSEMENT* OF 1666

Colbert's earliest project in Marseille, the urbanization project of 1666, triggered heated debates over the correct protocols for realizing commercial expansion. As Béatrice Hénin has shown, urbanization during the Sun King's reign "imposed the political concept of the national state and its corollary, the absolute monarchy." Gutting Paris, Sète, Brest, and Rochefort of their medieval traces, the Crown transformed their cityscapes to conform to uniform guidelines. Similar city plans and standardized architectural themes would represent the cohesiveness and breadth of the French state.[12] Colbert's aspirations for France to emulate imperial Rome found physical expression in urban expansion, in the construction of neoclassical public buildings and in the restoration of antique monuments. He set up new institutions, such as the Académie royale d'architecture (1671), which offered public instruction in architecture, mathematics, mechanics, perspective, and hydraulics and provided students with opportunities to study in Rome.[13] Roman motifs were integrated into French public buildings, from the Dôme church at Les Invalides (1676) to the Chapelle de Versailles (1689) and St. Sulpice (1736) and later the church of St. Geneviève–Panthéon (1773) in Paris.[14] Striving for equilibrium between Roman antiquity and French modernity, royal architects built a state linked to the splendor of the past.

Louis XIV's architectural imperialism transformed Marseille as well. Colbert's letters patent of 10 June 1666 ordered the town to be redesigned as a clean, spacious city to facilitate commerce and accommodate royal administrators. From its founding to 1660, the city perched on the three hills above the Vieux Port faced the Mediterranean, with its back to the eastern marshes. Compact and cramped, the city's walls, narrow alleys, and squalid apartments, a royal informant observed, made Marseille a hotbed of disease.[15] Colbert decided that the new city would follow a gridline arrangement. A Grand Cours, 300 fathoms (549 meters) long and 14 fathoms (about 25.6 meters) wide, would extend from the main gates down the eastern side of the city. The Cours would intersect with another new boulevard (the present-day Canebière) at the Place Royale. The newly developed southern bank of the port would be the site of the Arsenal of the royal galleys. Conforming to the monumentality and classical symmetry characteristic of baroque urbanism, these renovations would convert Marseille into a French commercial metropolis.

Colbert tapped Nicolas Arnoul, the royal intendant of the galleys in Marseille, to direct the expansion. A commission consisting of Arnoul; Henri de Maynier, baron d'Oppède, *premier président* of the parlement de Provence and *conseiller du Roi*; and Dominique Guidy, *trésorier général de France*, was appointed to design the new city.[16] It focused on three priorities: first, to plan new neighborhoods for naval and other royal personnel; second, to devise methods to lure prominent merchants from the old city to the new; and third, to improve circulation of goods and people by engineering wider boulevards. By June 1666, the Crown had given the developer François Roustan permission to demolish the old walls and to collect taxes to support the project.[17]

Marseille's *échevins* "completely opposed the entire execution" of the *agrandissement*, which they saw as an imposition from outside and above.[18] They argued that decisions for urban development had to be deliberated in the city council; the Crown, they maintained, "could not execute [its plans] without hearing

Marseille in the mid-seventeenth century. *Courtesy Archives municipales de la ville de Marseille, 11Fi47.*

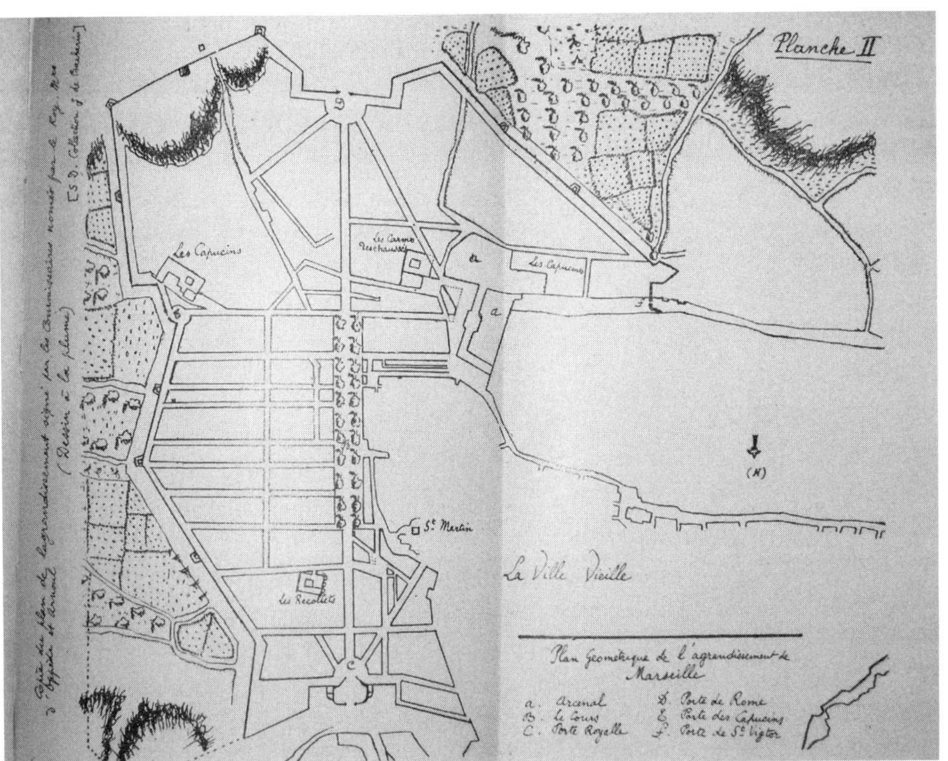

Nicolas Arnoul's expansion plan, 1666. *Courtesy Chambre de Commerce et d'Industrie Marseille-Provence.*

the appeal of the supplicants." The project would not only "greatly inconvenience" the Marseillais but spell their financial and moral ruin. New buildings would devalue older property. Expansion would create a taste for luxury, leading Marseillais to abandon entire quarters for new, "beautiful homes furnished with the furniture and paintings following the century's trends." As a result, they would "lose their entire fortunes" and eventually "desert" the city, inviting economic disaster.[19]

The *échevins* insisted that the expansion favored those least interested in Marseille; it catered to non-Marseillais. New plans, they claimed, were always "suspicious" and "harmful to the city and its commerce." The "most suspect" of these "foreign enterprises," they complained, were new taxes that introduced an "infinite variety" of "contentions" among Marseillais. Motivated only by their own interests, the partisans of expansion "would practice several violations in tax collection."[20] Landlords would face excessive burdens and become entangled in legal processes. As "protectors of the privileges of Marseille" the *échevins* were "obliged to represent to the Court, the general and particular interests, regarding the subject of the expansion [*agrandissement*]."[21]

Nicolas Arnoul derided the *échevins* for their audacity in claiming to represent the "general interest," depicting them as self-interested, defiant republicans. "Special interests oppose [the expansion],"[22] he complained; "the *échevins* still think they are ancient Roman consuls";[23] they did "not want to quit their ancient errors," but rather "behave freely and capriciously without submitting."[24] Climate and geography, Arnoul added, exacerbated the situation; "humidity" and "the heat of the land get the upper hand and reason comes to [Marseillais] too tardily."[25] Tropical conditions made the city's leaders and inhabitants shortsighted: "they abandon themselves to their work, working for bourgeois who have no other thought than their sole interest without regard to anything else." Marseille was a city where "the interests of [private individuals] are totally opposed to that of the king."[26]

The intendant of the galleys advocated a method of recognizing the public good that was consistent with traditional notions of absolutism. These saw the state as comprised of a multitude of corps, orders, and Estates; the king alone could discern the public good and maintain the state—a collection of disparate corporate bodies—by exercising his justice, reason, and will. As Keith Michael Baker has argued, "it follows from this definition of absolutism that the king, and the king alone, is a public person."[27] As members of diverse bodies held together only through the coordinative powers of royal will and justice, French subjects could only harbor partial interests. While Arnoul and the *échevins* commonly polarized general and particular interests, the *échevins*' claims on behalf of the general good remained, for Arnoul, the expressions of a particular corps.

Equating local resistance to the *agrandissement* with personal interest, Arnoul informed Colbert that it was necessary to impose the royal will in Marseille. "[I have] no other aim than the king's grandeur and the good of the city," he wrote to the controller-general, "Marseille will become . . . a great city that will not be able to defend itself against its master."[28] Arnoul asked the Crown for the power of force to silence the *échevins*: "the *échevins* cover their ears when you urge them to give up their old errors . . . they are accustomed to want the opposite of what they should want. It is necessary to cure these sick people by force."[29]

Ultimately, however, the Crown ignored Arnoul. On 6 March 1668, caught in a deadlock with the municipality, Colbert authorized the *échevins* to lead the expansion. Under their direction, it became a local project rather than one imposed from outside.[30] The *échevins* formed a Bureau de l'agrandissement com-

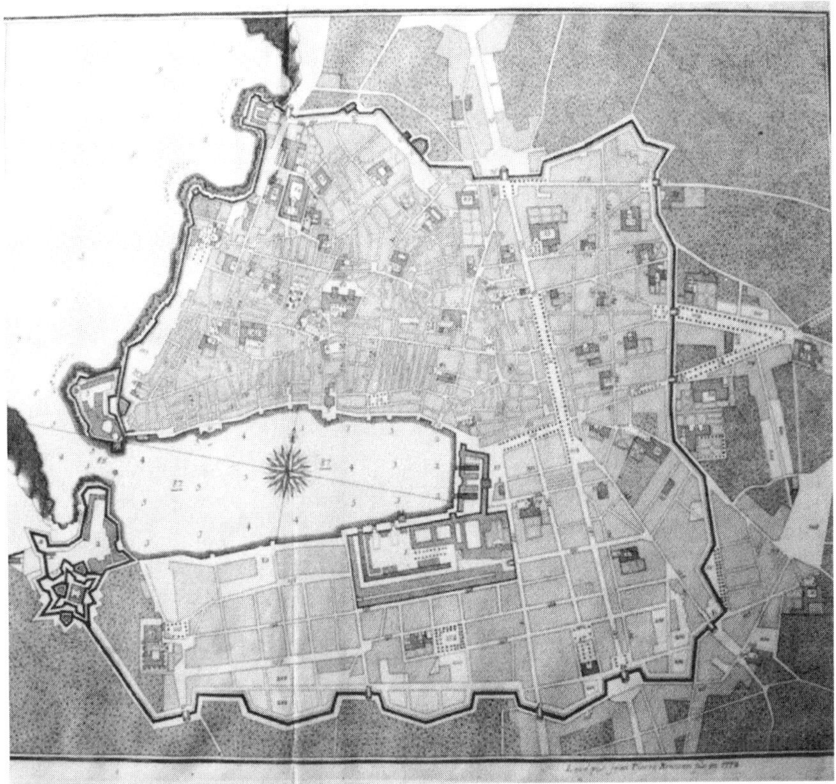

Marseille in the eighteenth century. *Courtesy Archives municipales de la ville de Marseille, 11Fi22.*

prised of the municipal magistracy and six (later twelve) elected directors. They drafted a revised proposal with two local architects, Gaspard Puget and Matthieu Portal, to triple the size of the city from 67 to 195 hectares and to create a new city center at the port by developing the eastern and southern areas beyond the old city walls.

The *échevins'* new expansion plan met royal calls for uniformity but integrated local traditions. While conforming to the grandiosity that Colbert imagined for French cities, the project incorporated regional and Italian styles. Gaspard Puget's brother, Pierre Puget, used his training as a sculptor and builder in Florence, Genoa, and Rome, to recast Marseille in the style of an Italian city-state.[31] Rejecting Arnoul's plans for an austere Cours flanked by apartments with identical façades, Puget envisioned a street "as wide as its length," similar to the Strada Nuova in Genoa. Apartment buildings would be adorned with

Ionic and Corinthian columns or with "nymphs, tritons and sea gods celebrating the maritime vocation of the city, while simultaneously evoking the gilded figures on the galleys anchored at the port."[32] The building blocks for the *agrandissement* came from Genoa, not France. Deliberations of the Bureau de l'agrandissement as late as 1687 show local architects requesting more Italian marble for the pillars along the Cours.[33]

The money and time spent on the new expansion suggest that the *échevins* disagreed with Arnoul and Colbert more over procedure than over the idea of the project itself. Arguments that the expansion would prompt inflation, depopulation, and financial and moral catastrophes tapered off once the Hôtel de Ville received authority to direct the expansion. Ultimately, it seems that the project worked favorably for many local merchants. Marseille's artisans and small traders found accommodation in the newer neighborhoods, undercutting Arnoul's plan to "separate the different social classes by creating a residential sector reserved for notables."[34] *Echevins,* officers of the galleys, and royal commissioners populated the new district, and it was only in the southwestern part of the

The Cours of Marseille. *Courtesy Archives municipales de la ville de Marseille, 11Fi26.*

agrandissement—the Paradis quarter—that Arnoul's original idea of an exclusive area restricted to imported elites was realized.

Architecturally and socially, the *agrandissement* played out in a way that privileged local needs and followed the *échevins'* methods of discerning the *bien public.* It mutated from a royal project into a local one. It transformed the city, not into a Paris in the south, but rather, into an Italian republic on French soil. The intendant of the galleys left Marseille before this materialized, but Controller-General Colbert authorized the modifications. However, he billed Marseille's *échevins* 100,000 *livres* for the privilege of directing the expansion.

COLBERT AND MARSEILLE'S CHAMBER OF COMMERCE: THE EDICT OF 1669

Tensions between Colbert and Marseille's *échevinage* and Chamber of Commerce reignited, however, when the controller-general unfurled his subsequent plan to restructure commerce under royal control: the edict of April 1669 that established Marseille as a duty-free port with a monopoly over France's Levantine trade. This edict prompted a century of unprecedented French commercial expansion.[35] It abolished all duties on goods landed in Marseille, attracting foreign merchants by the thousands to the city, which emerged as a global node for merchants from the Levant, the North Sea, the German states, Switzerland, Piedmont, the New World, Guinea, and the Indies. By the eighteenth century, vessels left the Vieux Port for Mexico, the Antilles, Martinique, and Peru, via Cape Horn. India, China, Guinea, and Mozambique also became frequent destinations.[36] Marseillais *négociants* accumulated incredible profits over the first decades of the eighteenth century. Jean-Baptiste Bruny, for example, who made a profit of 120,000 *livres* in 1700, doubled his sales to 200,000 by 1705, half a million by 1710, a million by 1715, and twice that by 1720.[37]

Historians credit the edict of 1669 with ushering in a period of major commercial success for France and Marseille.[38] Why, then, would the *échevins* and Chamber of Commerce voice opposition to this edict for two decades? If the edict established Marseille's monopoly in the Levantine trade and secured the city's position vis-à-vis domestic and international ports in the Mediterranean, why were there objections to it, and how were they expressed?

Two institutions, the *échevinage* and the Marseille Chamber of Commerce, opposed the promulgation of the edict. For the *échevins,* this project, like the *agrandissement* that preceded it, was an initiative imposed from outside. They challenged the liberalization of the port from the moment the idea of the edict became public knowledge. As of 1664, Colbert had not found a single collaborator willing to act as an intermediary in Aix-en-Provence and in Marseille to realize his dreams. Finally, he turned to Arnoul and d'Oppède.

Facing opposition from the *échevinage*, these royal administrators tried to court the Marseille Chamber of Commerce, hoping that its members would cooperate with the Crown. In 1650, the city council had separated the administration of commerce from that of the city, freeing the chamber from the authority of the Hôtel de Ville, and it thus wielded considerable power in Marseille.[39] It controlled its own activities, determined its budget, founded its own archive, and elected its treasurer without interference from the Hôtel de Ville.[40] The royal administrators hoped to exploit this separation between municipal and commercial administration to royal advantage: "There are two interests in Marseille," Arnoul wrote. "It is necessary to separate, one from the other, the *échevinage* and Chamber of Commerce, and treat them differently, discredit the former and authorize the latter."[41] Arnoul and d'Oppède initiated negotiations with the Chamber, without the participation of the Hôtel de Ville, which could not concern itself directly with commerce.

The Chamber of Commerce decided, however, that the edict did not suit the financial interests of Marseille's merchant community. Although it recognized in a *Mémoire dressé contre le port franc pour envoyer à Sa Majesté* that "Your Majesty would like to enrich your subjects," it asserted that the edict would invite "a contrary development." The abolition of all duties would be disastrous for the chamber. It would be deprived of the income that it spent to maintain the port, impose quarantines, police smugglers, and pay the stipend of the French ambassador in Constantinople. Commerce would be destroyed, firms would go bankrupt, and "Marseille would become desolate." Increased foreign traffic would augment the risk of illegal arms feeding into the market. Foreigners would take over real estate. The pressures of increased traffic and lack of funds would undermine the effectiveness of quarantines. Colbert offered to alleviate these pressures by imposing one new tax—the *cottimo*—but the chamber argued that a single tax would not generate enough revenue to support expenditures. The Crown's expectation that the chamber reimburse tax farmers whose services would be suspended in a free port added the final "unsupportable" pressure.[42] Ultimately, the chamber anticipated that these problems in Marseille would harm the kingdom at large.

While acting independently of each other, the *échevinage* and Chamber of Commerce presented a similar argument to the Crown. An initiative imposed from outside, it claimed, the edict catered to non-Marseillais interests rather than those of Marseille's merchant community. It ignored the city's budgetary needs. It released foreign merchants from the payment of duties needed to maintain the port and consulates in the Mediterranean. It promised foreign merchants the possibility of acquiring the status of French subjects and Marseillais citizens; indeed, Colbert imagined that adopted Frenchmen would play a major role in stabilizing France's growing market.[43] The chamber insisted that a free port would free foreigners from taxes, but the Marseille chamber would be burdened with new expenditures and the problem of confronting potential competitors—naturalized citizens—within the city walls. The chamber and the *échevins* saw in the edict the same inattention to the Marseillais *bien public* manifest in Arnoul's *agrandissement.*

Colbert reacted by stating that Marseillais merchants could not discern the general good: "there is," he insisted, "no greater enemy of general commerce and good order . . . than the merchants of Marseille." He reminded his intendants in Provence to "work hard for the particular good of this city and the general good of the kingdom," both which depended on the liberalization of Marseille's port. He warned that "the small-minded merchants of Marseille have no notion of any other trade than that between their shops . . . they ignore business in general for the sake of quick, small individual profits, which ruins them later."[44]

It would seem that the Crown defeated the *échevinage* and chamber when the parlement of Aix registered the edict in April 1669. Colbert wrote to d'Oppède in May 1669 describing how the positive effects of this edict would prove "most public" and "universal."[45] His ideas regarding the edict's universal application and publicmindedness, as well as his understanding of the Crown's exclusive authority to crush merchant self-interestedness, were echoed in the edict's language. It began by defining commerce as the glue that united people and states, and that would secure France's international power: "Commerce is the most proper means to reconcile different nations and entertain the most opposed spirits in great mutual correspondence,"[46] it asserted. "We oblige our subjects to apply themselves and carry [commerce] to the most distant nations to gather the fruit . . . to establish, in peace as in war, the reputation of the French name." Commerce, it continued, was good for all individual subjects: "it brings and spreads abundance by the most innocent of means, it renders subjects happy." The edict portrayed the Crown as the liberating force arrived in Marseille to crush personal interests manifest in the vexing tariffs that the city's administrators had levied: "The best and most profitable establishments for the public became degenerate and enfeebled, . . . and we found this city overburdened with import and export duties more than any other [place] in the kingdom, although ours [i.e., the Crown's] were not established there."[47] The edict reproached the Marseillais who had profited through superfluous duties and contrasted the Crown's public-minded, universalist position with the particularistic, self-interested one of local merchants.

The edict of 1669 abolished all duties previously levied by Marseille—the 1/2 percent tax used to pay the expenses of the French ambassador in Constantinople; another 1/2 percent tax, the *gabelle du port,* used to maintain the port; the *table de la mer*; the duty of 50 *sous* per ton on foreign ships; taxes on spices and medicine, oil, honey, and alum, a salted-fish tax, and many others. Foreigners could no longer be charged export duties.[48] The Crown imposed one new tax—the *cottimo*—on ships entering and leaving Marseille. The Chamber of Commerce would use the *cottimo* to compensate for what its former duties had paid: the ambassador's salary, the 25,000 *livres* required for the upkeep of the port, a new quarantine center, and the liquidation of debts to tax farmers.[49]

Colbert optimistically calculated that the edict and the liberalization of Marseille's port would generate profits that would quickly render the *cottimo* unnecessary. He projected that the chamber would be able to cover its expenditures from the surplus in revenue pumped into the city through increased trade. He insisted that the quick abolition of the *cottimo* was imperative to make Marseille a truly free port.[50] The Crown therefore reduced the *cottimo* three times in the first year of its imposition.[51] Meanwhile, royal intendants in Aix-en-Provence pressured the Chamber of Commerce to pay its debts punctually so that the *cottimo* could be eliminated.[52] The chamber protested against such developments, pleading that it was near impossible for one tax to cover all its expenditures. Besides paying 16,000 *livres* to the ambassador and 25,000 *livres* for port maintenance, the chamber was hounded by tax farmers asking for the liquidation of debts topping 211,508 *livres.*[53] The chamber also used the *cottimo* for emergencies; in 1682, for example, the French ambassador to Constantinople promised the sultan 250,000 *livres* in reparation for the French bombardment of an Ottoman city, and Colbert ordered the chamber to pay this sum.[54] The chamber found Colbert to be out of touch with the financial realities of Marseille.

The suppression of the *cottimo* was as impractical as it was impossible. Following Colbert's death, the chamber borrowed 250,000 *livres* from the Crown in 1685 to cover its outstanding balance; the Crown responded by introducing a "double *cottimo*" to help pay this loan back.[55] The *cottimo* was not abolished until 1766.

COLBERT'S DEFIANT MERCHANTS: ARGUMENTS ABOUT SAILING ESCORTS

Although Colbert's assumption that creating a duty-free port at Marseille would benefit the fisc suggests an optimistic faith in royally regulated commercial expansion, his other initiatives with regard to the city signal an underlying pessimism about merchants. Following the edict, he introduced a series of regulations to reform French commerce in the Mediterranean and to bring it under royal control. Over two decades, Colbert consistently stressed two points. First, he maintained that merchants, and Marseille's in particular, placed their financial interests over the public good. Second, he insisted that given such merchant egotism, unregulated trade in Marseille would endanger the state. Colbert believed that commerce required the guiding hand of the Crown to ensure that trade contributed to the public good.

Such assumptions prompted Colbert to require Marseillais trading ships to sail the Mediterranean in convoy under royal naval escort. This decision was provoked by France's ongoing conflicts with the Barbary Coast states, as a result of which pirates frequently attacked French merchant vessels.[56] In 1662, Colbert informed his intendant in Aix that His Majesty would maintain twelve galleys and other warships in the Mediterranean to escort merchant ships during peak summer trading seasons.[57] He ordered Nicolas Arnoul to build more galleys, which were to be equipped with cannon and carry infantry.[58]

The Marseillais merchants refused this royal protection, insisting that delays involved in waiting for escorts and leaving at designated times would put them out of synch with fluctuations in the market dictated by supply and demand.[59] Colbert criticized the merchants for placing their financial interests over those of trade in general. He warned his intendant: "every time you speak with the merchants of Marseille about these affairs, guard yourself against their arguments, which are all false and will lead to the destruction of commerce."[60] He noted that the Marseillais merchants' objections were consistent with their desire "to preserve for themselves complete liberty in their commerce."[61] From Colbert's perspective, a duty-free port would attract merchants who would benefit France, but also pirates, bandits, and smugglers who disrupted trade and attacked French subjects. The liberty of a duty-free port was contingent on it being royally regulated. The Marseillais *négociants*, however, understood commercial liberty as the absence of royal interference.

When pirate attacks continued, Colbert blamed the Marseillais merchants, rather than the corsairs: "[I am] not surprised that . . . kidnappings and . . . other parallel inconveniences befall those of Marseille who continue their commerce *sans escorte* and who choose not to profit from the powerful protection that His Majesty offers."[62] Over a decade later, when he observed that Marseillais merchants continued to be "kidnapped by the Barbary pirates," he ridiculed them for "never want[ing] to put in the least amount of effort or diligence to get themselves out of this mess."[63] Colbert could not comprehend how Marseille's merchants could refuse the Crown's protection, when their practices upset not only France's "general commerce" but, more obviously, their own.

COLBERT AND COINAGE: CONTROLLING CURRENCY IN MARSEILLE

Most galling for Colbert was Marseille's merchants' practice of depleting the kingdom of currency. "The source of all the abuses that are committed in regards to money in the whole kingdom is Marseille," he claimed, "because the merchants do not want to find a means to send French merchandise to the Levant, and they find it easier to send money in cash [out of the country]."[64] Colbert calculated that they exported two million coins annually.[65] He doubted the merchants' argument that the superior quality of Levantine textiles left them no choice but to pay cash for them. The British and Dutch, he claimed, had no problems trading with "absolutely no money."[66] The use of currency benefited foreign markets at France's expense and disrupted Colbert's plans to increase exports. He accused Marseillais merchants of trading in counterfeit coin at inflated rates: "The greatest disorder concerning monies consists of the 3 *sous* coin exchanged in Marseille . . . the Marseillais merchants in particular . . . introduce false coins in the Levant."[67]

Colbert depicted these activities as financial "crimes" of self-interest that violated the Crown's "universal" laws: "The Marseillais merchants, who care for nothing but the little profit that they can make, and who abuse the liberty that they have been given up to now to ship money as they like to the Levant, do so against . . . the universal and fundamental law of all states, which prohibits the transport of gold and currency on pain of death." He ordered the royal navy to randomly check Marseillais ships, confiscate money, and punish noncompliant merchants. Initially limited to four annual searches, seizures escalated to several per month.[68]

The conflicts between the controller-general and Marseille's *échevins*, Chamber of Commerce, and merchant elite suggest a consistent problem for Colbert: business was good, but merchants tended to be bad. They pursued their financial interests and disregarded the good of the state. This negative view of merchants was a remnant of traditional perceptions of commerce as a "public hazard" and of its practitioners as the antithesis of virtuous citizens, Amalia Kessler argues.[69] Notwithstanding Colbert's new vision of commerce as the foundation of society, his understanding of it was thus distinctly old-fashioned. He insisted that the Crown alone could contain Marseillais merchants' egotistical impulses, if not through regulatory systems, then by force.

TRANSPARENCY IN THE MEDITERRANEAN: COLBERTISM BEYOND MARSEILLE

Colbert's plans to oversee merchant activity were not limited to Marseille. If the edict of 1669 brought Levantine goods and merchants to Marseille, it also released Marseillais merchants in greater numbers to the Levant. Policing commerce required the cooperation of ambassadors, consuls, and merchants around the Mediterranean who would serve as Colbert's eyes and arms. Three projects were central to his endeavors: reforming consulates, educating new interpreters, and modifying French treaties with the Ottoman Empire.

That Colbert's reform of the consulates coincided with the edict of 1669 was no coincidence. The month the edict was finalized, Colbert wrote to French consuls abroad, stating that the king had named him secretary of state, and that henceforth all consulates fell under his control. He ordered them to supply him with information on their country of residence, including the form of government, merchandise, manufacturers, the quantity of caravans, European ships and merchandise entering and leaving port, the status of the army and navy, and running prices and currencies of other nations.[70] He requested an inventory of French five-*sous* coins so that he could curb counterfeit trading and the depletion of currency from France.[71] According to Colbert, such policing was essential to protect confidence in and the value of French currency in the global market.

Colbert stressed the need for paper trails to bring the consulates into the orbit of centralized governance. He ordered strict delivery of deliberation minutes from "assemblies of the nation" abroad. These were councils composed of merchants, captains, and shipowners, who convened regularly to debate over resolutions to be executed by the consuls. Traditionally, Marseille's Chamber of Commerce requested copies of these minutes, but, as Colbert noted, such copies were "neither signed by all the participating merchants nor registered in time."[72] He issued an *arrêt du Roi* demanding prompt delivery of the minutes of deliberations to Marseille's Chamber of Commerce.[73]

Colbert's reforms also involved transforming the practice of hiring interpreters, or *drogmans*, for the consulates. Until 1670, these *drogmans* were Ottoman subjects—often Jews and Greeks. Strained relationships with their French employers generated "frequent complaints by French merchants residing in Levantine ports [*échelles du Levant*] concerning the functions of these *drogmans*"; Colbert therefore decided that merchant assemblies would elect French nationals as interpreters.[74] Given the scarcity of multilingual Frenchmen in the Levant, he ordered "that every three years, six young Marseillais boys be sent to the convent of the Capuchins of Constantinople and Smyrna to be instructed in our religion and the knowledge of Levantine languages." In the interim, he sent boys annually to supply consulates with immediate linguistic support.[75] Known as *enfans de langue*—children of language—these students served "the king and the public in their capacity as interpreters for which they have been called." Under Colbert, the former job of Ottoman personnel was transformed into an exalted occupation for "king and public."[76]

Marseille's Chamber of Commerce reluctantly paid—with the *cottimo*—the cost of educating these boys. It objected to the annual 300 *livres* requisite for each student and to the monastic education, which seemed inappropriate for boys destined for careers in commerce. The Capuchins in Constantinople complained to Colbert that the chamber refused to pay its installments or sent them tardily.[77] It was only after 1681, when the effects of such education were finally felt that the chamber's protests abated.

THE *CAPITULATION* OF 1673

The new commercial treaty concluded between the Ottoman sultan and French king on 5 June 1673 was Colbert's crowning achievement with respect to France's Mediterranean trade. The odds were against such an agreement being reached. In 1669, reports from merchant deputies in Marseille and Lyon regarding Franco-Ottoman relations were overwhelmingly negative. Word that Sultan Mehmet IV had arrested French ambassador, Denis de la Haye, sieur de Vantalet, and imprisoned him in the Castle of the Seven Towers—the Yedikule fortress— at Constantinople had brought France and Turkey to the brink of war. Such reports, Colbert worried, would cause "disorders and bankruptcies in commerce, and . . . the most considerable loss to commerce that there has been in Europe for the subjects of His Majesty." He planned to divert warships to the Levant to "reestablish the reputation of Your Majesty's armies."[78] He suggested to the chevalier Antoine de Valbelle, *chef d'escadre de galères*, that he reinforce his supply of gunpowder and grenades. At the end of 1669, right after the promulgation of an edict to bolster Levantine commerce, France was poised for war with the Ottoman Empire.

War was, however, averted. Louis XIV recalled his ambassador and dispatched Charles François Olier, marquis de Nointel, *conseiller du Roi* in the parlement de Paris, as new ambassador in August 1670.[79] Nointel's first impressions of Constantinople did little to ease the Crown's anxieties, but Colbert shied away from war. News circulated among Constantinople, Smyrna, and Paris that the French were the most abused foreigners in the Turkish capital. The Ottoman court treated the French ambassador "without regard for the dignity of the king," and, against rules laid out in former *capitulations*, prosecuted and executed a French national in front of Nointel.[80] The grand vizier, Ahmet Cuperly, agreed to the renewal of ineffective old treaties, but refused to sign a new agreement. While such news led Marseille's Chamber of Commerce to encourage war, the controller-general stalled. France could not afford to open another front when it had just ended the War of Devolution against Spain (1667–68) and was poised for the Franco-Dutch War (1672–78). A war of words ensued, with Colbert threatening to recall his ambassador and to suspend trade. Verbal threats worked; the sultan agreed to a new *capitulation*, formalized on 5 June 1673.

The *Capitulation* of 1673 strengthened French commerce in the Levant by establishing physical security for French nationals, commercial privileges that topped those of the British and Dutch, and consular sovereignty over French nationals. In flamboyant rhetoric, its preamble announced the friendship between "the emperor of emperors and distributors of crowns . . . protector and governor of . . . the largest parts of Asia and Africa . . . Mehmet IV" and Louis XIV, "the greatest monarch of the land of those who believe in Jesus, chosen among the glorious princes of the religion of Christ, the conqueror of Christian nations, seigneur of majesty and honor, patron of glory, emperor of France."[81] Its clauses guaranteed ambassadors, consuls, merchants, pilgrims, and French nationals in general protection in the Ottoman Empire. French ships and nationals could not be seized by Ottoman pirates; those taken prisoner had to be released, and the Crown could legally punish pirates by destroying their ports. Churches could not be vandalized, and previously burned Capuchin convents were allowed to be rebuilt.

The *capitulation* extended the definition of French nationals to include subjects of "nations that do not have their own ambassador in [Ottoman ports] and therefore trade under the banner of France," including Portuguese, Sicilians, Castilians, and Messinians.[82] Any European lacking protection of an ambassador could enter Ottoman territory as a Frenchman. European traders who did not speak French and had never set foot in France could thus trade as French nationals to benefit French commerce.

Beyond physical security, the *capitulation* established commercial advantages and the French Crown's extraterritorial authority. French merchants secured the privilege of trading whatever goods they pleased in the empire. French nationals were exempted from Ottoman taxes; the currency they brought with them from France could not be confiscated "under the pretext of converting it to Ottoman money." Import and export duties were reduced from 5 percent to 3 percent. The last category of clauses established French sovereignty over French nationals: Ottoman courts could not try, prosecute, or execute French nationals. French laws trumped Ottoman ones within French "nations" abroad.

The most important clause for Franco-Ottoman relations and for a pro-French international balance of power in the Levant was clause 19 of the 1673 agreement:

> The emperor of France is among all Christian kings and princes, the most noble of the highest family, and the perfect friend that our sultans have acquired among the kings and princes of the believers in Jesus . . . we command that his ambassador who resides in our happy Porte have precedence over all the ambassadors of other kings and princes, whether at our public divan [council of state] or in other places that they may find themselves.[83]

Like the edict of 1669, the 1673 *capitulation* introduced a framework whereby the Crown could maximize its authority over its merchants while enhancing French commercial activity. Underlying Colbert's commitment to centralized control of commerce were the assumptions that it was beneficial to state power, but that in the physically dangerous and financially volatile market world, the merchant needed to be protected, guided, and even punished by the king, who was the sole guarantor of the public good.

The many kinds of royal interventions that Colbert introduced—from *capitulations*, edicts, and *arrêts* to regulations regarding escorts, interpreters, and embassies—were intended to supplant traditional local trading arrangements. Louis XIV and Colbert's form of state-building was predicated on the understanding that statist authority would override and replace local forms. Paradoxically, however, it increased communication between royal and local administrators and provided a space where regional voices were amplified. Unwilling to sacrifice participatory methods of determining what was good for the public, the *échevins*, members of the Chamber of Commerce, and elite Marseillais merchants insisted on retaining their freedom to trade. Depending on context, this freedom meant many things: the *échevinage*'s power to convoke its own urbanization bureau; the Chamber of Commerce's freedom to decide on commercial edicts, regulations, and duties; merchants' ability to determine independently when to set sail with their merchandise and currency. Traditional civic definitions of liberty butted heads with statist, monarchical ones.

These meanings, however, were open to change. Following Colbert's death, some Marseillais elites began seeing him as a champion of liberty. Revisionist views of Colbertism offered by Marseille's new generation of merchants praised the controller-general's dedication to commercial freedom and the city's monopoly in the Mediterranean. "Commerce is the child of liberty . . . [which] alone can render [it] powerful and profitable," wrote Auguste Chambon, a Marseillais tax farmer (*receveur des fermes*), "the great Colbert, whose patriotic vision enriched France, saw how Marseille's situation could be profitable to domestic and foreign commerce, once he cleared the city of the troubles and hindrances that suffocated it."[84] Chambon celebrated Colbert's accomplishments for freedom of trade, while associating Marseillais merchants' activities prior to 1669 with the "abuse of liberty," and "too much liberty." Patriotism and civic excellence, in Chambon's view, required a form of liberty, such as Colbert's, that trumped older, local forms of liberty, which generated anarchy. A contemporary Marseillais remarked that resistance to the controller-general was indicative of "personal interests prevailing" over the general good, while the controller-general "disentangled the general interest from particular interests and placed the latter in service of the former, for the establishment of the Levant trade."[85] This is not to say that resistance to Colbertism went underground; throughout the eighteenth century, many Marseillais administrators and merchants continued to try to get rid of the regulations the controller-general had imposed on the city. It is telling, however, that between 1700 and 1703, the Marseille Chamber of Commerce and its deputies in the royal Council of Commerce strove to restore Marseille as a duty-free port, and protect Colbert's reforms, which the previous generation of *échevins* had nearly refused. Had Colbert still been alive, nothing would have made him happier.

TOWARD RECONCILIATION: PONTCHARTRAIN, CHAMILLART, AND A NEW ERA OF MERCANTILISM

Colbert died on 6 September 1683, at a time when Europe was again plunged into the throes of war. A week after his passing, King Jan III Sobieski of Poland broke the Ottoman siege of Vienna, initiating the eventual Turkish withdrawal from much of southeastern Europe. Louis XIV took advantage of the Wars of the Holy League and staged French advances into Luxembourg and Strasbourg. His rivalry with the Spanish and Austrian Hapsburgs led to the wars of the Grand Alliance (1688–97) and the Spanish Succession (1701–13). Meanwhile, though his military engineer, Marechal Sébastien le Prestre, marquis de Vauban, warned that war and religious intolerance undermined the army, navy, and commerce, Louis revoked the Edict of Nantes in 1685, triggering the exodus of nearly 300,000 Protestants from France.

Against this backdrop, new characters took center-stage as Colbert's successors. In contrast to his one-man show, this ensemble led by successive controllers-general, Michel-Robert le Peletier, comte de Saint Fargeau (1683–89), Louis Phélypeaux, comte de Pontchartrain (1689–99), and Michel Chamillart (1699–1708) divided the management of commerce and the navy. They shared commercial administration with state officials and former intendants promoted to the offices of directors-general of commerce. The expanded scope of war, commerce, naval activities, and colonization made one-man control impossible. These successors, whether for lack of Colbert's dedication or for the sake of practicality, brought his level of multitasking and micromanaging to an end.[86] Under Pontchartrain, who became chancellor in 1699, naval affairs passed to his son, Jérôme Phélypeaux, while the administration of commerce was divided between his cousin, the *conseiller d'état* Henri-François Daguesseau, former intendant of Languedoc, and his nephew, the *conseiller d'état* Michel-Jean Amelot, marquis de Gournay. With these men, the Marseille *échevinage* and Chamber of Commerce succeeded in developing more conciliatory relationships with Versailles.

Historians have been divided over the direction mercantilism took following Colbert's death. Some have downplayed the changes introduced by Colbert's successors arguing that "the machinery that Colbert had created . . . was continued and enlarged"; others have shown that pragmatic concerns led Pontchartrain and Chamillart to shrink royal interference in the administration of commerce and colonial enterprises.[87] Meanwhile, recent studies have shed light on transformations in the positioning of local leaders, go-betweens, and patrons.[88] A focus on the linguistic practices of the local and royal elites—particularly the new Council of Commerce's modified expressions of how to govern diverse commercial interests—can offer insight into how this era of mercantilism was characterized by change and continuity. While royal and local administrators deployed traditional expressions to articulate their ambivalence about merchant self-interest, they also adopted new conceptual approaches to understanding commerce. These practices obscured the tensions between absolutist and civic ideologies. Municipal representatives to the Crown in the Council of Commerce oscillated between their uses of absolutist and civic idioms, while combining new utilitarian principles that valorized commercial activity with ideals of political virtue stemming from the city. The remainder of this chapter will focus on two things: how these representatives imagined themselves as participants of royal administration, while maintaining their local affiliations, and how, through them, the Crown adapted civic idioms for royal use.

JOSEPH FABRE AND THE COUNCIL OF COMMERCE

The Council of Commerce (1700) was instrumental in repairing the relationship between the Marseille Chamber of Commerce and royal representatives. Several negative developments, however, preceded its founding. Wars and changing royal administrative personnel initially damaged the Marseille chamber's relations with Versailles. Pressured to fund its skyrocketing war expenditures, Versailles revoked the tax-exempt status that Colbert had granted Marseille; from 1686, it issued and raised new duties on cotton, sugar, and coffee. By century's end, Marseille was a duty-free port in name only. The imposition of new taxes strained Marseille's Levantine trade and its relationship with other French cities. Foreign traders diverted their business to other cities in France, Holland, Italy, and England, endangering Marseille's monopoly. While this benefited other French cities, it generated tension among them as they sought to discontinue Marseille's duty-free status permanently and achieve duty-free status for themselves.

Amid these developments, Colbert posthumously became a champion for Marseille's freedom of trade. Marseille's Chamber of Commerce appealed to the Crown to reinstate the edict of 1669, nudging royal delegates with gifts. The royal intendant Thomas Morant became a favorite of the chamber, which paid him 6,000 *livres* annually to serve as inspector of Marseille's Levantine commerce. The chamber also offered gifts to Controller-General Pontchartrain.[89] Royal agents at Versailles proved inconsistent patrons, however. Initially, Colbert's son Jean-Baptiste-Antoine Colbert, the marquis de Seignelay, secretary of the navy, and Jean-Baptiste de Lagny, director-general of commerce, urged Pontchartrain to "defend the cause since . . . the interest of Marseille is united to that of the state."[90] Lagny's support floundered, however. For reasons that remain mysterious, he supported French cities whose administrators wished to discontinue Marseille's monopoly. Lagny resurrected Colbert's vilification of Marseillais merchants' self-interested behavior: "It seems to the inhabitants that the freedom of the port gives them permission to do anything to the detriment of the state," he charged; "few want to reduce this freedom within limits fitting the *bien public.*" The Marseillais screamed for liberty, he continued, but did not govern themselves in "the spirit that had prompted the king to privilege them," ruining their own trade, expending financial resources, and "introducing goods whose sale is ruinous to the public."[91]

Marseille's Chamber of Commerce faced a tough challenge: to get the edict of 1669 reinstated, it had to convince Versailles and representatives of other French cities that what was good for Marseille was good for the country as a whole. It had to prove that Marseille's merchants were motivated not by self-interest but by the desire to benefit France.

The opportunity to make such claims materialized when Pontchartrain and Daguesseau created the Council of Commerce on 29 June 1700,[92] stating that "protecting the commerce of [Louis XIV's] subjects inside and outside of the kingdom," was "most important for the good of the state."[93] The council included six royal officers (*commissaires*), and thirteen merchant deputies—*négociants* elected by municipal officers—from leading French cities.[94] Because Marseille had a Chamber of Commerce, it elected its deputy to Paris. The Council of Commerce was responsible for advising the controller-general on French domestic and international commerce. The ministers of state forwarded petitions regarding commerce received from intendants and manufacturers. The *commissaires* reviewed the dossiers; the deputies convened at the home of Henri Daguesseau to deliberate the council's decisions.

Marseille's Chamber of Commerce asked the council to restore two privileges: Marseille's free-port status, and its monopoly in the Levantine trade. Meanwhile, it nominated Joseph Fabre (1634–1717), son of the Marseille *négociant* Jourdan Fabre, as its delegate to the council.[95] Joseph Fabre had served as consul, was a banker, manufacturer, diplomatic agent to the prince of Savoy, naval treasurer in Marseille, director of the Compagnie de la Méditerranée, and director of French consulates in the Mediterranean.[96] He was favored by the current controller-general, Chamillart.[97] The sixty-six-year-old Fabre arrived at the capital in January 1701 and presented himself at Versailles, his valet and horses wearing the colors of Marseille and his carriage blazoned with the city's coat of arms. He communicated to Marseille's Chamber of Commerce that "diverse deputies have made propositions that are not suitable to our commerce," and promised to fight them "for the good of the *patrie* and satisfaction of our commerce."[98]

Thomas Schaeper has applauded Joseph Fabre for leading "the most successful and resourceful lobbying campaigns in early modern French history."[99] Dis-

1700
29 Juin

ARREST
DU CONSEIL D'ESTAT DU ROY,
PORTANT ESTABLISSEMENT D'UN CONSEIL DE COMMERCE.

Du 29. Juin 1700.

Extrait des Regiſtres du Conſeil d'Etat.

LE ROY ayant connu dans tous les temps de quelle importance il eſtoit au bien de l'Etat, de favoriſer & de proteger le Commerce de ſes Sujets, tant au dedans qu'au dehors du Royaume, Sa Majeſté auroit à diverſes fois donné pluſieurs Edits, Ordonnances, Declarations & Arreſts, & fait pluſieurs Reglemens utiles ſur cette matieres. Mais les Guerres qui ſont ſurvenuës, & la multitude de ſoins indiſpenſables dont Sa Majeſté a eſté occupée juſqu'à la concluſion de la derniere Paix, ne luy ayant pas

Founding *arrêt* for the Council of Commerce, 1700. *Courtesy Chambre de Commerce et d'Industrie Marseille-Provence.*

mantling the claims of deputies who wished to reduce Marseille's commercial privileges, and rendering fruitless their alliances with councilors of state and farmers-general, Fabre persuaded the Crown to issue the *arrêt* of 1703 that reaffirmed his city's privileges. He accomplished this by maneuvering between two identities. First, by portraying himself and the other delegates of the council as vital components of centralized power, Fabre claimed, in effect, to be part of the royal government. The council was more collaborative in nature than similar institutions founded by Colbert; the delegates were advisors to the controller-general rather than mere administrative subordinates. Mastering this function, Fabre insisted on the role of the delegates as impartial protectors of France's commercial interests: "[We must] know the commerce of each province, their problems, their remedies, and [we must] protect them. And we must not change or measure the practice of one province against the other."[100] He downplayed his local ties and stressed that he was interested in the universal welfare of French commerce. Inclusion in the council gave him, as a local representative, an opportunity to buy explicitly into the king's rhetoric of the public good. Fabre maintained that the delegates to the Council of Commerce served as the eyes the Crown, which alone could discern the *bien public*.

At the same time, however, Fabre was a representative of Marseille's Chamber of Commerce. He studied its 445-page memo that requested the following: the suppression of bureaus established in Marseille by tax farmers; the transfer of these bureaus to locations outside the city, at the "entry to the kingdom"; freedom of transit—toll-free passage—for merchants carrying goods from Marseille to Geneva; restriction of direct Levantine trade to Marseille.[101] Fabre justified these requests to the council by mobilizing a civic idiom. Marseille's merchants, he insisted, exhibited the best model of citizenship, harmonizing their personal interests with the public well-being of France. Marseillais commerce was an invaluable asset to the kingdom: its fair prices encouraged trading, its bread and oil market fed the kingdom, and its duty-free market encouraged consumption.[102] Fabre produced calculations to dispel the argument that Marseillais merchants' custom of paying foreign manufacturers with gold and silver (the *écu d'or* or the *pistolle d'Espagne*) depleted France's funds. He maintained that such money was used to buy bread and oil from the Levant, "indispensable necessities for the kingdom."[103] Marseillais merchants provided the state with money, food, and service. They were not merely self-interested.

Meanwhile, Fabre highlighted the moral bankruptcy of delegates and merchants from cities other than Marseille, accusing tax farmers, contraband dealers, and deputies from other regions of placing their own interests over France's general good. Fabre's primary adversaries were tax farmers who infringed on Colbert's edict by setting up *entrepôts* in Marseille to collect duties on coffee, tobacco, and sugar. Fabre's Paris lawyer and secret agents provided evidence to show that these tax farmers encouraged contraband trading that benefited foreign markets.[104] Sellers wanting to evade taxes used illegal means to smuggle goods out of the city, while buyers turned to foreign markets rather than pay taxes. Contraband smuggled in from quarantined ships in Marseille amplified the risk of contagious disease. Vilifying tax farmers and contraband dealers for making "the public suffer for their particular interests,"[105] Fabre insisted that such self-interested acts of "disorderly" conduct and "tyranny" be punished for the "good of the state."[106]

Fabre also disparaged the deputies who wished to discontinue Marseille's monopoly in the Levant trade. These deputies, who understood *liberté du commerce* as opening duty-free Levantine trade to all French ports, maintained that prices for Levantine goods in Marseille were 33 percent higher than prices in English and Dutch markets; they called for the suspension of the 20 percent duty on Levantine goods acquired from ports other than Marseille.[107] Against those who maintained that "[we] are not assembled here for Marseille alone, but rather to consider the general good of the state,"[108] Fabre responded that such men craved a "good market for their own merchandise, advantageous for their own manufacturers."[109] Fabre argued that universal direct trade with the Levant would lead to an oversupply of Levantine goods and generate large trade deficits.[110] Deputies who wished to enhance profits in particular cities at the expense of general freedom of trade were "devils" and "imposters," he fulminated.[111]

Both Fabre and his adversaries climbed a slippery slope. Wearing their royalist hats, the deputies maintained that they were there to protect "the general state of commerce"[112] and to help the Crown impartially regulate French trade. They concurred that strengthening French commerce required the *liberté du commerce, liberté générale,* and *entière liberté* of the market. Each deputy, however, understood "liberty" to mean the maintenance of local privileges, often at the expense of other municipalities.[113] Fabre expressed his commitment to restoring Marseille's free-port privilege by arguing against universal laws. Against motions for uniformity, Fabre called for the preservation of particular privileges: "we shall fail if we want to render all the provinces uniform. The difference of situations creates differences in commerce."[114] Fabre argued for "general interest" and "universal liberties," but he did not want general laws. The Crown had established the Council of Commerce to cut through the labyrinth of privileges and to introduce universal laws to govern French commerce. The council's deputies, however, did not wish to see that happen.

The difficulty for the deputies lay in the fact that they could not argue for their privileges as privileges. Each utterance on behalf of privileges placed the speaker at risk of being implicated for harboring self-interest. Fabre described this challenge to Marseille's Chamber of Commerce, explaining that arguments for privileges—by definition particular laws for corporate bodies—had to be couched in terms of the "general interest of the state." "I have some difficulty regarding things that pertain . . . to policy and the general interest of the state," Fabre wrote. "I must not ask for things contrary to politics or to the interests of the state that the king, the minister, and the council will never grant."[115] One consistent argument worked in his favor: what happened to be good for his city was good also for France: "the kingdom's most useful commercial establishment is the free port [of Marseille.]"[116] Fabre used the utility of Marseille's free port to negate the fact that it was a privilege; defending Marseille's free-port privilege against encroachments from privileged trading companies, his brother, Matthieu Fabre, went so far as to maintain that "all privileges are contrary to the public good . . . the liberty of the port [of Marseille] is opposed to all exclusive privileges; it is necessary to leave a free port entirely free."[117]

The strategy of arguing for a privilege by denying privileges, combined with massive amounts of gift-giving, produced results for Fabre and Marseille.[118] The Crown reinstated Colbert's edict of 1669 on 10 July 1703.[119] The *arrêt* redesignated Marseille as a completely free port; no other French port could receive goods directly from the Levant. It reimposed the 20 percent duty on Levantine goods purchased outside of Marseille. It ordered tax farmers out of the city's limits; all duties imposed on coffee, sugars, and tobacco were withdrawn. It reestablished free transit to Geneva.

Fabre's victory came at a price, however. Marseille's Chamber of Commerce complained that royal officers in Paris and Versailles had influenced him for the worse; he was now too invested in "the general interest" and the "public good." These men, the chamber insisted, made Fabre "too republican."[120]

What does this comment suggest? Fabre had become, in a sense, bilingual. He mastered the royal rhetoric of the public good to legitimate himself as an impartial deputy to the council, while mobilizing the civic idiom of public good to legitimate Marseillais commerce. His depiction of himself as part of a monarchical institution that would regulate the commercial interests of French subjects was rooted in the absolutist ideology of the sovereign gaze; his characterizations of Marseillais merchants as citizens harmonizing their private interests for the public, and his vilification of his enemies as morally decrepit abusers of the public, were founded on civic conceptions of the body politic. Both traditions, royal and civic, posited a tension between public and private interest. Both valorized individuals—in the first case, the king; in the latter, the citizen—who channeled private interests in service of the public. The chamber failed to distinguish when Fabre slipped between his use of absolutist and civic idioms.

More important, this confusion suggests that new opportunities for participation in discerning the public good had emerged since the discussions among Colbert, Arnoul, and Marseille's merchant elite in 1660. Arnoul and Colbert distrusted the Marseillais' administrators and merchants' aptitude for recognizing their own interests, let alone those of the state; as Henry Clark has shown, Louis XIV "operated on a radical distrust of the ability of ordinary people to understand their own interest [while] counter[ing] this deformity with a supreme confidence in the sovereign's ability to discern and understand all the interest of all his people."[121] Clouds of mistrust of merchants still hovered over the Council of Commerce, but its discussions reveal a very different dynamic. Local delegates and royal counselors fluctuated between their uses of the traditional concepts of royal authority and civic spirit and the more modern idiom of utility. This utilitarian argument was a powerful tool for local and royal proponents of commercial expansion; as historians have shown, "a traditional conception of commerce as a public hazard that had to be carefully regulated increasingly . . . gave way to a modern conception of commerce as free private exchange naturally redounding to the social good."[122] At the turn of the eighteenth century, the Council of Commerce still subscribed to the idea that merchants were a threat to the state. It deemed government regulation crucial for commercial and political stability; its deputies, meanwhile, accused one another of self-interestedness. Its members also, however, began using utilitarian arguments to valorize cities, subjects, and merchants useful to French commerce.

These new ideas that defended commerce and merchants as useful to the state could be bridged with absolutist and civic traditions. Merged with absolutist language, it held that through regulated commerce, the Crown would create social conditions whereby merchants' personal gains generated wealth for the royal coffer. Combined with local idioms of civic excellence, this utilitarian argument formed the basis of the emergent commercial civic spirit. Advocates of commercial civic spirit viewed commerce contributing to the public good because participation in commercial activity allowed merchants to duplicate and practice the kind of virtues that citizens cultivated in the political *res publica*: "commerce was a synecdoche for 'the public sphere.'"[123] Such arguments presented an alternative to the traditional concept of the merchant as a morally suspect, self-interested threat to republics and kingdoms. From this perspective, commerce stabilized society.

CHAPTER TWO

Between Republic and Monarchy

Debating Commerce and Virtue

From Colbert's tenure as controller-general through the convocation of the Council of Commerce, methods for overseeing Marseillais merchants drew on the notion that they required royal guidance. Underlying this idea was the assumption that commerce was potentially beneficial to state and society but involved dangers: fluctuations in the market, physical and political threats associated with Ottoman trade, and the merchants' alleged proclivity for favoring their own interests over the general good.

Discussions over policies, however, also undermined the traditional view of the corruptible merchant and fostered a new notion of merchant civic excellence. This chapter explores, in three parts, this reconciliation of exemplary civic spirit with mercantile activity. First, it demonstrates how supporters of commerce revised definitions of republican virtue and noble honor, blurring the distinctions between the two. It analyzes how royal policy makers like Jacques Savary and ecclesiastics such as André de Colonie argued that *négociants* practiced the virtues requisite of a citizen in the *res publica*. They equated merchants with citizens, the market with the public, and trading with civic participation. Expressed in a language that focused on political virtue, participation in public affairs, and citizens' alignment of personal interests with the public good, this understanding of the merchant-citizen rehabilitated classical republican idioms.

The positive spin on *négociants* linked virtue with another characteristic not part of the classical republican tradition, honor. Associated with the nobility, the concept of honor became central to the reworked assessment of elite merchants. This conflation of honor with virtue mirrored two social changes in France.

First, social differences between *négociants* and retail merchants became entrenched over the late seventeenth and eighteenth centuries, splitting merchant society into two tiers. As *négociants* emerged as "an aristocracy of commerce,"[1] attributes of honor traditionally used to characterize the second estate were incorporated into positive evaluations of the elite merchant. Second, the social upgrading of the *négociant* occurred simultaneously with the "downgrading" of certain members of the nobility, who began participating in commercial opportunities traditionally closed off to the second estate.[2] Due to this participation, the lines between *négociants* and nobility were increasingly obscured and the nobles' concept of honor began to be applied to them.

The valorization of the *négociant* thus resulted from the adaptation of both the classical republican vocabulary of virtue and the language of noble honor to a new commercial aristocracy. These old languages could also be mobilized to support emerging concepts of universality and inclusion. Ideally, any meritorious citizen might rise to the status of a *négociant,* viewed as the model citizen in a commercial *res publica.* This emphasis on merit and virtue as the determinants for inclusion into the market undermined traditional concepts of privilege and blurred social hierarchies. As shown by Amalia Kessler, the concept of honor, once reserved for nobles privileged by birth, was increasingly applied to *négociants,* who demonstrated their honor not by lineage but by participation in commerce and their utility to the state.

The Crown itself strengthened such concepts of universality and inclusivity through new methods it devised to oversee *négociants.* By the 1670s, the Crown began departing from its practice of issuing particular laws for different *corps,* guilds, and merchant institutions. As demonstrated in Colbert's *Code marchand,* or Commercial Ordinance (1673), and Jacques Savary's *Le parfait négociant* (1675), the monarchy generated reforms that applied to merchant institutions and individuals regardless of affiliation, background, or trade. Introducing universalist laws to govern commerce, the *Code marchand* and supporting publications underscored the new understanding that *le négoce* was an activity open to a wide range of meritorious citizens and subjects.

How did Marseille's nobility respond to these new perceptions of *négociants* and to the central place that they occupied in civic administration and leadership following the conquest of the city by the French Crown in 1660? The second part of this chapter argues that the Provençal nobility of the robe supported Marseille's commercial expansion. Having bought into the nobility after accumulating wealth through mercantile activity, these new-blood aristocrats were socially positioned closer to *négociants* than to the nobility of the sword, who resisted social mobility and participation in commerce. Antiquarians who belonged to the robe nobility vocalized their enthusiasm for "new Marseille" by publishing local histories that credited the monarchy with resurrecting the aristocratic republic of Massilia, classical Marseille. Mobilizing what I term a new kind of "republican historicism," they rehabilitated the notion of the republic's cyclical historical trajectory—its perfect founding, the corruption of its mores, and its regeneration—but adapted this narrative to commercial expansion and royal intervention. These writers, however, also used their histories to temper their acceptance of royal centralization with local particularism and Marseillais patriotism. Their narratives of the founding, decline, and resurrection of Massilia disrupted the story of French centralization; they maintained that despite the city's colonization by Colbertist regulations and French administration, Marseille was fundamentally Greek. Like the merchants who constituted Marseille's *échevinage* and Chamber of Commerce, these historians from the robe nobility were accommodators of, not collaborators with, the Crown.

The last segment of this chapter discusses how the Provençal robe nobility's support of commerce differed dramatically from the "republican historicism" fostered among the French sword nobility. Most famously in the northern Burgundian circle, sword nobles reiterated their exclusive claims to aristocratic honor and civic virtue. The classical republican tradition allowed them to articulate their criticism of absolutism and to resist social mobility and royally driven commerce. Reclaiming noble honor as uniquely characteristic of the second estate, writers like François Fenélon, Henri de Boulainvilliers, and Jean du Pradel argued that only the old nobility could restore to France the virtue destroyed by self-interested rulers, administrators, and merchants. Patriotism, virtue, and honor, they contended, were cultivated only in a society that rejected commerce and royal aggrandizement.

What we find, then, are several contrary developments. By encouraging people across estates to participate in commerce, and by extending universal laws to these participants, the Crown nurtured positive ways of thinking about commerce and merchants. While this process undercut traditional hierarchies, it introduced new forms of social stratification within estates. *Négociants* emerged as elites distinct from retail merchants; meanwhile, the gulf separating the sword and robe nobilities became fixed. These divisions were not solely based on wealth. Particularly among the nobility, their understanding of commerce, their political assessment of monarchical aggrandizement, their historical visions, and their very definitions of virtue, honor, and utility diverged in profound ways. Moreover, while royal administrators and those who participated in commerce disengaged from long-standing negative portrayals of commerce and merchants, new political and religious arguments against commerce gained force across France. Particularly among the sword nobility, these criticisms became discursive weapons to discredit and disrupt royal aggrandizement and, simultaneously, the demographic mobility that the Crown, in part, supported.

SELLING COMMERCE: THE DEVELOPMENT OF COMMERCIAL CIVIC SPIRIT

Historians have used the term "commercial humanism" to describe the ideology adopted by some supporters of mercantilist expansion under Louis XIV and Jean-Baptiste Colbert. Commercial humanism, these argue, developed through two combined processes: the disruption of the Christian philosophy that denigrated the pursuit of worldly goods as sinful, and the adaptation of the secular, civic concept of the general good to a defense of commerce. Writers argued that merchants were citizens dedicated to the public good; merchants practiced the virtues of the *vita activa* requisite of a citizen in a republic. In short, "the commercial inflection of the humanist movement could view commerce as itself an adequate paradigm for the public sphere."[3] Henry Clark argues that this commercial ideology appeared in the 1500s. His argument builds on studies of how the vocabulary of virtue that developed in Italian city-states during the Renaissance continued to shape debates on the commercial state. Combining J. G. A. Pocock's analysis of political virtue with Jürgen Habermas's study of the public sphere, he points to humanist-inspired defenses of commerce in late sixteenth-century France.[4]

This study accepts Clark's assumption that parts of this commercial ideology as it appeared in Old Regime France picked up on classical republican vocabulary. It did not, however, derive solely from the classical republican tradition. This ideology came together in tandem with state-sponsored reforms in mercantilist activity, and through demographic transformations among the aristocracy and merchant communities. Moreover, I shy away from characterizing it as humanistic. Like the Italian humanists, seventeenth- and eighteenth-century Frenchmen looked to classical antiquity for intellectual, political, and moral exemplars. They celebrated elite merchants' commitment to the public good and extolled their service to the state. Unlike Italian humanists, however, these French supporters of commerce were not motivated by a desire to disengage from Catholic scholasticism or to win the support of secular rulers who patronized the arts and sciences in pursuit of a *vita activa*.

I therefore use the term "commercial civic spirit" to discuss favorable views of merchant public engagement expressed through the combined use of the classical republican idiom of virtue, the noble language of honor, and the new statist vocabulary of utility. This commercial civic spirit materialized in several contexts: at state and local levels, in religious discussions, and among the robe nobility. State officials and local apologists justified commercial expansion, hailing the market as a hotbed of civic and moral virtues and encouraging merchants to participate in the Levant trade.

At the state level, new legal codes intended to monitor the market energized this commercial civic spirit. Most important in this regard was Colbert's *Code marchand,* created to "suppress . . . the abuses committed in trade."[5] Universal laws that were applicable to all merchants were a novelty in France. Traditionally, each corporate body or guild had its own privileges, distinct from those of others, but this system was inconsistent with a regime that progressively allowed nobles to make foreign investments and *négociants* to be wholesale traders without belonging to a mercantile guild.

Two years after the appearance of the *Code marchand,* its main contributor, Jacques Savary, published the authoritative textbook on commerce for aspiring *négociants, Le parfait négociant, ou Instruction générale pour ce qui regarde le commerce des marchandises de France et des pays étrangers.* Born in Anjou on 22 September 1622 into the robe nobility, Savary arrived in Paris and cultivated relationships with his uncle Guillaume Savary, "who had made a great fortune in trade," and his cousin Jean Savary, *secrétaire du Roi.*[6] With such connections, Jacques Savary rose to be a *procureur au parlement* and then *notaire au Châtelet.* By the time he married Catherine Thomas, daughter of one of Paris's wealthiest *négociants,* Savary himself was a successful *négociant.* He quit the profession at age thirty-six, and between fathering seventeen children and serving as primary advisor for the *Code marchand,* he penned *Le parfait négociant.*

Savary made two arguments in the opening chapter of his book. God willed commerce; commerce was useful to king, state, and individuals. God "dispersed his gifts so that men could trade together, and that their mutual need to help one another would sustain friendship among them." Savary praised Louis XIV for strengthening his state through commercial reform: "[The king] has accorded great privileges to *négociants* and, to bring to an end the disorders and abuses committed in trade, he made a rule that seeks more than ever to establish good faith, prevent fraudulent transactions, and lead more subjects to engage in commerce."[7] Encouraged from on high, monitored by the king, commerce benefited France and its subjects.

The *Parfait négociant* followed in the spirit of the *Code marchand*. Ignoring legal distinctions among merchant *corps*, Savary addressed a general population of merchants who "wanted to instruct themselves and to embrace the mercantile profession." He intended his text as a guidebook for all potential merchants, regardless of birth, fortune, *corps*, or guild. Savary's trader "cut across the corporate and geographic barriers that had long divided merchant entities," Amalia Kessler observes; he "engaged in no particular type of commerce, residing in no particular community."[8]

Savary began by addressing the parents of the future merchant, guiding them through the steps necessary to mold a commercially minded adult. He then addressed the child, explaining how to enrich himself and his country:

> I take a child leaving his father and mother and begin to instruct him in his apprenticeship, then I lead him through retail sale of merchandise, wholesale, currency exchange, manufacture, and fairs; I lead him through foreign countries and distant places, and in so doing, I make him see all the maxims he must observe, the things he must avoid, and I make him learn . . . all that concerns whatever sort of commerce or trade that might be, directly or indirectly, down to the most particular circumstances, including the application of the royal ordinances, and above all the ordinance of March 1673, so that he can conduct himself happily in this profession that is so *useful* and so *honorable* [emphasis added].[9]

Savary's merchant-child required two features, an imaginative mind and a strong body, neither of which the author attributed to a particular class or rank. The child required a "natural disposition" for "the arts, manufacture, and negotiation." The perfect trader also needed "a strong and robust" frame to withstand the hardships associated with travel. Savary urged parents of such children to "encourage the desire for this profession, more by reason than by paternal authority or threats."[10] Once this child reached the age of eight, he would undergo technical training and moral disciplining. Studies in mathematics, bookkeeping, the Italian, Spanish, German, and French languages and foreign history, travel, and commerce would prepare him for the cosmopolitan life of a *négociant*. At fifteen, he would begin apprenticeship. Further schooling in Latin, grammar, rhetoric, and philosophy, Savary explained, was "useless" and "harmful." Aristocratic *collèges*, he argued, only created libertines. Savary, therefore, encouraged apprenticeship that developed the virtues of fidelity, obedience, and camaraderie. "The happiness of *négociants* proceeds from their perfect knowledge of commerce," he wrote, "from the great experiences they acquire in serving under other merchants" and by observing "good order . . . in their books," "prudence," "vigilance," "thrift and economy," "strength and courage." The merchant-child required technical training, but above all, he needed virtue.

Savary devoted the remainder of his volume to facts useful in all areas of commerce. He elaborated on different systems of measurements used in France and abroad and currency exchange rates. He suggested methods for receiving assistants, keeping books, selling merchandise, and formulating inventories. He provided examples of fraudulent transactions, including royal *arrêts* against merchants who contracted them. The second section of the manual focused on foreign commerce, with individual chapters on each specific country, its history, geography, trading regulations, and customs.

Savary's guidebook, like the ordinance he helped create, addressed all French merchants and *négociants* as a unified audience. Savary's *parfait négociant* was "perfect," not because of his corporate affiliation or inherited rank, but because of his innate qualities and general virtues, potentially possessed by all.

COMMERCE AND CIVIC VIRTUE: A RELIGIOUS ARGUMENT ON BEHALF OF THE MARKET

While the Crown invented general laws for French merchants and depicted *le négoce* as an honorable and useful undertaking, local apologists argued on behalf of commerce and merchants, insisting that the market stabilized society by fostering virtue. Commerce strengthened social links; it was a useful activity for exemplary citizens. Such was the argument in the ecclesiastic André de Colonie's *Eclaircissement sur le légitime commerce des intérêts.* A treatise that defended commerce on theological and moral grounds, this was one of the most popular texts on the subject and was repeatedly reprinted in the late seventeenth century (1675, 1677, 1682).

De Colonie opened his *Eclaircissement* with endorsements from Parisian and Marseillais professors of theology who maintained that the author's contentions "conformed to the Catholic faith . . . and promoted spiritual health." Furthermore, he quoted Pope Innocent III's "moral assurance" that commerce benefited society, understood as the unity of human wills.

The book—a compilation of maxims—demonstrated that commerce was not only "useful and universal" but also "contrary to neither natural law nor divine law." It taught that "commerce is essential to human life, and society is as natural to man as is reason." De Colonie argued that merchants who worked for the betterment of society were virtuous citizens. God, he recounted, had given each individual his allotted portion; it followed that "the right to dispose of one's portion . . . by handing [it] over to society, in changing, selling, or giving" was "a law of nature and nations," and "a civic virtue."

Legal contracts, de Colonie explained, guaranteed virtue in commerce. Contracts bound together vendors and buyers, who were thus "embraced by a common will." The signing of contracts was an "act of prudence and justice; . . . it could only be necessary to life, because it was an act of virtue." The merchant simultaneously advanced his own welfare and contributed to the well-being of his fellow traders. Far from isolating the trader in a vacuum of self-interest, commerce integrated him into society and ensured his utility to others. Understood in this manner, commerce was the building block of society. Commercial links formed society; the more links, the more virtuous the society.[11]

De Colonie's defense of commerce based on social utility and moral unity places him as a precursor of more radical eighteenth-century proponents of commercial society such as the abbé Gabriel-François Coyer. De Colonie was far from revolutionary; he dared not think of supporting commerce that did not conform to divine law. He simply showed how social and religious virtues converged. For him, the market fostered the active life idealized by both religious and civic republican authors; virtue and commercial interest did not operate in diametric opposition.

THE *NÉGOCIANT*: SOME DEFINITIONS

Who, exactly, was the *négociant* whom Savary and de Colonie described as a virtuous and honorable contributor to society? He was "a new breed of commercial player" dedicated to international business, banking, and wholesaling.[12] Unlike merchants committed to the local retail trade, the *négociant* did not strictly belong to a mercantile *corps*. In 1698, the intendant of Provence estimated that "the number of 'merchants of consideration' in Marseille was around two hundred."[13] By 1710, it exceeded three hundred, and by the mid eighteenth century, the city's merchant elite numbered close to a thousand.[14] These numbers point to a contradiction. Although authors like Savary argued that any man, regardless of social hierarchy, could become one, *négociants* became members of a privileged elite, distinct from retailers. While the *négociants'* disruptions of traditional corporate limits highlighted unprecedented inclusive trends in commercial regulation and participation, the definition of the *négociant* as a wealthy wholesaler underscored monumental social inequalities developing among merchant populations. Although anyone could become a *négociant*, it took a lot of wealth to be considered one.

In his *Parfait négociant,* Savary observes that wholesale trading (*commerce en gros*) is "more honorable and extensive" than retail (*commerce en detail*).[15] The *négociant* elite, comprising the wealthiest of merchants, spread "to all the provinces of the kingdom and to foreign countries." Moreover, this class began to include nobles, whose participation in mercantile activity had traditionally been unimaginable. As wholesale and international ventures became profitable for merchants and the state alike, the Crown encouraged nobles' involvement, assuring them that it would not jeopardize their titles: "The king's edict . . . permitted nobles to partake in wholesale commerce . . . and . . . still enjoy the privileges accorded to the nobility."[16]

The *négociant* elite was thus an exclusive group composed of wealthy, socially climbing merchants and of nobles embracing mercantile activity. The involvement of the nobility had a profound effect on the concept of commerce. As early as 1646, the Breton Jean Eon infused commerce with noble values in his *Commerce honorable;*[17] Eon argued that commerce helped inculcate "virtues normally associated with the noble ethos—such as honor, loyalty, fidelity, courage, boldness, and generosity."[18] Savary echoed these arguments when he depicted *négociant* activity in noble terms. Wholesale and international commerce involved "risks" and "dangers in negotiation" and could only be managed by "the noble and honest."[19] The ideal *négociant* combined the best traits of an aristocrat and citizen; his character demonstrated nobility and his actions were motivated by virtue.

The terms *négociant* and *marchand* were used interchangeably into the eighteenth century, but during Colbert's tenure, the distinction between the two became pronounced in the world of trade. In Marseille, the uniqueness of the *négociant* emerged as early as 1660 when Louis XIV constituted the *échevinage.* Restricting the office of *premier échevin* to "men of the *Loge* [the Chamber of Commerce], bankers or *négociants,*" the monarchy contributed to the growing distinctions among the ranks of the merchant population.[20] By the late eighteenth century, the *négociant*'s elite status clearly distinguished him from retailers. *L'encyclopédie méthodique* (1782) clarified that "the term *négociant* can be compared to the *négociateur,* which [the *négociant*] can be considered [to be]: like him, he has relations, views, large interests; like him, he has to be acquainted with the spirit of nations, their laws, and their mores, and to know how to identify with their interests to his great advantage." *Négociants* were devoted to "external trade, maritime, international, colonial, and global commerce, insofar as this term can be used of the eighteenth century," Charles Carrière notes.[21] This emphasis on the *négociant*'s dedication to global business and dangerous missions reinforced the notion that elite merchants could be honorable; like the military nobility who risked their lives for the king, the *négociant* undertook hazardous tasks for the state. The first edition of the *Dictionnaire de l'Académie française* (1694) defines *négoce* as "traffic, trade in merchandise, or in money," but also specifies that an individual who participates in *négoce* is "a man who involves himself in something shameful, or dangerous." The 1762 fourth edition echoes this emphasis on danger: the *négociant* is "a man who involves himself in an affair that endangers him." While *négoce* could be seen as a shameful activity (*vilain négoce, un étrange négoce*), it could also be understood as a risky one (*bon négoce, grand négoce, dangereux négoce*) that amplified the honor of the *négociant* who braved all to benefit king and state.[22]

The relationship between danger and merchants was a complicated one in early modern French discussions of commerce. On the one hand, as we saw earlier, Colbert articulated how the dangerous environment of the Mediterranean and Levantine market threatened to hurt French commercial interests; worse, as the following chapter describes, the controller-general feared that French merchants might succumb to the moral, physical, and political sicknesses that early modern Frenchmen associated with the Ottoman Empire. If the Turkish Empire was regarded as morally perverse and corrupt, it was particularly dangerous for merchants, traditionally regarded as morally questionable, self-interested creatures. On the other hand, the language of danger and risk could be marshaled to create a rather positive assessment of *négociants*; it was precisely the hazardous environment in which they operated that provided elite merchants with opportunities to show themselves to be honorable, brave, noble, useful servants of France.

The cosmopolitan *négociant* who allegedly risked the perils of international commerce inhabited a marketplace defined not by place but by common interests. He identified himself as "closer to foreigners of his rank than the *boutiquier* of his own street." A Marseillais *négociant* described himself as "a natural inhabitant of all parts of the world where he has his goods and his correspondences."[23] Elite merchants traveled extensively in the early parts of their career, not only to ports such as Algiers, Alexandria, Istanbul, Salonika, Smyrna (Izmir), and Tunis, along "les échelles du Levant et de Barbarie," but to the inland cities of Aleppo, Cairo, and Edirne. Living in European communities—often consisting of no more than fifteen *négociants*, their assistants, doctors, and a consul—they traded with the help of go-betweens who spoke Turkish, Arabic, and European languages. Isolated from neighboring populations in their own areas to avoid the pestilential diseases that were endemic in Ottoman territory, they were governed by treaties ensuring that they "benefited from extraterritoriality."[24]

Négociants' internationalism might seem inconsistent with civic commitment to a "hometown" or fidelity to a monarch. National and civic loyalties, however, were not measured by physical presence in France; *négociants* did not have to reside exclusively in Marseille to be considered good Marseillais citizens or French subjects. Patriotism as a citizen and subject was measured by utility, not by presence or even by ethnicity. Moreover, upon returning to France, *négociants* demonstrated their civic commitment by occupying prominent administrative positions. In Marseille, *négociants* held administrative offices in the *échevinage*, the Council of Sixty, the Chamber of Commerce (comprised of *échevins* and twelve *négociants*), and the Bureau de la santé (comprised of sixteen *négociants*, of whom two were *échevins*). Understood by advocates of commercial civic spirit, *le négoce* remained a useful, honorable, and virtuous activity; and in a commercial entrepôt like Marseille, *négociants* occupied the echelons of civic governance.

MASSILIA RISING: HISTORY AND KINGS IN SERVICE OF THE COMMERCIAL REPUBLIC

How did Marseille's nobility respond to the perception that commerce and *négociants* formed the crux of Marseille's body politic? Given that the municipal regime that Louis XIV installed in 1660 excluded the possibility of noble participation in politics, it would seem that the aristocracy would view the city's commercial makeover and administrative elite with contempt. While sword nobles did utter grievances against the composition of the new civic regime in the decades following the conquest, their appeals fell on deaf ears until well into the eighteenth century.[25] Meanwhile, Marseille's robe nobility was favorable to the new regime. The overwhelming consensus among texts penned by the robe nobility following the conquest was that the Crown injected political, moral, and economic vitality into the Mediterranean port. Materializing most often in historical accounts of Marseille's ancient and recent pasts was, curiously, a narrative steeped in republican language that celebrated royal intervention, commercial expansion, and commercial civic spirit. These local histories written by Marseillais and Provençal robe nobility set the tone for a historical understanding of the events that transpired from 1660 to 1683 (corresponding to Colbert's tenure as controller-general) that later became the dominant Enlightenment reading of Marseillais history.

Nowhere is this historical narrative more clearly captured than in the Enlightenment manifesto *L'encyclopédie, ou dictionnaire raisonné des sciences, des arts et des métiers,* which included an article on Marseille. Classified under geography and listed with *Massilia,* Marseille is described as "an ancient and strong maritime city, the wealthiest, most commercial and populated in Provence, France." The encyclopedist then devoted half of the article to the history of the rise, fall, and revitalization of Massilia, a republic of Greek origin. "This city founded five centuries before Jesus Christ by the Phocaeans of Ionia was from its origins the most visited in the West," he began, "Born of the best Greeks, who dared to risk long voyages and whose ships took routes through the Adriatic gulf and the Tyrrhenian Sea, the Marseillais naturally turned to commerce." Governed as a republic, Massilia flourished, respected by the Roman Republic for its commerce, laws, virtuous citizens, and their sciences and arts. Massilia was "as urbane as though she were situated in the middle of Greece, which is why the Romans raised their children there."[26] Massilia thrived for six centuries.

Republics, however, corrupted, and Massilia fell to Julius Caesar. The Massilians "renounced their virtues and frugality, and they abandoned themselves to pleasure until their mores passed into the proverbs." Renamed Marseille, a republic was established in 1226, but the city's glory faded. It took French kings—Louis XIV and Louis XV—to raise it from its ashes. The Sun King "subjugated the Marseillais, deprived them of their rights and liberties," but revived their commerce, providing "exclusive privileges to the Levant," and installing royal galleys. Accompanying commercial expansion, intellectual and cultural vitality helped recover Marseille's classical reputation. In 1726, Louis XV authorized the rededication of Marseille's Academy of Letters. Committed to Eloquence, Poetry, History, Physics, and Mathematics, the Academy chose for its emblem a phoenix rising from the ashes, before a dazzling Bourbon sun. Massilia owed its resurrection to the French Crown.

That the conquest of 1660 signaled commercial growth is uncontestable. Why, however, did the Marseillais robe nobility and, later, encyclopedists depict this growth in terms of republican revival? What allowed them to imagine a "liberating conquest?" How did positive depictions of commerce and merchants factor into this narrative? What purpose did such a narrative serve for its aristocratic authors?

A steadily popularized narrative, the story of Massilia rising from its millennium-long sleep was developed in the late seventeenth century by local historians, mostly hailing from the robe nobility, who sought to make sense of royal interference in their city's political life. As waves of political crises shook

Marseille between the sixteenth and seventeenth centuries, local intellectuals imagined a glorious past to help their city reclaim lost status. Faced with monarchical intervention, historians invoked Massilia and spoke of the French monarch in service of the Greek city-state. They represented the conquest of Marseille in a way that obscured the city's vulnerability in face of absolutist state-building. Their republican historical revisionism stabilized the conquest of 1660 by depicting it in a manner palatable to Marseillais patriots.[27] If the perfect republic had declined through the Middle Ages, historians saw both the benevolent and brutal moments of royal involvement in civic politics as a series of attempts to resuscitate Massilia. This "prism of antiquity" allowed them to extol a conquering monarch as liberator while providing "symbolic compensation" for a defeated republic.[28] Republican historicism sustained a fantasy of liberation and allowed Marseillais elites to obscure the conquest. While the physical residue of a republic, manifest in the crumbled walls of Porte Reale demolished by Louis XIV, could be swept away, the linguistic traces of the republic could not be scrapped easily. As Reinhart Koselleck has argued, "language changes more slowly"[29] than events, and in Marseille, this deferral allowed its historians to rewrite unsavory events. By the end of the century, what had been a conquest was no more. Marseille's robe aristocracy played an integral part in this mnemonic erasure.

The French Crown reacted positively to this case of Marseillais amnesia.[30] If Marseille's aristocrats underscored their region's links to classical antiquity, French kings could use this to their advantage. The more prestigious the republic being resurrected, the more commanding the monarchical ally and liberator appeared: both king and republic emerged triumphant. Republican and imperial traditions from classical antiquity could be marshaled to strengthen local and statist claims to power, and their relationship with one another. Marseille's Greco-Roman past and its aristocratic intellectuals' "republican historicism" could support a new French empire reminiscent of classical Rome.

The French monarchy, therefore, extended its powers by building upon Marseille's long-standing commercial identity, and by exploiting the ambiguities of Marseillais republicanism. Downplaying the lost political freedoms that once signified the republic, it focused on the commerce that also formed the city's republican identity. Even while conquest brought political autonomy to an end and new projects stamped royal presence in Marseille, the Sun King did not destroy all vestiges of the old republic. De-emphasizing political rupture, highlighting economic expansion, and encouraging the myth of republican liberation, the Crown extended its control by creating a new political assembly, the *échevinage* and Council of Sixty, that it draped in metaphorical togas, and a city that it swathed in its Greek past.

By 1660, Marseille and the French monarchy were familiar with the theatrics of liberation. The Crown had repeatedly exercised its influence and military strength to reestablish order in Marseille; each time, the king emerged as the savior who rescued the city from factional divisions. Sixteenth- and seventeenth-century precedents, including Henry IV's victory over the Marseillais despot Casaulx and Louis XIII's involvement in establishing the *Règlement du sort*, made the casting of Louis XIV's conquest as liberation more convincing.

Besides repeated spectacles of political restabilization, the ambiguity of the terms *république* and *républicain* allowed Marseillais historians to imagine alliances between republics and monarchs. The first edition of the *Dictionnaire de l'Académie française* (1698) provided an assortment of contradictory definitions. *République* was "a state governed by many," such as "the Roman republic, the Athenian republic, the republics of Venice, Genoa, Holland." The term also meant "all sorts of States," synonymous with "government." *Républicain* could mean "one who lives in a Republic," "one who loves the government of Republics," and finally "one . . . who is mutinous, seditious, who has sentiments opposed to the monarchical State in which he lives."[31]

Eric Gojosso has recently charted the transformations in the definitions of the term *république* over the early modern period. In the sixteenth century, apologists for absolutism still described monarchy as a republic or spoke of the ideal marriage of republics to monarchies. Jean Bodin spoke of monarchy as the republic par excellence. Barthélémy de Chasseneuz invoked Cicero to emphasize the "mystic marriage of the king and the *république*." The latter maintained that "the prince is in the republic and the republic is in the prince . . . as the man is the head of the wife, the wife the body of the man . . . so is the prince the head of the republic and the republic his body."[32] In the seventeenth century, however, the term *état* became more closely associated with "the notion of sovereignty," while the term *république* became "confined to the definition of a political regime."[33] Religious wars and the Fronde saw the monarchy using the term *républicain* to implicate heretics and rebels; the royal chancellor d'Aguesseau accused Protestants and Jansenists of "republican radicalism," and Cardinal de Bernis asserted: "Parlements tend toward republican principles.[34] The monarchy divorced itself from the term *république*, opting for *état*.

In Marseille, however, writers kept alive the old uses of *république* and *républicain*. They invoked Marseille's ancient history to imagine the republic as an autonomous municipal body politic ruled by virtuous citizens. They also cast their city's mergers with France, under Louis XI and Louis XIV, as the beginning of marital bliss between a republic and monarchy. While the Sun King might have conquered Marseille to punish its seditious "republican" nobles, Marseillais writers insisted that their restored *république* was that same king's grateful ally.

ANTOINE AND LOUIS-ANTOINE DE RUFFI: HISTORIANS OF MARSEILLE

Who were these aristocratic seventeenth- and eighteenth-century Provençal historians of commercial Marseille, and to what notions of republicanism did they subscribe? Some were antiquarians.[35] The renowned Aixois parlementaire Nicolas-Claude Fabri de Peiresc, for example, was one of several Provençal nobles who collected Greek, Roman, and Egyptian antiques, not only to showcase wealth, but to comprehend the region's connections to the classical past.[36]

Marseille's most famous seventeenth-century historians, Antoine de Ruffi, and his son, Louis-Antoine, provide emblematic examples of how linguistic ambiguity and commercial development could be marshaled to shape a narrative of republican regeneration. Born in 1607, Antoine de Ruffi hailed from a noble family who served for generations in Marseille's administration.[37] His grandfather, Robert Ruffi (1542–1634) was secretary to Marseille's "dictator," Charles de Casaulx; his father, Pierre de Ruffi, a captain of the *corps-de-ville*, arranged the royal arrival of the duc de Guise into Marseille in 1618 and served a term as Marseille's consul. Antoine de Ruffi himself became a member of Marseille's *sénéchaussee* in 1631, helped prepare the royally patented civic constitution, the *Règlement du sort*, in 1652, and became *conseiller d'etat* in 1654. Meanwhile, he dedicated himself to a literary career: the first edition of his *Histoire de la ville de Marseille* appeared in 1642, followed in 1654 by the *Règlement du sort, contenant la forme et la manière de procéder à l'élection des officiers de la ville de Marseille.* Ruffi's *Histoire des comtes de Provence depuis 934 jusqu'en 1480*, and a biography of Gaspard de Semiane, *chevalier* of Lacoste, were published the following year. Ruffi died in 1689, having begun a second edition of his *Histoire de Marseille*, which his son Louis Antoine completed in 1696.

Both the elder and the younger Ruffi legitimated the monarchy's presence in Marseille and extended the symbolic life of their republic. The Ruffis offered stories of continuity, not political rupture. They insisted that the monarchy did not conquer, but rather resuscitated, the republic. For the elder Ruffi, the republic restored was a political one; for his son, it was commercial.

The first edition of the *Histoire de Marseille* was intended, according to the author, "to inform posterity" of Marseille's greatness.[38] It covered the city's history from its founding to "the year 1596 when [the city] was reduced in obedience to the King."[39] Ruffi began with Massilia's mythical founding by seafaring Phocaeans, following the marriage of their leader Protis to the Ligurian princess Gyptis, whose father ruled the territory. The Massilians "vanquished the Carthaginians, helped the Romans, civilized the ancient Gauls, taught good letters to Italy, and enjoyed the happiness of being the first in France to receive the Christian Religion." Massilia became a model republic, with "the most beautiful and advantageous port for navigation and commerce." The Massilians established colonies along the coast to extend their commerce: Monoikos (Monaco), Olbia (Hyères), Athenopolis (St. Tropez), Antipolis (Antibes), and Nikaia (Nice).[40]

Massilia, in Ruffi's description, was a "perfect aristocratic republic, where the small group of the most virtuous citizens commanded all the general followers." Virtue, reason, and liberty sustained the republic for six centuries. The *timouchos*, an aristocratic council of six hundred led by three presidents, rivaled the consuls of Rome. Commerce bred neither luxury nor corruption; the inhabitants remained frugal.[41] The Massilian Academy, the Athenopolis Mabiliorum, was esteemed through Greece, Rome and Italy.[42] Massilia's reputation earned the respect of the Romans, who "exempted the Massilians of all charges and subsidies, giving them first rank among the Senators in the theaters and public festivals, and made an alliance with all equal conditions." In Ruffi's imagination, the Romans, like French kings a millennium later, honored Marseille's autonomy. Expanding empires did not crush republics. They allowed them their liberties.

Fortuna, however, disrupted Massilia's perfect politics, commerce, citizens, and alliances: "All things are subject to the reversal of fortune; . . . the same tempest that ruined the Roman Republic caused the decadence of this flourishing city." Famine, plague, and Caesar laid siege to the city. Marseillais leaders and citizens tried to recover the city's ancient reputation. Local elites invoked the city's Greek and Roman heritage to reestablish a republic. Before submitting to the counts of Provence in the Middle Ages, they formed the Podestat, a government modeled on Italian republics.[43] Marseille's consuls, so-named in the Roman tradition, continued wearing the ermine, symbol of their republican heritage. Nonetheless, Marseille fell prey to its megalomaniacal tyrants.

Marseille finally recovered when republican freedom fighters allied with the French monarchy, Ruffi recounted. In one famous alliance, Henry IV forged a pact with the Marseillais patriot Pierre de Libertat, a captain of Porte Réale and "a brave and solid Citizen of great probity,"[44] to topple the Marseillais dictator,

Casaulx. While the duc de Guise and his army arrived in Provence in February 1596, Libertat lured Casaulx to Porte Réale and assassinated him to secure the "Liberty of the Patrie." The duc de Guise, meanwhile, "entered Marseille through Porte Réale, where he found Libertat who took the oath for the conservation of the Privileges of Marseille." When Guise marched through Marseille "with Libertat at his side, the people who accompanied them [wept] tears of joy, crying *Vive le Roi, Monsieur de Guise, vive Libertat.*" Marseillais patriots and French king together restored the republic.

Written two decades before Louis XIV's conquest, Ruffi's text introduced two themes that would resurface after 1660. First, the falling republic: virtuous republics fell prey to contingency, and attempts at restoring ancient perfection brought further turmoil and tyranny. Second, monarchical intervention: the king restored liberty to Marseille. Extending the life of the republic by having monarchy resuscitate it, Ruffi proved a son of Marseille; it was not so much the liberator he focused on as the liberated. Glorifying the monarch was a means to restore and glorify Marseille. With Henry IV's and Libertat's victory, the story of decline came full circle, back to the free republic.

This theme of republican resurrection reemerged in Ruffi's *Le Règlement du sort, contenant la forme et la manière de procéder à l'élection des officiers de la ville de Marseille* (1654). Ruffi wrote this text having witnessed monarchical involvement in Marseillais politics. As in 1596, the king appeared, though without force, to heal a fractured community by patenting a new constitution, the *Règlement du sort* (1652). This new order instituted the casting of lots for municipal offices to quell the divisions splintering Marseillais politics. When the king ordered this rule that hearkened back to ancient traditions, Ruffi saw monarchy allied with republic. His own personal gains must have contributed to his growing monarchist leanings. In 1654, he was rewarded for his participation in crafting the *Règlement du sort*; he was appointed *conseiller d'etat*.

In his preface, Ruffi described the electoral process in the Venetian republic, then ruled by the Doge, a *consiglio grande*, a *consiglio de' pregati*, and a *collegio*. Ruffi lauded the Venetian aristocratic republic and its system of election by lot. Venetian magistrates, Ruffi explained, were chosen "by fate" and "by the large concurrence of citizens." Ruffi saw the Marseille *Règlement* as an imitation of Venetian republicanism: "We have borrowed the wisdom of the Venetians in our recent *Règlement du sort*."[45] Through it, "the Inhabitants of this flourishing City have entirely sacrificed their passions and their interests." Marseille was no longer a "true republic," but casting lots allowed the citizens to sacrifice personal interests for the common good.[46]

Following his Preface, Ruffi included municipal deliberations leading to the institution of the *Règlement du sort* and the king's letters patent. The municipal deliberations fostered reconciliation "by forgetting things past."[47] Exhausted by factionalism, the consuls convoked a general assembly that voted unanimously to reinstitute election by lot, "as was practiced in ancient times in this city."[48] The *Règlement*, Ruffi described, created a government modeled on the ancient republic: united, virtuous, and free. Meanwhile, the king's letters patent told a different story. Unlike the municipal deliberations that underscored Marseille's glorious past, the royal letters patent invoked the past to demonstrate Marseille's dependence on the throne: "the subjects of our city of Marseille, who have been several times divided, but who have always rested in obedience to us, unite in agreement." This, the king recalled, evoked similar "disorders and confusions that appeared in our city in the year 1585," when Henry III "diverted the dangers of cabals and emotions" by ordering the city's consuls to create a new constitution. Marseillais citizens, the royal letters patent made clear, tended toward "usurpations" and "frauds"; only "the certain science and plain power of Royal authority" could restore fractured municipalities.

Despite divergent historical perceptions and narratives, the Crown and municipality pieced together a new civic constitution to bolster their respective powers. Municipal elites and the king established what appeared to be a mix between a democratic and aristocratic republic. The *Règlement* instituted "a perpetual council of three hundred men."[49] Lots determined the selection of its members. The council was open to all citizens who were Catholic, "native and original citizens or married to a daughter of the city," aged at least thirty.[50] Selection by lot and alphabetical roll calls underscored political equality.[51] Nonetheless, the *Règlement* also instituted aristocratic elements. The offices of *viguier*, consul, captain of the Corps de ville, and the captain of the artillery were restricted to gentlemen who met financial requirements. Lots chose all three consuls from among aristocrats possessing 30,000, 20,000 and 10,000 *livres*.[52] The captain of the Corps de ville, the city's magistrates, secretaries, and treasurers were not chosen by lot; five approvers chose from a pool of men nominated by a committee. Finally, the consuls nominated nine "gentlemen possessing fiefs, original inhabitants of the Province," selected by lot, for the position of *viguier*.[53]

Ruffi concluded by listing French kings and local patriots who had reestablished Marseille's autonomy throughout the city's history. Claiming that royal statutes "contributed to the lives of [Marseille's] principal citizens, the advantages for the King, and to the glory of France," Ruffi imagined royal power restoring citizenship and liberty to Marseille. Both Marseillais and monarchist, Ruffi provided a history of the *Règlement* that accommodated ancient republican glory, decay and revival, and monarchical heroism. The monarchy resuscitated republican liberty; this message, he reminded, was etched on Marseille's gates, in "the remarkable inscription under the Porte Royale, under the statue of the king: SUB CVIUS IMPERIO SUMMA LIBERTAS."[54]

The younger Ruffi's *Histoire de Marseille* (1696) told a similar story of republican revival. While his father's edition was a story of the virtuous political republic, this second edition paid homage to Marseille as a commercial republic. The younger Ruffi, moreover, proved more royalist than his father. Published after Louis XIV's conquest, this edition began with a letter from the *échevins* to the Crown that began, "Dear Sire, the *History of Marseille* composed by one of our most dignified citizens, can only be dedicated to its August Master, and by those whom Your Majesty has agreed to be its magistrates." They described a "heroic representation of Your Sacred Person" in their Hôtel de Ville, where "the figure of the City of Marseille prostrates at Your feet to render homage." An illustration of the aldermen on bended knee before the monarch accompanied the letter. Local patriotism, however, tempered deference. The *échevins* described, "this most glorious city that has submitted to your laws, has been the sister of Rome, and has partaken with her all the respects of the universe."[55]

Descriptions of commercial and royal grandeur filled the pages of the book from beginning to end. "This port that Mela named Halycidon . . . was the most secure of the Mediterranean Sea: the premier port of the world," Ruffi began; he then compared this ancient hub to his contemporary Marseille, where "forty-two well-equipped galleys attest to the glory and magnificence of our invincible monarch LOUIS LE GRAND."[56] He described the urban expansion projects along the port, quays, and citadels.

The younger Ruffi used commerce as the signifier of Marseille's republican identity and shifted the city's position vis-à-vis the monarchy. Like his father, Louis-Antoine began with Massilia. He closed his history, however, lengthened by four chapters, with Louis XIV's birth in 1638. The narrative's center of gravity shifted from the city to the monarchy. The story of French grandeur eclipsed that of the independent republic. The author attributed his city's magnificence not to its political republican history, but to French commercial expansion.[57] Commercial Massilia had crumbled; the Sun King prompted its rebirth. A robust commerce and a royal governor who "gave evidence of his zeal and his sage conduct in all occasions that presented themselves for the service of the king and for the good of his *patrie*," restored Marseille's magnificence. Ruffi ended with an homage to the *viguier* Alphonse de Fortia, *chevalier de l'Ordre militaire du Roi, lieutenant en Provence* and *chef d'escadre des galères de France.* With de Pilles, he wrote, "Marseille has, like ancient Rome, men who are capable of governing and defending her." Such a man exuded "all faithfulness as subjects should to their sovereign, and all the love that citizens should have for the *patrie.*"[58] Imagining the royal governor as model subject and citizen, Louis-Antoine de Ruffi believed that the monarchy restored the commercial republic.

The Ruffis' arguments for the rise, fall and resurrection of the Marseillais republic reverberated over the late seventeenth and eighteenth centuries. Joseph Haitze's *Dissertations sur divers Points de l'histoire de Provence* (1704), the abbé Aillaud's *De l'ancienneté de Marseille,* and a Monsieur Ricaud's *Conformité des moeurs et des lois avec les anciennes* described the resurrection of the Marseillais republic.[59] The Provençal *parlementaire* Jean-François de Gaufridi's *Histoire de Provence* (1694)[60] focused on Marseille's "natural" inclination toward republicanism; its "grandeur of birth, establishment of great laws and mores, the introduction of the arts and sciences among the Gauls" easily "animated . . . the memory of her first government." Like the Ruffis, he discussed how the French Crown helped Marseillais elites remember their republicanism and described how the republic's heroes knelt at the feet of the royal liberator. These works indicate a crescendo of royalist tones in the eighteenth century; this did not, however, materialize at the expense of Marseillais republican historicism. Monarchy and republic were not inversely related. The more idealized the ancient republic, the more generous the monarchy appeared. The narrative of republican renewal was elastic enough to reserve for kings a leading role in resurrecting ancient Massilia.

Commercial expansion and the alteration of memory made conquest imaginable as liberation and helped reinforce Marseille's distinct Greco-Roman identity. Marseillais historians' representations of their distant past and their depictions of contemporary events tamed a long series of disruptive events and created a rather seamless story of republican renewal. They deleted memories of Louis XIV's troops entering Marseille and the confrontations between royal and municipal administrators. The conquest was rarely discussed without mention of Marseille's commercial recovery and grandeur. The myth and reality of commercial expansion fed and were fed by the remembrance of things long past and the forgetting of things recent. "Republican historicism" stabilized the political regime and commercial society brought into existence in 1660. Greek Massilia administratively metamorphosed into French Marseille, but in literature French Marseille continued to metamorphose into Greek Massilia.

THE ITALIAN GAZE: PROVENÇAL RELICS AND THE GRECO-ROMAN PAST

Intellectual elites used more than Marseille's Hellenic founding and history to establish their city's links to the classical past. Greco-Roman relics preserved in Marseille and Provence also authenticated the region's record in antiquity and bolstered "republican historicism" by offering tangible proof of it. Provence, imperial Rome's first *provincia*, in the words of Pliny, had been "another Italy."[61] Following the discoveries of Herculaneum (1709) and Pompey (1738), travelers went to Italy to visit them, but the French could find relics of Julius Caesar and his successors in ancient Roman cities in their own kingdom such as Arles, Nîmes, St. Rémy, and Marseille. Both Ruffis devoted entire chapters to tombs, urns, plates, lamps, medals, and "all sorts of antiques"[62] unearthed in Marseille dating to Greek, Roman, and medieval periods. Ruins were rich resources for monarch and provincial administrators; archeological treasures were concrete links between antiquity and the present, between the grandeur of Rome and that of France. Monarchs and regional elites scrambled to claim ownership of them.

The connection with antiquity benefited both the state and the *patrie*, an antiquarian wrote in the eighteenth century.[63] Provence and Marseille were privileged to own what many other provinces in France did not: a wealth of tangible pieces of the ancient world. Their intimate connection with Rome, evidenced in their relics, was a historical privilege unique to the area. But as Louis XIV and his intendants restored these remains, they claimed them as state possessions. Antiques unearthed in Provence held a dual identity: as Provençal treasures, they called attention to a particular region, while as royal property, they forged the Crown's links to Roman grandeur. Antiquities served as a prism that cast light on local claims and royal ones.

Nowhere is the tension between national and regional claims to artifacts more visible than in the reconstruction of Arles' Roman obelisk. On his way to subdue Marseille in 1660, Louis XIV discovered two separated parts of a ruined obelisk on the outskirts of Arles and remarked that they were "the most beautiful gems in my kingdom." Municipal leaders subsequently reerected the ancient monument "in honor of the king." The obelisk was hauled to the Hôtel de Ville on 20 March 1676. The dedication of the obelisk involved pageantry broadcasting Louis XIV's glory. Spectators watched as the renovated obelisk was revealed to the sound of trumpets, tambours, announcements by the city's consuls, and cries of "Vive le roy!" Adorned with symbols of absolutism, a terrestrial globe and sun, the obelisk testified to the absolute power of Louis XIV.[64]

Arles Obelisk, Hôtel de Ville back right. *Photo by author.*

Or did it? Arlesian administrative elites, like those in Marseille, looked for opportunities to showcase how their city, likewise a former republic, had been the "Rome of Gaul" allegedly founded by Hercules. The monument's new home in front of the Hôtel de Ville offered a story that conflicted with the Crown's narrative. Claiming that the obelisk was a priceless "ornament of the city," the consuls had four lions, ancient symbols of "the city, its power, and its courage," erected at its foot. The monument's placement in front of the ancient city hall, home to the city's "autonomous political body," emphasized Arlesian independence and

Arles Obelisk, close-up. *Photo by author.*

connection to a Roman past. The panegyric to the city read under the obelisk eulogized how Provence and Arles had been autonomous entities in the Roman *provincia.*

The restoration of antiques bolstered regional patriotism while contributing to the myth that monarchs resurrected republics. The spectacle of Marseille's *agrandissement,* the dedication of Marseille's Academy, the restoration of Arles' first-century obelisk, and the Crown's other restoration projects of Roman columns, pillars, arches, temples, and aqueducts around Nîmes, St. Rémy and Avignon lent credence to the idea that monarchs allied themselves with ancient republics.[65] Though overseen by royal administrators, these projects that depended on municipal cooperation and a workforce empowered *échevins*, consuls, local assemblies, and communities. This empowerment could be understood as local "resurrection."

VIRTUE, MYSTICAL PIETY, AND DESPOTISM: PERSISTING DILEMMAS OF COMMERCIAL SOCIETY

Marseille's aristocratic antiquarians mobilized a republican historical vision in the context of Bourbon state-building and commercial expansion to speak of their city's revival, rather than decline. In so doing, these writers gave value to the idea of commerce. Departing from Christian and classical republican traditions that condemned the marketplace as the source of self-interest, they adopted the notion that commerce was ideal for individuals, former republics, and growing states. Those who adopted the vocabulary of commercial civic spirit saw merchants as ideal upholders of civic ethos (de Colonie), equated *le négoce* and *négociants* with honor and nobility (Eon and Savary), and offered a revised republican myth that understood commerce as the engine propelling France forward and Marseille back to glory (Ruffi).

Such ideas of virtuous and honorable merchant-citizens dedicated to republics and states did not, however, go unchallenged in France. In particular, the sword nobility recovered the classical republican vocabulary of virtue to warn that republics were prone to decline; they offered a dramatically different assessment of commerce and royal expansion. If royal intervention and state-supported commerce jump-started citizenship and republican grandeur, according to some Marseillais writers, there were also aristocrats who saw them as corrupters of cities and states.

As Jay Smith and John Shovlin have analyzed, such ideas were particularly prominent in northern France, among the Burgundy circle, where "displeasure over the spread of venality of office and the rise of the *noblesse de robe* had led various spokesmen of the old nobility to decry the declining fortunes of the second estate."[66] Blaming the aristocracy's political and social decline on luxury, royal aggrandizement, and commerce, noble writers contrasted the ideal of virtue against the specter of despotism. Seeing virtue through classical republican lenses, they wrote that whereas the ancients had aligned their personal interests with the public good and expressed "love of the *patrie*," in their own age,

Colbertism and Louis XIV's warmongering extinguished that virtue. In *Traité contre le luxe des hommes et des femmes, et contre le luxe avec lequel on élève les enfans de l'un et de l'autre sexe,* Jean du Pradel argued that luxury needed to be abolished to restore virtue in France; Henri de Boullainvilliers' *Essai sur la noblesse de France, contenans une dissertation sur son origine* charged French kings with having softened mores, introduced luxury, and destroyed noble virtues. In their view, the sword nobility, not *négociants,* were the state's patriotic, morally sound, virtuous leaders.

In the late seventeenth century, the most ardent aristocratic critics of commercial luxury and war-centered state-building began courting Louis XIV's grandson, the duc de Bourgogne, to offer a unique notion of virtue that combined republican notions of citizenship with a mystical understanding of spiritual piety. This circle included conservative French Jesuits; Louis XIV's advisor the duc de Chevreuse; the duc de Beauvilliers, head of the Royal Council of Finance; and, most notably, the archbishop of Cambrai, François de Salignac de La Mothe Fénelon, who was Bourgogne's tutor, and spiritual advisor to Madame de Maintenon.[67]

When the death of Bourgogne's father made him immediate heir to the French throne, Fénelon penned his epic *Télémaque* in an effort to teach the future king better methods of rule that would curtail the excesses of Louis Quatorzian absolutism. The epic tells of the experiences of Telemachus, the son of the Ithacan hero Ulysses, as he traveled the Aegean and Mediterranean with his tutor, Mentor. Mentor used their encounters with different governments and societies to teach the prince how to be a wise ruler. Fénelon's story did not endorse a ban on commerce; as his disquisition on the commercial city of Tyre demonstrated, commerce could strengthen society. "The Tyrians are industrious, patient, laborious, clean, sober, and frugal," Fénelon wrote; "they have a well-regulated administration; there is no discord among them; never was there a people more firm and steady, more candid, more loyal, more trusty, or more kind to strangers." Commerce, however, could produce the conditions that generated luxury: "Should discord and jealousy once prevail among them; should luxury and laziness get a footing; should the first men in the nation begin to despise labor and frugality . . . you will soon see this power, that now is so much the object of admiration, dwindle away to nothing."[68] Luxury created the "contagious" and "moral poison" of "effeminate pleasure," the "abuse of power," and "idle ambition" that established despotism.[69]

Urging his charge, Bourgogne, to reconcile "monarchical *rule* with republican *virtues,*" Fénelon advocated a political system that prioritized the moral qualities of "disinterestedness."[70] He used the model of a Christian's disinterested love for God over the self to formulate his ideas regarding a citizen's disinterested love for the (re)public. The archbishop argued how French subjects could emulate the civic virtue of the ancients, and elevate it to a higher level with their religious knowledge of God, to produce the kind of disinterestedness requisite for a renewed agriculturally based state.[71] For Fénelon, republican and religious morality went hand in hand. Disinterested love, in other words, served as the foundation for relationships between man and God, man and man, and man and the body politic; in the first case, it manifested itself as "charity," in the second, as friendship, in the last, as civic virtue.[72] Such ideas were repeated in Fénelon's more overtly theological writings, such as the *Explications des maximes des saints* (1697) and his writings on education, most notably the *Traité de l'éducation des filles* (1687). He called upon his readers to emulate the simplicity of the ancient Romans, while practicing the "truths of Christianity," "sincerity," "modesty," "disinterestedness," "fidelity . . . and above all, piety."[73]

Fénelon's emphasis on mystical disinterestedness, and on the assumption that life was a passage extending from sin and concupiscence to "pure love," whether of God, fellow man, or the body politic, may appear to have much in common with the Jansenist variant of Augustinian theology. Fénelon, however, remained highly critical of Jansenism, emphasizing that man's spiritual and secular journeys toward disinterested love rested on free will, something that the Jansenists denied. Ultimately, it was not the charge of Jansenist heresy that landed Fénelon in trouble; rather, it was his support of Madame de Maintenon's religiously unorthodox acquaintance Jeanne-Marie Bouvier de La Motte, Madame Guyon, which led to accusations that he accepted Molinism and Quietism. Fénelon, Bishop Jacques Bénigne Bossuet and the philosopher Nicolas Malebranche charged, promoted a heretical understanding of disinterested love that excused the "elect" from morality and denied any hope of salvation or divine punishment.[74] As a result, Louis XIV banished the archbishop from court in 1697; the papacy followed suit by placing *Télémaque* on the Index of banned books in 1699. Meanwhile, the exiled Fénelon continued to try putting his ideas for political and spiritual reform into practice; he drew up his *Tables de Chaulnes* (1711), endorsing a program that proposed to restore the nobility to positions of power at court and in the provinces, abolish the intendancy, and eliminate universalized taxes like the *capitation*.[75] The duc de Bourgogne died in 1712, extinguishing Fénelon's dreams of a reformed monarchy and French state, and he himself died in January 1715, but *Télémaque* would become the most widely read book in the kingdom in the eighteenth century. Aside from Jean-Jacques Rousseau's

The Social Contract (1762), it was to be the most important political text in prerevolutionary France.

From Fénelon to Boulainvilliers, noble and religious critics of luxury and absolutist aggrandizement shared several points in common with the robe nobility who adhered to the new commercial civic spirit. Like the robe nobles of Marseille, these sword aristocrats located models for virtue in the classical Greek and Roman republics. Like them, they also blurred the lines between "honor" and virtue"; Fénelon's aristocrat and Savary's *négociant* both practiced the honor worthy of an aristocrat and the virtue requisite of a citizen. However, for critics of luxury, commerce was fundamentally connected to social mobility, the confusion of social hierarchies, and royal despotism.[76]

Debates over despotism, understood as the nonexistence of liberty, had initially emerged in the sixteenth century, most notably with Jean Bodin's *Six Books of the Republic.* Sword nobles became increasingly preoccupied with the issue of royal despotism in the seventeenth century as they saw Bourbon state-building during Louis XIV's reign involving too many illegitimate extensions of royal sovereignty. This discussion of Bourbon despotism did not resonate in a commercial port experiencing a long-awaited economic revival like Marseille. There was, however, one discussion concerning despotism that did take root among some observers in Marseille during this period: that of "oriental despotism." As debates over despotism strengthened, some royal critics deployed the concept of "oriental despotism" to compare the unlawful extension of French royal authority to non-Western forms of arbitrary rule that many European observers associated with the Ottoman Empire. This comparison between "oriental" and French despotism gained currency in part due to intensified diplomatic contacts between France and the Ottoman Empire, first between François I and Suleiman the Magnificent in the sixteenth century and later between Louis XIV and Colbert and Mehmet IV in the seventeenth (evidenced in the *Capitulations* of 1673).

The vocabulary of "oriental despotism" functioned to define the limits of absolutism.[77] Many royal critics feared that the allegedly tyrannical, corrupt, slavish, and perverse politics of the Ottoman Empire could infect France as French monarchs allied with the Ottomans to fight their common Hapsburg enemies. The king, these worried, was becoming a sultan, and the monarchy was becoming "oriental." Such arguments registered among many observers in Marseille, due to the city's geographical location and commercial identity, which rendered it open and vulnerable to non-French, and particularly Ottoman, Armenian, and Jewish merchants and migrants. Even while Marseillais elites and robe nobility praised the French *négociant* for the virtuous, honorable activities he pursued in the market, they remained ambivalent about the foreign merchants who increasingly served as business associates, and often, competitors in Marseillais and French commerce. Louis XIV and Colbert's commercial initiatives opened Marseille to more foreign traders, merchandise, and immigrants from the Levant. French commercial expansion resurrected the Massilian phoenix out of the ashes, but, according to many observers in Marseille and beyond, it could trap the city in a graveyard of foreign vices and disease. Virtues would be lost, citizens would forget their civic duties, Marseille would become an "Ottoman," "Armenian," or "Jewish" city on French soil.

The political and commercial alliances that the French monarchy forged with the Ottoman Empire to amplify royal power, strengthen the state, and bolster the French market threatened to undermine the tenuous faith that controllers-general, royal intendants, historians, and local elites developed in commerce and *négociants*. Could the foreign merchant serve as reliable business partner for French and Marseillais merchants? Could Levantine Jews and Armenians become Marseillais citizens, or would they threaten the moral and political fiber—the virtue and honor—of native Marseillais merchants and their families? Chapter 3 turns to these questions and to the persisting mistrust of commerce and merchants.

CHAPTER THREE

France and the Levantine Merchant

The Challenges of an International Market

"Trade is a Pandora's box," the Marseille *négociant* and *académicien* Pierre-Augustin Guys protested in 1786.[1] While royal administrators and aristocratic Marseillais historians provided positive evaluations of honorable and virtuous *négociants*, the traditional view that commerce fostered political and moral instability persisted through the eighteenth century, largely due to the transnationalism of the market. Two circumstances—increased traffic between French and Turkish merchants, and Ottoman immigrations to Marseille—disrupted the argument that commerce benefited the public good. How did French elites perceive the Ottoman Turks, Jews, and Armenians who traded with French merchants and arrived in France in growing frequency and greater numbers during Louis XIV's reign? What kinds of languages did they employ to understand the Ottomans and their interaction with French nationals? What policies did the French Crown generate to manage Ottoman merchants and immigrants, and how did Marseillais administrators react to them? Did worries over the political, financial, and moral risks allegedly presented by the Ottomans dampen commercial civic spirit?

As scholars have demonstrated, early modern French perceptions of the Turkish Empire were "overwhelmingly negative." Apart from their admiration of military prowess, French elites ascribed to stereotypes that depicted Ottomans as lascivious, violent, and corrupt.[2] Ottoman merchants, many French administrators and writers concurred, were doubly dubious; Ottomans were politically and religiously bankrupt, while their merchants were self-interested and avaricious. This chapter, however, challenges the monolithic model of the self-other dynamic previously presented by some historians of Orientalism. While Edward Said has shown that the "West" constructed its counterpart, "the East" as its polar opposite, recent scholarship has established that there were many "selves" and "others" projected on to one another.[3]

Indeed, this chapter will demonstrate how the French Crown, aristocracy, supporters and critics of commerce, Catholics and Huguenots employed an array of Orientalist tropes in conversations that often had more to do with French politics and society than with the Ottoman Empire.[4] Members of different political bodies, social ranks, and religious denominations adopted Orientalist discourses that would help secure them positioning over rivals and adversaries in France and Europe. Depending on such contexts, French elites alternated between adopting derogatory symbols of Ottoman subjects and merchants, and other tropes that stressed the "Asians'" moral, spiritual, and cultural superiority over Frenchmen. The generalizations they formulated helped them define social and political hierarchies, intra-estate and intra-personal relationships within France, while they also served to classify Ottoman peoples vis-à-vis the French.[5]

This chapter examines variations in French Orientalist utterances during the reign of Louis XIV then explores how these tropes helped sustain inconsistent policies toward Ottoman subjects in Marseille. First, it analyzes the works of authors patronized by the Crown—ambassadors, noblemen, ecclesiastics, doctors, professors, *parlementaires,* and knighted military personnel. These traveled to the Levant (generally "lands of the rising sun," or *soleil levant,* east of Venice) and gathered geographical and historical information for merchants and missionaries. The assessments of the Ottomans that these authors generated were intended to render the Turkish Empire appealing to French travelers to get them to extend their activities in the Levantine market. In the context of mercantilist expansion, the Crown had little to gain from disseminating knowledge of the Levant that concentrated exclusively on physical danger and political, cultural, and religious depravity.

Second, this chapter explores Orientalist texts penned by the French Crown's critics. Troubled by the monarchy's mishandling of statecraft—demonstrated by religious intolerance, court intrigues, and commercial luxury—these writers extolled the virtues of "oriental" rulers, contending that Turks, Persians, and other Levantine peoples were culturally, religiously, and politically superior to Europeans. Most famously, the baron de Montesquieu created his literary character the Persian monarch Usbek to criticize, among many things, the corruption and luxurious tastes of the French population. Montesquieu was not alone in mobilizing the Islamic other as a device to evaluate French politics and society.

Much prior to the 1721 publication of his *Lettres persanes,* French Protestants praised the religious pluralism of the Ottoman Empire in contrast to Louis XIV's intolerance. Other writers, such as the Comte de Boulainvilliers, compared the wisdom of Muslim prophets and leaders to virtues found among France's sword nobility.[6]

French policies established during the reign of Louis XIV to police Levantine merchants and immigrants mirrored inconsistencies in French Orientalist literature. The Crown initially extended a welcome to Levantines who were attracted to Marseille by the 1669 Edit sur la franchise du port de Marseille, which "urg[ed] foreigners to frequent . . . Marseille, come establish themselves therein," and become naturalized French subjects.[7] Such an open-door policy was an extension of Colbert's mercantilism. He recruited Ottoman merchants—mostly silk and textile traders—to Marseille to conduct commercial warfare against France's Dutch and British competitors. Naturalized Frenchmen of Levantine origin could help France produce its own silks, while their fabrics could compete favorably in other European markets. Colbert obscured the distinction between French and foreign subjects, native Marseillais citizens and naturalized ones, by imagining Marseille as a melting pot of diverse Frenchmen. By turning foreigners into French subjects, he would deactivate the financial threats they posed to the kingdom; their activities and goods would be used for France's profit, rather than their countries of provenance. While Marseillais *échevins* objected to his policies, Colbert insisted that naturalized Ottomans benefited the public good and French commerce.[8]

Ultimately, however, the Crown discontinued such open-door policies. Generating derogatory stereotypes of Jewish and Muslim merchants, royal and Marseillais administrators argued that foreign merchants posed a threat to the state and city. Using a combination of the statist language of utility, the civic vocabulary of virtuous citizenship, and derogatory Orientalist tropes, these argued that naturalized subjects neither relinquished their ties to their countries of origin nor set the general good above their personal interests. Following the Edict of Fontainebleau (1685), these discussions focused on the impossibility of certain others—Jews, Armenians, Muslims, and Protestants—aligning their personal religious inclinations with the commercial interests of France. While parlementary magistrates occasionally contested such claims and came to the aid of immigrant supplicants, exclusionary policies from the latter half of Louis XIV's reign curtailed the participation of religious others and naturalized subjects in French commerce.

STATE-SPONSORED ORIENTALISM AND THE OTTOMAN EMPIRE

From its beginnings in the sixteenth century, early modern court-sponsored French Orientalism was fraught with tensions. On one hand, French monarchs hoped to extend their territorial holdings into Asia and pursued their dream of a Gallia orientalis by energizing Christian anti-Muslim rhetoric in circulation since the Middle Ages. Such negative stereotypes flared across Europe as Suleiman the Magnificent set a tone for Ottoman expansion with his conquest of Hungary and siege of Vienna in 1529. On the other hand, France's political alliance with the Ottoman Empire, made official by François I's treaty with Suleiman in 1536, jump-started Franco-Mediterranean commercial expansion and introduced a pro-Ottoman sensibility at court. The alliance that resulted in the capture of Nice from the Holy Roman Empire (1543) strengthened Franco-Mediterranean commerce in Marseille, Montpellier, and Narbonne.[9] As France's first Renaissance king, François I extended court-sponsorship to scholars and linguists of the Orient, and initiated France's diplomatic relations with the Ottomans with the first French embassy to Turkey.

Louis XIII and XIV inherited the French Crown's complicated relationship with the Ottomans. Louis XIII and Richelieu capitalized on the commercial foundations François I had laid down for Franco-Ottoman trade, revising French laws and allowing noblemen to participate in overseas commerce. Aristocratic diplomats and successful merchants such as Laurent d'Arvieux and Jean-Baptiste Tavernier confirmed that Eurasian, and specifically Ottoman, trade was a lucrative business for the *noblesse commerçante*; their published works helped circulate stereotypes of Eastern luxury, opulence, and lavishness. At the same time, however, while the battle of Lepanto (1571) signaled the end of Ottoman naval hegemony in the Mediterranean, Turkish aspirations to push against the Hapsburg frontier continued to alarm Europeans. At the French court, Cardinal Mazarin, Anne d'Autriche, and their Catholic *dévot* supporters rallied against the monarchy's tradition of allying with the Ottomans. Together with French missionaries, whose many travel writings contained negative portrayals of Barbary corsairs, Muslim barbarism, and religious fanaticism, these naysayers continued to ignite Christian, anti-Islamic vocabulary.

Under Louis XIV, the French Crown's relationship with the Ottomans became more complex, as did French "Orientalisms." During his reign, the Köprülü viziers reactivated the Ottomans' drive to push to Vienna, fueling the Wars of the Holy League that involved the Hapsburgs, the Ottomans, Poles, Venetians, and Russians over the last decades of the seventeenth century. In the meantime, French-Mediterranean trade soared, as the Ottomans exported textiles (silk, wool, angora, and cotton), dyes, foodstuffs (dried fruits, oil, and wheat) and tobacco to the French in exchange for manufactured products (brocade, caps, and paper) and colonial goods (indigo, sugar, and coffee).[10] These tandem developments—renewed Turkish offensives in Europe, and intensified Franco-Ottoman commerce—generated confused utterances regarding the compatibility between French and Levantine populations. Meanwhile, Louis XIV's determination to preserve amicable relations with the Ottomans for the purposes of commercial aggrandizement and personal glorification generated new currents of Orientalisms in science and culture. Institutions such as the Académie des sciences encouraged the gathering of information on "the East," while at court, French royals and high nobility helped produce the vogue of *turkerie*, masquerading as Turks, Persians, and Indians in royal carrousels, following "Oriental" sartorial trends, and consuming coffee and tea with imported and imitated porcelain, to exhibit political, social, and economic power.[11]

State-subsidized studies of Levantine, Mediterranean, and Asian languages, geography, religions, histories and populations were crucial for a monarch who hoped to use such research to establish advantageous political and commercial relationships with the Ottoman Empire. Authors who participated in such information-gathering presented two prominent narratives. On one hand, they presented the standard metanarrative of Eurocentric Orientalism, insisting that the Turkish religion, politics, culture, and physical environment were diametrically opposed to those of Europeans. They described that the Ottoman Empire bred corrupt societies—diseased in politics, religion, mind, and body—and threatened to spread malaise to Europe. On the other hand, the same writers occasionally favorably depicted territories ruled by the Turks. They imagined that populations in the eastern Mediterranean shared common Hellenic and Roman histories with Europe until Asiatic powers had usurped them from "civilization." These authors argued that Ottoman politics, not fundamental "ethnic" differences, rendered the people of the Ottoman Empire incompatible with the French. This perception that Greeks, Cypriots, Slavs, and Persians were neither different nor averse to the West reassured French audiences. Eastern Europeans and subjected Levantine populations became buffers against the encroaching Turks. If navigation and commerce made the Levant more accessible and brought the Ottoman Empire closer to France, imagining eastern Mediterranean and Levantine peoples as semi-European allowed the French to push back the putative borders of the enemy. By stretching elastic discursive European borders and characterizing the Levant as demi-European, writers assembled a linguistic defense that protected France when European physical ramparts proved vulnerable.

One of the most distinguished seventeenth-century traveler writers of the Ottoman Empire was the Aixois botanist Joseph de Tournefort. Studies in Montpellier and Barcelona and voyages around the Mediterranean brought him fame, and Madame de Venelle, the undergoverness *(sous-gouvernante)* of the royal children, invited him to Paris in 1683. He became professor of Botany at the Jardin des Plantes and a member of the Académie des sciences in 1691. Hearing that Tournefort was an "excellent voyager," Louis XIV ordered him on a mission to collect information on Levantine and Mediterranean lands.[12] Between 1700 and 1702, Tournefort traveled the Greek archipelagoes, visited Constantinople, and toured Ottoman Armenia, Georgia, and North Africa until plague in Egypt forced his return to France. His *Relation d'un voyage du Levant fait par ordre du Roy,* originally written as letters to Secretary of the Navy Louis de Pontchartrain, "who had procured all the permissions for his voyage," appeared soon thereafter.[13]

Tournefort's understanding of the Ottoman Empire was Euro- and Francocentric. The further east he traveled, the more he observed politics deteriorating, women becoming uglier, and animals fiercer. Tournefort focused on the concept of "Oriental" or "Turkish despotism," attributing the degeneracy of the Ottoman Empire—its people, religion, animals, plants—to Turkish politics: "From its origins," he wrote, "the Turkish government has been tyrannical." Turkish despotism spanned four centuries and three continents; it began in the sultan's seraglio, where eunuchs "gave themselves over to ambition and the care of their fortunes."[14] Despotism infected the population in multiple forms. "Ignorance . . . one of the miseries of slavery," deteriorated Ottoman minds, and the plague, their bodies. The Ottoman world, Tournefort concluded, was deranged in mind, body, spirit, and politics.

Such depictions of Turkish despotism and corruption abounded in French travel literature. The Levantine travel journal (1668) of a Sieur Poullet asserts that "the Ottoman Turks who possess the most beautiful parts of the world were initially a troop of vagabond shepherds descended from the Tartars of Asia Minor around the year 1200." Through twenty-two generations of sultans, the Ottomans, Poullet recounted, had extended their empire with their Janissary militia, "winning more land in four centuries than the Romans managed to acquire in eight hundred and fifty years."[15] The Janissaries "forced their Sovereigns to abandon their treasuries to their avarice, will, caprice . . . and conspiracies."[16]

The Norman *parlementaire* Gilles Fermanel elaborated on the Janissaries' luxurious tastes that gradually rendered them "cowardly," "weak," and "effeminate."[17] Their degeneracy reflected the sultan's: leaving governance to viziers, "the Great Lord locked himself up with his women in the Seraglio, where he forgot the care of his affairs."[18] Turkey, these French writers confirmed, was a declining empire.

How could such a purportedly depraved, self-destructing empire pose a threat to Europeans? Travel writers argued that Ottoman despotism could turn friends into foes, trading partners into enemies, Europe into Turkey. Turkish expansionism was a perverse form of imperialism, where a corrupt, weak, effeminate, "barbarous" empire destroyed strong states. The Islamic religion, these writers claimed, served as a major weapon in this perverted version of state-building. The sultan sent his eunuchs to Asia and Europe to spread the Islamic religion.[19] According to Poullet, "there [was] nothing more contrary to reason than *Mahometisme*."[20] "Christian children paid as tribute [to the Ottomans] are raised from an early age in *Mahometisme*; they have an extreme horror of all that regards Christianity; [they] hate their parents, they never want to recognize them, they consider the sultan as their father . . . and would rather die than contravene his commands."[21] The Islamic faith, writers insisted, generated moral decline, depopulation, wars, and disease.[22] Islamic attitudes toward disease prevented them from protecting themselves against epidemics. The Turks let the plague run rampant; placing their faith in predestination, they did "nothing to preserve themselves, if a person died, another slept in his bed unconcerned and wore his clothes."[23]

Writers warned that commerce brought "Asian" despotism, disease, and immorality closer to Europe, particularly through ports that served as open doors to "Asian" mores, habits, and illnesses. Gilles Fermanel observed that commerce "brought terror" to Marseille and Toulon, even while these cities became wealthier than Malta, Tunis, Algiers, and Tripoli. Administrative leaders, he wrote, "cried for help" to stop trading with Ottoman neighbors.[24]

Writers who disparaged the Turks nonetheless favorably judged Levantines, whom they saw as sharing Europeans' Greco-Roman heritage. Positive evaluations of Marseille's historical otherness—manifest in the city's connections to ancient Greece, Rome, and Carthage—became very relevant in these discussions that pointed to historic, geographic, and cultural similarities among Mediterranean and Levantine peoples and lands.

That France's premier Mediterranean port shared affinities with its eastern neighbors was not difficult to imagine for writers, given that the sea route between Marseille and Constantinople was 730 leagues, traversable in less than a month.[25] The journey led from Provence to Sardinia, between Malta and the Barbary Coast, and then via the Aegean to Constantinople.[26] Gilles Fermanel and Sieur Poullet, the same writers who provided negative evaluations of the Turks, maintained that the whole of Asia Minor shared a common Greco-Roman heritage. Smyrna and other cities had been founded as Ephesian colonies; the Georgians descended from "the Spanish and the Argonauts."[27] Meanwhile, these writers described Constantinople, Smyrna, Erzurum, Rome, and Marseille as geographically and culturally comparable. Their histories traced to classical Greece, and their city plans were reproductions of Greek models. The Jesuit Père Avril noted how the Turkish city of Erzurum's "grandeur is similar to Marseille's." Its ancient walls, spacious neighborhoods, and excellent air and water made it "one of the best cities in the entire Ottoman Empire."[28] Fermanel, meanwhile, compared Constantinople to Rome. "This city built to command the entire world," was "a copy of Rome, built on seven hills [and] bathed by the sea." In Smyrna, he continued, "Christians lived freely . . . and accommodated themselves easily with the Turks, who are ordinarily good men." Avril described how "the mores there are so sweet that we French live there comfortably."[29]

Commerce, Avril continued, rendered Mediterranean peoples even more similar and well-adapted to one another. Armies, sailors, and merchants, he wrote, "carried their humors with them into the land of the Levantines," until Mediterranean peoples increasingly resembled one another. He particularly noticed similarities between Venetians and Turks: "the ways they prepare their meats and make their pastries are similar, their restraint in opening themselves up, never rendering a blatant response, and in counterfeiting seriousness are nearly completely parallel."[30] While these authors conceded that politically, the Ottoman Empire "was the most dangerous land for the French,"[31] they suggested that Mediterranean mingling and hybridity—evidenced in culinary overlaps and behavioral similarities—was not altogether negative. These were the benefits of transnational cosmopolitanism.

Other French authors rejected depictions of a corrupt Turkish Empire. In *Bibliothèque orientale, ou Dictionaire universel contenant généralement tout ce qui regarde la connoissance des peuples de l'Orient*, Barthélemy d'Herbelot stated: "The term 'Turk' is so decried that it is understood to signify a barbaric, crude nation that is utterly ignorant, and by their name, one understands similarly all who are under the domination of the Ottoman Empire." He corrected: "One does them injustice to charge them with such calumnies. Without going so far as to justify barbarism or crudeness . . . one can report that with regard to ignorance, [the Turks] yield neither to the Arabs, nor the Persians in the sciences and in good letters." The *Bibliothèque orientale,* Herbelot insisted, would correct such "unjust" stereotypes.[32]

The first in France to produce a collection of knowledge on the Turkish Empire in the form of a dictionary, Barthélemy Herbelot (1625–1695) mastered Hebrew, Latin, Greek, Arabic, Persian, and Turkish before the Crown tapped him to produce a French version of a *Bibliotheca orientalis* (1658) completed by Johann Heinrich Hottinger in Leyden. Following two extended excursions to Italy, where he befriended professors in "oriental languages," Herbelot returned to France, where then *procureur général* of the parlement de Paris and *sur-intendant des finances* Nicolas Fouquet provided him with a pension. Fouquet's banishment from court did little to damage Herbelot's career; following several audiences with Louis XIV, he became royal professor in Syriac and competed his *Bibliothèque orientale* in return for an annual pension of 1,500 livres.[33]

Dedicated to His Majesty as a dictionary of "the most excellent things nature has produced in one of the most beautiful parts of the earth; the most useful things art has invented; and the most marvelous events history has told," the *Bibliothèque orientale* was organized, not in the narrative and subjective form of published travel journals, but in alphabetical order. Topics included sultans, religious leaders, empires, cities and towns, geographic formations, historic events and battles. In this regard, the *Bibliothèque orientale* presaged the rational organization of the Enlightenment *Encyclopèdie.* "The alphabetical order of its organization does not invite confusion, as one might imagine," the author asserted, "to the contrary, it facilitates the [author's] intention to insert several things that are not part of the general history that he provides, but that support it to render things more intelligible." Herbelot presented his work as an unbiased, comprehensive collection of data.

Herbelot traced the Turks' origins to the Greeks and Romans and pointed to the common biblical heritage of Europeans and Turks. The Turks, he explained, traced their lineage to Adam and Eve. In his article, "Turc," Herbelot discussed Noah's grandson, Turk, who "governed his family and subjects with great prudence and justice" and taught his sons "about religion, government and the discipline of their families." His descendants established colonies and became rulers "of the greatest nation in the world." Eventually, this clan divided into forty-eight tribes; some of these became nomadic vagabonds. Consequently, the Persians and Arabs grew to hate these nomads and characterized them as "barbarians," "bandoliers," and "robbers."[34] Herbelot encouraged his readers to be skeptical of such stereotypes of Turkish barbarism that derived from prejudiced accounts.

The author who prided himself for objectively analyzing the Turks, however, could not remain unbiased in his assessment of Islam. Herbelot derided the Islamic prophet and faith, explaining that Turkish history declined after the introduction of Islam.[35] He began his article on "Mohammed Al Nabi, the Prophet" by describing "the famous imposter Mahomet," as "the author and founder of the heresy that has taken the name of the religion we call Mahometane." "The interpreters of the Koran and other doctors of the Muslim law," he continued, "have applied to this false prophet all the praise that the Arians and other heretics have attributed to Jesus Christ and have dared to establish his divinity." Suggesting that Mohammed could "neither read nor write," Herbelot claimed that the prophet was guided by erroneous knowledge of Jewish and Christian doctrines. Herbelot questioned the prophet's virtue, recounting that while Mohammad was allegedly untainted by original sin and concupiscence, he took twenty-one wives, disregarding the law that only permitted four.[36] He then characterized Islam as a religion of unreason, ignorance, and superstition. The Muslim pilgrimage to Mecca, he wrote, was nothing more than idolatry.

Herbelot's text was just as Orientalist as the journals of Tournefort, Avril, Fermanel, or Poullet. For Herbelot, what "othered" Turkey was not its politics, culture, or history; it was Islam. While he rejected stereotypes of Turkish barbarism and tyranny, he subscribed to the notion that non-Christian religions were irrational cults. While he argued that Europeans needed to temper their accusations of Turkish political and cultural inferiority with a rational investigation of Turkish texts, he failed to extend this methodology to his analysis of the Turks' religion.

ORIENTALISM AND THE CRITIQUE OF ROYAL ABSOLUTISM

French writers did not, however, unanimously condemn Islam as a signifier of Turkish ignorance and depravity. Many critics of Louis XIV rejected such assumptions. Like other French observers, they assumed that Islam defined the Ottoman Empire; for them, Islam was *the* signifier of Ottoman otherness. The first French translation of the Koran (1647) helped underscore this relation between the Turkish Empire and Islam. But these critics of absolutism used favorable discussions of Islam to praise Turks and Muslims for their tolerance, rationality, and virtue. The analysis of Islam became a rhetorical tool that allowed them to expose religious and political problems not in the Ottoman Empire but in France. As Mohammed Arkoun observes: "Islam represented either fanaticism or contrarily, a tolerance ignored in France and in Catholic lands. In all cases, good or bad, the Muslim was not seen for what he was, but for how it could serve in ideological struggles" in Europe.[37]

The earliest positive French assessments of Islam came from Protestant critics of the monarchy. The botanist-linguist Jean Thévenot (1633–67), the merchant Jean-Baptiste Tavernier (1605–1689), and Jean Chardin (1643–1713), a Protestant critical of the Catholic worship of saints and the Virgin Mary, published their travel journals of the Levant, Persia, and Turkey and lauded the Ottomans for extending to them the religious tolerance lacking in France.[38] Thévenot commented that the Turks "were better Christians than Christians themselves," and Chardin thought that the Shiites possessed better qualities than Christians.[39] "[T]he infidels the Christian missionaries try to convert . . . are more rational [than they are], because they do not close their eyes to *les lumières naturelles*, adore God alone, and are averse to the idolatry to which the missionaries are inclined," Chardin wrote.[40] To him, the Muslims were "the best deists of the world."[41]

Henri de Boulainvilliers (1658–1722), best remembered for his *Essai sur la noblesse de France* and *Histoire de l'ancien gouvernement de la France*, is perhaps the most famous of Louis XIV's domestic critics. Boulainvilliers described how the Frankish ancestors of the sword nobility had by right of conquest ruled the Gallo-Roman ancestors of the Third Estate until miscegenation between the Franks and Gauls weakened the conquerors. However, he reserved his strongest criticism for royal absolutism and the Crown's policy of commercial mercantilism. He insisted that the Crown sapped the sword nobility of power by supporting *négociants*, social-climbing financiers, and venal officeholders. The royal court and its luxurious decadence corrupted noble virtues and degraded France. Though superficially a discussion of the history of Arabia and its famous prophet, Boulainvilliers' *Histoire des Arabes avec la Vie de Mahomet* (published posthumously and translated into English in 1731) contained all of these themes and was a partially veiled condemnation of absolute monarchy.[42]

Like Herbelot, Boulainvilliers began by questioning Western misconceptions of the Levant, and Islam in particular. Frenchmen, he admonished, being ignorant of "Oriental languages" and uninformed about Arab history, "consider the Mahometan religion only as a monstrous fiction, settled by force of arms among weak and unwarlike nations, and maintained by ignorance and prejudice." They failed to recognize "the courage, virtue and sentiments," of Mahomet and his followers. Boulainvilliers credited Herbelot for revealing "the virtue of Arabians, whom we are led to regard as a barbarous people because of their distance from us and difference in religion."[43]

Boulainvilliers began with a comparative geographic and historical discussion of Jews and Arabs. Arabs hailed from "the nation sprung from Joktan, who was the younger brother of Heber, the father of the Hebrews." Consequently, he traced several similarities between Jews and Arabs in customs, language, and government. Both were initially nomadic peoples who had adopted monotheism and rejected kingship. Boulainvilliers applauded their establishment of governments without "absolute chiefs capable of suppressing the liberty of others." In place of kingship, they instituted "councils of particular tribes," similar to aristocratic councils in medieval France.

Boulainvilliers thought Arabs superior to the Jews, however. The Jews settled in fertile lands where they did not have to learn to cultivate the arts, sciences, or commerce; "destitute of navigation and commerce, unskilled in arts and sciences, without politeness, or any other manners than what were prescribed to them by their law," they existed "without politics, and were equally ignorant of the means either of cultivating peace or carrying on war." The Arabs lived in inhospitable deserts and survived by practicing "the most noble and exalted sciences." Unlike Jews, they were physically robust; they lived in the wilderness, preferring solitude and liberty, "disdain[ing] riches and pleasure," and developing "mastery over their passions."[44]

Boulainvilliers' depictions of Arabs resembled his imaginings of the Germanic Franks he so admired. His subtext suggested that Arabs were morally and physically comparable to the European "noble savage," the Frankish ancestors of the French nobility. "The solitude of the Arabians," he wrote, "was the principle of all their best qualities." Whereas solitude "produces nothing but stupidity in our monks," it stimulated virtue in the Arabs, who shunned riches and became "masters of themselves." Their isolation produced "hardness," "a barbarous scorn," and "contempt for life," but these, he explained, were admirable qualities. The Arabs' "coolness" and their "severity and firmness" led them to be "regulated by the consideration of justice and public security." Such moral vigor contrasted with "the soft and lively passions so common in our climates," where "ambition, love, jealousy, and politics" multiplied with the progress of civilization.[45]

In Boulainvilliers' historical worldview, however, aristocrats and noble savages lost their virtues, physical strength, and political power. As in France, where luxury had corrupted the Frankish nobility, the Arabs had declined with the development of commerce. He lamented "that the fatal desire of private convenience, which soon degenerates into luxury, found the way into these prodigious deserts." "The lust of wealth," he bemoaned, "triumphed over the love of liberty." The Arabs, "hurried on by the desire for riches, carry [coffee] into the ports of the Levant, in order to bring home money for it, of which, at length, they will make the same wise use as we do, and like us, to the irreparable loss of that inestimable liberty, whose price is far above gold and every other transitory pleasure."[46] The engine of historical decline was consistent in Louis XIV's France and in Arabia. Commerce exterminated moral and physical vigor and destroyed liberty.

Boulainvilliers appended a biography of Mahomet to his account of Arabia. Mahomet emerged in his narrative as a nobleman from the wilderness who restored virtue to a world overrun with "avarice and luxury." Abandoned in the mountains as a child, Mahomet developed "strength" and "dexterity" chasing "the fiercest savages, lions, and tigers." As a young adult, he joined some trading caravans and became a merchant. Mahomet's experience as a merchant did not, however, corrupt him. It provided him with the opportunity to observe fraudulence in government, politics, and religion. He found kings and merchants bent on personal aggrandizement and commercial expansionism usurping political power from the ancient nobility.[47]

Boulainvilliers projected onto his reading of Persian and Syrian history the problems he saw in Louis XIV's France. He described Mahomet's Persia as a state in decline. "The end of the monarchy" drew near, as power-hungry kings overturned "ancient laws" and "abandoned themselves" to "extravagance." "The nobility knew themselves no longer." A similar situation plagued Syria, where a state overrun by "tyrannical usurpation" had become "a mere shadow of what it once had been." Courtiers, priests, and military personnel cared only for money and luxury. Mahomet, Boulainvilliers continued, was particularly shocked at the corrupt practices among Christians: "he regarded the bishops, priests and secular clergy chiefly as a political combination of men, united for the purpose of making religion subservient to their passions, their concupiscence, avarice, pride and dominion." Sickened by such "abuses," Mahomet created a new religion free of controversy. Such a calling to restore virtue, Boulainvilliers asserted, was not developed out of "ignorance," "imposture," or fanaticism. This was the result of "deep meditation . . . upon the state and condition of the nations of the world at the time, and upon the reconciliation of the objects of religion with reason." For Boulainvilliers, Mahomet was a hero comparable to Alexander the Great and Caesar.[48] He restored the Arab nobility, curtailed royal aggrandizement, and preached against luxury.

The texts of Tournefort, Poullet, Avril, Fermanel, Herbelot, and Boulainvilliers reveal the many iterations of French Orientalisms in the seventeenth and eighteenth centuries. Reflected in these views of "Arabia," "the Levant," and "Turkey" were the French authors' own evaluations of, and ambivalence about the French monarchy, commerce, and Catholicism. French administrators relied on these inconsistent perceptions of Turks, Islam, and the Levant to develop equally inconsistent policies toward Ottoman traders both in France and in the wider French commercial world.

"SIRENS WHO ENCHANT US": FOREIGNERS IN EON'S *COMMERCE HONORABLE*

While dissonant Orientalist utterances on the Levant shaped royal and local administrators' attitudes to Ottoman merchants and immigrants, policy-makers were also informed by another set of discussions: political treatises that outlined how the Crown should handle foreign commerce, merchants, and immigrants in France. These texts are overwhelmingly xenophobic. In the mid sixteenth century, Jean Bodin and other jurists maintained that alien workers in France suffered from a "vice" that rendered them incapable of inheriting or passing on possessions to heirs; these arguments provided the basis for anti-immigration and anti-naturalization policies through the early modern period. The mid seventeenth century saw authors putting a new spin on such arguments, particularly in the context of discussions of international commerce.

One of the most important theorists in this regard was a Carmelite monk, Mathias de Saint-Jean, known as Jean Eon. Advisor to the maréchal de la Meilleraye, governor of Brittany, who was related to Richelieu, Eon published his *Commerce honorable, ou Considérations politiques* in 1646. The book defined how commerce was important for the state, but described the French market as embarrassingly weak and presented ideas for its improvement. It blamed France's lamentable situation on the "nonchalance" of Frenchmen and the "artifice" of foreigners and promoted the idea that commerce was an "honorable" and "useful art."[49]

Eon began by differentiating commerce's public-minded supporters from its self-interested enemies. The author lauded Meilleraye and Richelieu for their accomplishments "for the public good." He praised Richelieu for extending France's frontiers, and for founding companies for commercial and naval expansion. He criticized individuals who sabotaged the further development of French commerce. Such "declared enemies of the good of the state" were "foreigners and their compatriots," "the indifferent and the self-interested," "the critics and the ignorant," and all who "by their diverse interests ruin [the public good]."[50]

Commerce, Eon argued, was "an honorable art" that spread peace and prosperity. French subjects, however, neglected commerce. The French market languished, while foreign ones strengthened. France's chief outlets, the ports of Marseille (specializing in trade with Italy and the Levant) and Normandy (focused on trade with Spain, Portugal, and Britain) generated mediocre profits. The Dutch and British overwhelmed Marseille's Levantine market, while overpowering French colonies in the West Indies and Canada. Sniffing "on every side and discover[ing] the smell of profit," they out-earned France by 21,445,520 to 16,701,466 *livres*. In short, Eon claimed, "there is no commerce [in France]."[51]

Eon attributed this crisis to internal and external factors. Domestically, the French continued to believe that commerce was "dishonorable." Nobles shunned commerce as too base for their status. Members of the Third Estate preferred to procure venal offices and discouraged their children from commerce. Parents sent their sons to *collèges*, where they "abandoned themselves to love" and led "idle lives useless to the public."[52] Foreigners, Eon wrote, took advantage of French inattention to trade and applied themselves vigilantly to commerce. Boys began careers in trade at a young age, helping distribute merchandise, exchanging money in *bureaux de change*, conducting business in the markets, and mastering languages.[53]

Eon described foreign merchants and workers as enemies who disguised themselves as allies, while plotting to destroy the French: "They say that they work to give us rest, and that they are exempting us from the dangers of the sea; they provide us with the riches of the Orient and the Occident by these and other arguments that are like the voice of the Siren; they know how to enchant us and charm our senses, they leave us in a disgraceful and damaging nonchalance to the detriment of commerce." French administrators, Eon lamented, encouraged such foreign deception. "Free access" allowed foreigners "excessive liberty." Consequently, they "become arbiters and dispensers of the value of our goods, and reduce us to shameful servitude."[54]

Eon accepted that the French Crown could neither categorically exclude foreigners nor continue its open-door policy. As a civilized nation, Eon argued, France had a responsibility to extend compassion to less-fortunate foreigners. France moreover relied on foreigners to populate emptied cities. This method, Eon commented, had historically met much success; Romulus had built Rome, Theseus had expanded Athens, King Richard had strengthened London, and François I Normandy with foreign workers. France needed guest-workers and immigrants; they "bring us the things we lack, provided we reciprocate by giving them what they need."[55]

Ideally, Eon wrote, universal laws would regulate the comings and goings of people. Merchants and migrants, regardless of their countries of provenance, would work toward "the common and universal good of man." In reality, however, interests did not converge among people of different origins. "The intention of the foreign *négociant* who lives in a country other than his own," Eon insisted, "is never to enrich the host country or favor the indigenous inhabitants." Foreigners could never align their interests with the public good of France because they retained too many contacts with their homelands. It followed from natural laws that "the foreign merchant is more inclined toward the profit and utility of those of his *patrie* than those of another country."[56] Foreign merchants sold more than they bought in France, foreign intermediaries profited from commissions and returned to their countries, others counterfeited money. Marseille, Eon noted, suffered most from such damaging activities.

Eon outlined three strategies to confront the foreign menace. First, the Crown could implement protectionist regulations prohibiting foreigners from buying property and acting as intermediaries and agents for other foreign merchants.[57] Second, the Crown could develop commercial companies and a merchant marine. Finally, the Crown could promote the view that commerce was an "honorable and useful art." State-sponsored education would help recruit French merchants. Commerce, Eon said, was profitable for public and particular welfare. It guaranteed as much adventure and danger as did war, so there was no reason for the nobility to shun it. The commoner, meanwhile, could improve his means of subsistence. Authors from André de Colonie to Jacques Savary, who likewise labeled commerce "noble," "virtuous," and "honorable," would echo Eon's arguments.

Eon's *Commerce honorable* offered a range of ideas that administrators, from controllers-general to *échevins,* could adopt to forge policies on immigration and naturalization. Colbert would employ Eon's protectionist approach while discarding his pessimistic notion that foreigners could not care for the French good. Marseille's administrators would accept exclusionary rules imposed municipally, while rejecting centralized regulations. The dilemma for royal and Marseillais elites was deciding if foreigners and immigrants—particularly from the Levant—could align their interests with France's public good.

THE KING'S ADOPTED CHILDREN: NATURALIZATION IN OLD REGIME FRANCE

What were the procedures for naturalization in seventeenth-century France? Unlike modern processes, those by which early modern aliens became Frenchmen were not contingent upon cultural, religious, or political assimilation, but only on the exercise of the king's sovereign will. The alien was not required to adopt Catholicism or speak French. As Peter Sahlins has shown, the Crown mobilized two metaphors to understand naturalization: that of a legal contract, and that of adoption. Royal theorists saw naturalization as a contract between the alien and the king, and emphasized bureaucratic protocol in processing naturalization requests. They also understood naturalization as a process of adoption. A potentially inclusive metaphor, the idea of the king as father to his children blurred the distinction between natural and unnatural subjects.[58]

The early modern immigrant only needed to "express desire to live and die in the kingdom" to become naturalized. Foreigners requesting letters of naturalization were rarely refused. Tremendously high costs, however, restricted naturalization to wealthy aliens of considerable social stature. While the Crown saw naturalization as the king's free gift to the alien, the process of receiving a naturalization letter signed, registered, and sealed by the Chambre des comptes was expensive. Sahlins writes that the sum levied on the seals of the letter itself climbed from 74 *livres* 9 *sols* in 1674 to 106 *livres* in 1704. It was expected that the recipient would offer a compulsory "gift" to the Chambre des comptes and the Chambre du domaine et du tresor; these funds were earmarked as "donations" for hospitals and churches. By the mid eighteenth century, the cost of naturalization could total six hundred *livres*, amounting to two years of earnings for an artisan, or ten seasons of earnings for a laborer. At the end of the seventeenth century, less than a tenth of registered immigrants listed in French tax records were naturalized. Still, around fifty immigrants naturalized annually from the sixteenth century to the end of the Old Regime. Artisans and retail merchants numbered among them. While aliens from territories bordering France numbered highest, Provence became the most popular destination for aliens from the Ottoman Empire. A quarter of registered Ottoman immigrants to France, most of them merchants, settled in Provence.[59]

Why become a Frenchmen as opposed to residing in the kingdom as a resident alien? The myth of the good father who dispensed gifts to aliens was contradicted by the reality of a king who legally restricted aliens from several privileges. Aliens were excluded from participation in municipal politics and barred from holding public or religious offices. They could not participate in certain professions. Furthermore, the alien was saddled with the *droit d'aubaine*. Upon the death of an alien resident, the king claimed his property; the alien's heirs could not inherit the parents' assets. The legal inability of the alien to pass on his wealth stemmed from a tradition that the French monarchy adopted during the thirteenth century: as kings secured control over feudal seigneurs, they usurped the seigneur's ability to claim the possessions of aliens who died on his property.[60] Over the early modern period, the Crown expanded the *droit d'aubaine* to further limit the aliens' activities. Suspecting aliens of leaking money out of France, it prohibited them from banking and money-exchanging professions (Louis XIV reactivated this prohibition with the *Code Marchand* of 1673). Naturalization did not, however, guarantee complete protection from the *droit d'aubaine*. A naturalization tax of 1697 declared all former naturalizations null and void and imposed a tax on registered foreigners and descendants of immigrants who had arrived in France after 1600. In dire need of money to finance his wars, Louis XIV disowned his "adopted children" and ordered them to pay a tax to be readopted as Frenchmen.[61]

The *droit d'aubaine* and the naturalization tax of 1697 might suggest that Louis XIV fostered an unfavorable environment for immigrants and naturalized subjects. The Sun King embraced two contradictory policies during his reign, however. On one hand, the expansion of the *droit d'aubaine* placed financial burdens on aliens and naturalized subjects; alien merchants bore the brunt of these taxes. On the other hand, the Crown implemented pro-immigration policies that exempted aliens and naturalized Frenchmen from such burdens. Alien *négociants* and maritime merchants took advantage of the Crown's invitations to become naturalized; Colbert's Edict of 1669 was an example of such a policy taking effect in Marseille. Ultimately, in 1715, the Crown collectively exempted all alien maritime merchants from the *droit d'aubaine*. As the following discussions demonstrate, such inconsistencies were a product of the Crown's shifting commercial, political, and religious interests, as well as of the fluctuating perceptions of the alien's ability to contribute to French commerce and the public good.

OTHERING MARSEILLE: A SHORT HISTORY OF MIGRATION BEFORE COLBERT

Marseille was a destination for foreign merchants much before Colbert issued his edict of 1669. The port founded by Phocaean mariners established overseas commerce from ancient times, and its merchants participated in Levantine commerce from the Middle Ages. Marseillais administrators consistently faced the problem of balancing their city's dependency on foreigners and foreign trade, with the need to guard their own merchants, interests, and civic identity. Marseillais administrators juggled many concerns: demographically maintaining a favorable ratio of local to transplanted residents; preserving a Catholic civic identity in the presence of Muslim, Protestant, Armenian Orthodox, and Jewish merchants and migrants; withstanding the double pressures of French centralization and foreign diversification. Shutting its doors to outsiders was as illogical as leaving its port entirely open; as the historian Pierre Echinard has characterized it, "the Mediterranean world was, for [Marseille], at once a source of profits and of dangers."[62] Marseillais elites therefore permitted and prohibited certain categories of foreigners, depending on the financial, cultural, and political strains on the city.

Marseille attracted people from Provence, the Alps, and Lyon from within France, and Corsica, Genoa, and the Piedmont from without.[63] By 1485, King Charles VIII noted in the Etats de Provence that "every day, many merchants and peoples from foreign nations and countries come and go, from the Italian states, Lombardy, Savoy, the Piedmont and other areas, as well as from the Levant."[64] Short-distance migrations were supplemented by increased numbers of people from Spain, the German states, Holland, and the Levant. Migrations were welcomed after bouts of plague and depopulation. In the late fifteenth century, Marseillais consuls protested the Royal Council of Provence's decree to expel foreigners, complaining that "the city is almost entirely depopulated."[65]

Marseillais policies were inconsistent, however. The city's leaders often discouraged migration with the argument that it impoverished native citizens and drew money away from the city; "foreigners enrich themselves here, they return to their cities, and others come to take their place."[66] City officials directed such arguments most frequently at Levantine Armenians, who began arriving in the sixteenth century to trade in silk. By the seventeenth century, the municipality began introducing "draconian measures" to disrupt their activities.[67] In 1621, the City Council forbade Marseillais ships to transport Armenians; the parlement de Provence forbade Armenian merchants to take French currency out of France.

Non-Catholic immigrants faced the greatest difficulty in Marseille, whether Protestant, Jew, Muslim, or Armenian Orthodox. Magdalene myths that claimed Provence as the first landing point for Christians in France, in addition to the lengthy papal presence in nearby Avignon, and Marseille's alliance with the Holy League during the Religious Wars, rendered Marseille's Catholic heritage particularly potent. Consequently, the city remained hostile to religious others.

Marseillais authorities expelled Protestants in 1562. While Jews enjoyed relative peace in Provence under the Angevins, the province's union with France and the Jewish diaspora following their expulsion from Spain increased intolerance in Marseille. Muslims experienced similar repression. Their expulsion from Spain after 1492 led to the arrival of 275,000 Moors into Provence; the parlement reacted with its *arrêt* of 13 January 1611, evicting them from the territory. Marseillais administrators' positions regarding Muslims was particularly complicated by Barbary piracy; in one of the worst flare-ups of anti-Islamic sentiment, Marseillais inhabitants massacred forty Algerian diplomats in 1620 following the capture of a Marseillais ship.

Despite exclusionary regulations in Marseille, high-profile naturalizations took place throughout the seventeenth century. The early seventeenth century saw three successful Corsicans—Sanson Napollon, Antoine-Marie Francisco, and Marco Francisco—become Marseillais citizens; the first negotiated the city's treaty with the dey of Algiers and the other two were successful *négociants*. Jean-Baptiste Magy from Bologna, a *négociant* in the Levantine trade, was naturalized in 1635, and became an *échevin* in 1676. His son became director of the Levant Company. Levantine *négociants* also naturalized and found administrative positions in municipal governance. The Armenian Antoine Arméni became a Marseillais citizen in 1625, while under less tolerant circumstances, Chain Chelebi and his son Jean were naturalized in 1694.[68]

All told, despite the influx of foreigners in the pre-Colbertist era, Marseille remained a small town until the mid seventeenth century. Figures from the thirteenth through sixteenth centuries show the population remaining fixed between 15,000 and 20,000; it rose to 30,000 by 1550 and 50,000 by 1650.[69] After Colbert's rise to power, the city's population suddenly soared; by 1720, Marseille was a bustling metropolis of 100,000. An untold number among them were of foreign origin.

ARMENIANS, JEWS, AND PROTESTANTS IN MARSEILLE: COLBERT, IMMIGRANTS, AND THE PUBLIC GOOD

Colbert's 1669 edict was an open invitation to immigrants. Its stipulation that silks from Italy, Levant, Africa, and countries ruled by the Turkish sultan or the shah of Persia could enter France only through Marseille or Rouen encouraged Ottoman traders to use the southern port. Moreover, it specified that any non-French foreigner could become a naturalized Frenchman and a *bourgeois* of the city if he worked in Marseille and married a Marseillaise; if he bought and lived in a house "within the walls of the new *agrandissement*" worth more than 10,000 *livres* for three years, or bought and lived in a house worth 5000 to 10,000 *livres* for five years; or if he spent twelve consecutive years in Marseille to "do commerce," without acquiring a house. Naturalization, obtained through certificates signed by Marseille's *viguier* and *échevins*, rendered the applicant "a participant in all civic laws, privileges and exemptions."[70]

The edict of 1669 visually transformed Marseille. By the eighteenth century, the city acquired the look celebrated in Joseph Vernet's tableaus of the Vieux Port. As engravings show, merchants, sailors, women, and slaves from different countries all frequented the port. Sketches of Marseille depict men in tunics and turbans negotiating with French merchants, while Levantine women in veils and furs lounge on traveling trunks on the quays.[71] Meanwhile, the city also witnessed the arrival of a less glamorous crowd. Colbert transferred the royal galleys from Toulon to Marseille and ordered the construction of an arsenal at the port in 1660. Subsequently, galley slaves, or *forçats*—French convicts, Protestants, and Turks—arrived in the city from Paris, Rennes, and Bordeaux through Marseille's main gates, the Porte d'Aix, and were housed at the Hôpital des forçats. The port population tripled. Historians have determined that over three thousand criminals—conspicuous in their red bonnets and shaved heads—appeared on the port daily, commuting to work along the quays.[72] While these chain gangs disappeared under the galleys when they took to sea, they worked at the port when the vessels anchored in the city for weeks at a time. By 1700, close to a hundred master craftsmen employed *forçats* for cheap labor; estimates from 1703 show that a third of the galley slaves were able to bribe officers to extend their stays at port. The historian Ina Baghdianz McCabe goes as far as to characterize late seventeenth-century Marseille as a Turkish town during the winter season.[73]

Levantines—Armenians and Jews in particular—and Protestants benefited most from Colbert's edict. The controller-general's welcome to Levantine merchants was reminiscent of open-door policies toward Armenians initiated by Cardinal Richelieu, who in June 1636 had overridden municipal decisions made by the consuls and Chamber of Commerce and permitted "Armenian merchants to come at liberty from their countries to ports and cities in Provence and others in the kingdom with whatever quantity of silk and other merchandise."[74]

Following Colbert's edict, Armenians and Jews—*négociants*, retail merchants, and priests among them—again began arriving in Marseille, where they formed a colony, comparable to the populous Italian one, of over 400 people.

Many of them were "already Europeanized."[75] Such developments delighted Colbert. In 1671, he wrote the *président de parlement* in Aix, Oppède, that "it is a great advantage for us . . . that the merchants have abandoned Leghorn [Livorno] and that the Armenians have brought silks to Marseille." He guaranteed Armenians protection "from all the chicanery of the city's [administrators]."[76] Through similar protection, an Armenian founded Marseille's first café—the first in France—in 1672. The same year, encouraged by Colbert, Armenians founded the city's first Armenian publishing house in the city.[77]

A number of Marseille's citizens reacted negatively to the influx of Armenians and Jews. An anonymous writer wrote a memoir on behalf of the "public benefit" to the *échevins* describing how Jews ruined Marseillais commerce and the mores of the citizens. They participated in usury, traded in counterfeit currency, and "made purchases at prices infinitely ruinous to sellers and extremely advantageous to themselves." Jews ruined virtuous Marseillais women by tempting them with finery. They corrupted inexperienced Marseillais merchants, buying merchandise from them at prices 60 percent below their value. They traded real estate at unfair prices. The overwhelming Jewish presence—evidenced by their homes, real estate, and synagogues—"Judaified" young Marseillais to the "disgrace of our Holy Religion."[78] He called for their expulsion.

Colbert rejected such arguments against Armenian and Jewish immigration. He criticized the city's citizens for their lack of interest in the public good; the Marseillais, he charged, "do not care about commercial expansion, but only that commerce remains in their hands and on their terms." Marseillais self-interest threatened to spread a "bad reputation through all of Europe," he warned. "There is nothing more advantageous for the general good of commerce than to augment the number of those who can do it; and in this regards, that which is not advantageous for the particular inhabitants of Marseille is for the general strength of the kingdom," Colbert insisted. Since "for religious reasons aside, we have never forbidden Jews from trading," he decreed that "it is not necessary to listen to the propositions [the Marseillais] have made against these Jews."[79]

In Colbert's view, Jews and Armenians benefited the public good more than the Marseillais, whose interests, he believed, contradicted the Crown's. For Colbert, race, ethnicity, color, or religion were not grounds for exclusion.

The Crown, however, ultimately reneged on its patronage of Ottoman Jews and Armenians. By the 1680s, the political and commercial situation in Marseille and France had changed dramatically. Louis XIV's Revocation of the Edict of Nantes (1685), proclaiming France's policy of religious intolerance, had disastrous consequences for foreign implants in Marseille and the kingdom.

The earliest traces of the Crown's intolerance taking effect on Jews in Marseille emerge from Colbert's writings to intendants in Aix in 1681. He wrote to Thomas Morant, asking him to inform him of the number of Jews in Marseille; "as the king no longer allows them in the country . . . you will examine secretly, if the people are useful or not in Marseille." Colbert ordered the expulsion of the Jews if they were proved useless to the French public good; the private interests of the Marseillais, however, were not to factor into royal decisions. "Commercial jealousy always leads merchants to advise you to expel them," he warned. He ordered his intendant to disregard "particular interests" and objectively analyze "whether they are advantageous for the state, what these advantages are, and if the same commerce cannot be supplied by Frenchmen, in which case, they will be expelled."[80]

Marseillais administrators' local initiatives to expel the Jews gained force once the Crown initiated these efforts to limit Jewish commerce in France. Marseille's Chamber of Commerce had opened a dossier against the Jews as soon as they began arriving from Leghorn in 1670. Since then, the chamber had unsuccessfully tried to curtail the "Israelite community" of Joseph Villeréal and his brother-in-law, Abraham Attias, elite merchants with contacts in the Levant, Barbary, and Leghorn. For over a decade, the chamber accused them of usury and corrupt practices. Memoirs asserted that the Jews harmed the "glory of God" and commerce by ruining Marseille financially and morally. The chamber alleged that in a large city like Marseille, the poverty of a large number of inhabitants provided the Jews the right environment for "corrupting mores" and exercising their lawless influence.[81]

The chamber cooperated with the royal intendant to show Colbert that Jews posed a threat to France. It presented a memoir steeped in the language of public good detailing a conspiracy among the Jews of Algeria, Leghorn, and Marseille. Jews threatened the state, it claimed; they consorted with Barbary pirates and profited from the sale of French prisoners. In a letter to Colbert's son Jean-Baptiste, marquis de Seignelay, a chevalier de Beaujon claimed that "the Jews of Marseille had caused the last war between the French and the Algerians." Jews tipped off Algerian pirates as to the whereabouts of French ships, and the pirates sold their French captives to the Jews.

In 1682, the king expelled Marseille's Jews for illegally operating a synagogue out of Villeréal's home, and for conspiring with Barbary pirates.[82] The battle against the Jews, however, continued when the parlement de Provence in Aix came to Villeréal's aid. It decided that the Jewish plaintiffs who requested parlement's aid were "advantageous to Marseillais commerce." The profits Villeréal accumulated in Marseille over the years had contributed over 16,000 *livres* to the king's coffers. Marseillais merchants, parlement contended, were "jealous of the [Jews'] *négoce*"; their expulsion, they ruled, was "contrary to His Majesty's justice."[83] Parlement allowed the Jews to reenter Marseille. The Chamber of Commerce protested, claiming that the parlement had violated the royal ordinance.[84] This struggle between Marseillais administrators and the parlement continued into the eighteenth century, and numerous parlementary *arrêts* allowed Jewish merchants to reestablish themselves in Provence. The Crown issued an ultimatum in 1710 decreeing that "the king annuls the *arrêts* rendered in the Chambre des vacations du parlement de Provence and prohibits parlement from rendering such *arrêts* in the future."[85]

The participation of Jews in French commerce led to heated debates among different sources of local and state power: Versailles, Marseille's Chamber of Commerce, and the parlement de Provence. More than a question of religious intolerance, the Jewish issue became a political matter that saw agents of local power competing to assert influence vis-à-vis the Crown and one another. Given the parlement's history of intolerance, it is unlikely that its decisions on behalf of the Jews were prompted by a sudden dose of tolerance. Rather, parlement perhaps recognized an opportunity; *arrêts* against the Crown's ordinances were political strategies that undercut Versailles' growing interference in local governance, as it was a way to remind the Marseille Chamber of Commerce of its subordinate status vis-à-vis the parlementary court. Meanwhile, the alliance between Marseille's chamber and Versailles over the Jewish question suggests how a locality that traditionally opposed centralizing initiatives found its interests furthered by collaboration. Whatever their levels of tolerance or intolerance, these administrators used the Jews as pawns to further their political and commercial interests.

Following Colbert's death, the Crown and local administrators developed exclusionary policies toward Armenians as well. Controller-General Pontchartrain initially continued his predecessor's early policies of inclusion by enrolling several young Armenians in French royal *collèges*, but by 1687, Seignelay prohibited Armenians' silk trade in France.[86] He determined that sales of *ardasses*—cheaper and allegedly inferior Armenian silks sold in Marseille as French silk—"entirely ruined" French manufacturers. He ordered the confiscation of *ardasses*; ships found carrying them were fined 3,000 *livres*.

Marseille's Armenian colony disintegrated following Seignelay's decree. Those who stayed or returned to Marseille faced detainment and harassment; their goods were often confiscated.[87] When Armenians like Oandjy and Ibraham

Barsan disembarked in Marseille on their way from Alexandria to Spain in 1716, the Chamber of Commerce and royal intendant confiscated their goods, accusing them of illegally selling silk.[88] In 1720, two Armenians from Smyrna, Abro and Serpuis Georgi, requested permission to trade in Marseille. They hoped that their credentials would protect them from exclusionary policies; they had served as honorary interpreters for the French nation in Smyrna, and their father had been awarded the king's protection by the French ambassador in Constantinople. Versailles initially began the process of providing them with letters of protection, motivated by the desire to prevent the French consul in Smyrna from facing "any inconveniences." Ultimately, however, the Crown agreed with the Chamber of Commerce's "just reflections" to reject their petitions. The Crown had to balance exclusionary policies toward foreigners in France with its responsibility to stabilize favorable conditions for French expatriates abroad. In this sense, Versailles was prone to act inconsistently toward foreigners in France, granting allowances when it estimated that leniency toward foreigners at home might ease tense Franco-Turkish situations abroad. The city's Chamber of Commerce, however, remained consistent in its exclusionary tendencies.

Difficulties for all foreign nationals escalated under Michel Chamillart's tenure as finance minister (1699–1708); in 1697, he promulgated the naturalization tax, and in 1704, he attempted to extend it to all naturalized Frenchmen.[89] Naturalizations and migrations dropped in Marseille. The Crown also began clamping down on absentee naturalized subjects. Versailles revoked letters of naturalization from foreigners who retained homes abroad or failed to establish residence in France.[90] It restricted naturalized subjects' participation in certain professions. Royal ordinances in 1681, 1689, and 1725 called for naturalized subjects to present naturalization certificates to *échevins*, complete two three-month apprenticeships, serve on a ship belonging to His Majesty, and serve a minimum of five years on a French merchant ship before they could become captains or pilots.[91]

Despite these exclusionary regulations, the Crown and Marseille Chamber of Commerce consistently welcomed one category of alien trader: expatriate renegades who had "gone Turk" but were willing to reconvert to Catholicism and trade in France. Alphonse de Fortia de Pilles, the royal governor of Marseille, wrote to the *échevins* in 1687 describing how renegades from Tunis had arrived in Marseille, wanting to reembrace Catholicism. The captain and lieutenant of the Tunisian ship, Pierre Terragon (become Ali Raix) and Jean Guedon (become Ramadan) were originally Majorcan and Marseillais, respectively. Likewise, two Greek renegades on the same vessel, Dmitri (become Ali) and George (become

Mahemet) expressed a desire to reconvert to Catholicism, while a Moor, Mahamet, expressed an interest in becoming Catholic. The governor responded favorably and noted that treating such renegades tolerantly was a great advantage to the state. France, he insisted, should welcome them before rival countries took them in and benefited from their commerce.[92]

The cases of the Jewish Villeréal community and the Tunisian renegades demonstrate that the politics of exclusion and inclusion was a complicated matter that required a balancing act between power and authority, commercial interests, and religious difference. French authorities, whether Crown, controller-general, governor, or parlement, might choose to ignore or allow religious difference if they prioritized the commercial benefits of inclusion. Likewise, renegades like Ali Raix and Ramadan might weigh their religious convictions against their financial interests and find conversion a useful strategy to maximize their commercial privileges at different ports of call. Ultimately, it seems that amplified official religious intolerance did not completely limit personal agency; Jews could find advocates in the parlement, renegades could persuade governors to open city doors, and Chambers of Commerce and parlementary bodies could resist or accommodate Versailles' will on their own terms.

The Crown was less pragmatic, however, in its decisions concerning Protestant merchants in Marseille following the Revocation of the Edict of Nantes. It discontinued its policy of allowing "the liberty of commerce" and restricted would-be Protestant expatriates from trading overseas. Traditionally, the Crown's "liberty of commerce" allowed Frenchmen to trade without passports in neighboring states that had signed peace treaties with France. Following the Revocation, the Crown decreed (October 1685; 26 April and 7 May 1686; 12 October 1687; 11 February, 13 September and 5 December 1699) that "newly converted" Catholics could not leave France. A royal ordinance from 1711 limited "freedom to commerce" to Catholics; it prohibited Huguenots from misinterpreting "the liberty of commerce" to establish their families in Protestant nations. Such "abuses," it defined, amounted to "criminal disobedience."[93]

French Protestants were treated more severely than alien ones. The king's goal of "one king, one law, one faith" applied to fostering unity among French subjects; he was less interested in seeing foreigners subscribe to the same rule. He guaranteed freedom of religion to foreign Protestants as long as they did not naturalize. Seignelay wrote in 1685 that "for the advantage of commerce in Marseille, [the Crown] leaves the British, Dutch, and Swiss entirely free in their religion; but in regards to those who have taken letters of naturalization, His Majesty desires that they be regarded as his subjects, therefore they must be of the same religion and conform to the will of His Highness."[94] Foreign Protestants could live in France. Frenchmen, however, could not be Protestant. In 1680, Colbert wrote to the intendant of the galleys at Marseille, informing him that the king had "resolved to remove from his galleys all those [officers] who are of the *religion prétendue réformée*, and would like to be informed whether there are any Huguenots among the officers who serve at port." He instructed the intendant to "pleasantly inform the officers of this religion" that if they "continued in their errors," the king would discontinue "his service toward them."[95]

The Revocation was disastrous for the kingdom. Rather than generating mass conversions of Protestants to Catholicism, it prompted the Huguenot exodus to Great Britain, Switzerland, the Dutch republic, and the New World, and deprived the kingdom of a great portion of its merchant population.

THE EFFECTS OF COLBERTISM: POLICIES OF INCLUSION AND EXCLUSION

Louis XIV's controllers-general issued inconsistent regulations regarding foreigners and those of different religious orientations. Following the edict of 1669, Colbert saw foreigners and religious others as beneficial to France's general welfare. Contrasting recalcitrant Marseillais citizens who protested his immigration policies with the Jews, Armenians, and Protestants who benefited French commerce, Colbert called the Marseillais merchants bad subjects. However, given the king's growing desire for religious unity, the Crown mobilized the concept of public good to expel immigrants from Marseille and France. The services of immigrants were no longer seen as suiting the public good.

Initially, the idea of a free port filled with French subjects, adopted subjects from the Ottoman Empire, Armenians, Jews, and Protestants did not bother Colbert as long as he focused on the commercial benefits they generated. The overwhelming demographic diversification, however, disrupted the Crown's desire to establish administrative transparency and uniformity across the kingdom. While international commerce provided unprecedented opportunities for the Crown, local administrators, and merchants to fill their respective pockets and increase their political powers, it generated a profound sense of insecurity at all levels. Competition from foreign merchants put pressure on Marseille's status as a French port. Religious and cultural diversity obscured the city's native Catholic identity as much as it did the Crown's plans to construct a distinctively French one, defined by one king, one law, and one faith. Fears of Barbary piracy, Turkish expansion, foreign economic competition, and disease exhausted favorable evaluations of others and otherness and ended the openness that the Crown initially extended to foreign arrivals.

This book began with the observation that early modern French elites spoke of commerce in many ways. The new commercial civic spirit was founded on several claims: that commerce was beneficial to the state, and that merchants and elite *négociants* were honorable, virtuous subjects and citizens. These claims emerged out of new ways of applying statist concepts of utility and classical republican notions of participatory citizenship to the market. They helped jump-start commercial expansion during the reign of Louis XIV. But when the Crown extended opportunities for commercial engagement to aliens and immigrants, it met with local resistance. Seeing their commercial activities threatened by foreign competition, watching their neighborhoods opened to non-European populations, fearing their Catholic religion jeopardized by Islamic, Jewish, and Protestant "corruption," Marseille's merchants and citizens protested the demographic changes generated by Colbert. Ultimately, the Crown too, shared these local anxieties.

Commercial civic spirit, therefore, spawned both inclusive and exclusionary policies during Louis XIV's reign. The Crown extended to all merchants—French and foreign, noble and common—the opportunity to participate in French commerce. Intellectuals and travelers who described the cultural, historic and geographic similarities between France and other Mediterranean countries encouraged French traders to seek their fortunes and strengthen the state through the Levantine trade. But when "the foreign" made inroads into France, exclusionary arguments resurfaced and derogatory notions of commerce and "the foreign" reemerged. Ottomans were untrustworthy. Jews were usurers. Armenians were deceptive. Merchants were self-interested. Commerce was dangerous.

Such arguments would peak in 1720, when city and state administrators' worst fears were realized. The plague—the ultimate symbol of "Oriental" decadence—arrived on the *Grand Saint-Antoine*, a Marseillais merchant ship from the Levant, wiped out half of the city's population, and took tens of thousands of lives in Provence. With plague threatening to spread to the French heartland, evaluations of foreign commerce soured. Meanwhile, the city was thrown into civic crisis as administrators and leading citizens found themselves torn between accepting and rejecting commerce, their commercial links with the Levant, and their dependence on the French Crown. What happened to commercial civic spirit in this context? To this catastrophe, the following chapters turn.

CHAPTER FOUR

Plague, Commerce, and Centralized Disease Control in Early Modern France

Most early modern Europeans would have concurred with the physician Jérôme-Jean Pestalozzi that "Oriental plague" was the sum of everything "most contrary to life."[1] During his tour of the Levant, the Aixois botanist Joseph de Tournefort noted how frequently plague ravaged the Ottoman Empire and that the Turks refused to implement preventative measures. Ignorance and fatalism doomed the population to death. "Aside from fire, the plague and the *leventis* [undisciplined soldiery] are the two main scourges in Constantinople," he observed; the Turks tranquilly watched "up to five or six hundred people die daily of this cruel malady, without taking any measures to avoid or combat it." The Turks spread disease by continuing to trade during an epidemic: "the goods and merchandise of the plague-ridden are sold as easily as those people who have been murdered or have died in old age."[2]

Tournefort's descriptions of the connections between Islam, Turkish despotism, and disease were hardly original. Abbé Martin Gaudereau described how the "Orientals" rejected precautions against disease under "the tyranny of *Mahometisme*." "While the Christian Religion flourished in Armenia, Asia Minor, Mesopotamia and Syria," he wrote, "these Provinces surrendered to the purity of the air." They transformed, however, into lands "overshadowed by death . . . that devoured its own inhabitants" under the "force" and "ignorance" of the Turks.[3] By the eighteenth century, European writers agreed that "all plagues that have appeared in Europe have been transmitted by communication with the Saracens, the Arabs, the Moors and the Turks, and that plagues do not have our homes as a source."[4] They understood that merchants, soldiers, travelers, and their goods brought the "Oriental plague" to Europe. Plague—along with the sultan's janissaries, eunuchs, and harem—became symbolic of "Oriental" decadence. European accounts encoded plague within a matrix that equated corrupt states and societies with corrupt bodies.

Beyond expressing anxieties that the Ottomans would destroy French commerce by conspiring with pirates or trading inferior silks, French administrators remained particularly wary of the threat of plague they associated with the Turkish Empire. "Plague covers Turkey, and appears frequently in cities, following commerce and communication," the French physician G.-A. Olivier commented at the end of the eighteenth century. "It is always present in Constantinople because it is the city that communicates most with the rest of the Empire." Turkish ships carried plague to Alexandria, Asia Minor, and Europe.[5] Worried that international trade amplified the risk of outbreaks of this dreaded disease in France, physicians and administrators kept a nervous eye on merchants and merchandise from the eastern Mediterranean.

Plague was by no means the sole large-scale catastrophe that concerned early modern Europeans. As Stephen Tobriner has discussed, the "specter of earthquakes loomed large in the Enlightenment consciousness" as seismic activity under Lisbon, Sicily, and other parts of the Mediterranean killed over 130,000 people between 1693 and 1783.[6] Devastation caused by hurricanes found expression in various literature, from William Shakespeare's *The Tempest* to Daniel Defoe's *The Storm*.[7] Meanwhile, cold winters, bad harvests, and parasites in Europe and its colonies triggered famines. In early modern imaginary, these calamities traced to the same source; following ancient Hippocratic medicine, experts and lay populations believed that bad air, or miasma, "precipitated a radical imbalance between inner and outer states of being in humans and other life forms, from animals to seeds of grain."[8] However, it was only plague that they understood in relation to commerce and the Ottoman Empire: plague was an "Oriental" disease, it spread as a result of commerce, and it disrupted European commerce.

What medical knowledge did French experts generate to protect the kingdom from the ultimate "Asiatic" disease? What initiatives did the Crown and local administrators develop to safeguard commercial centers from catastrophic epidemics? This chapter argues that seventeenth- and eighteenth-century knowledge of plague was as inconsistent as French Orientalist discussions of the Ottoman Empire. On one hand, plague treatises, dictionary articles, and medical pamphlets exaggerated its terrible characteristics. They insisted that a plague-stricken city was the apocalyptic inverse of a properly functioning community. As Daniel Gordon and Colin Jones have shown, early modern writers used metaphors that depicted plague as religious, political, and social derangement.[9] They adopted Hippocratic theories to argue that plague resulted from disturbances of equilibrium and order in the human body and the environment. Such ancient interpretations jibed with early modern Orientalist visions of the Turks. French stereotypes of the Ottomans—political tyranny, sexual depravity, religious fanaticism, medical catastrophe—could be legitimated if medically rationalized as products of humoral derangement. The same writers who stressed plague's dystopic qualities and followed ancient medical formulas, however, adopted new interpretations of disease by claiming that plague was not so dreadful if examined rationally. They insisted that empirical science would counterbalance the plague's disruptive effects on body and society. Early eighteenth-century scientists and doctors—notable among them, Jérôme-Jean Pestalozzi and François Chicoyneau—understood disease as a product of irrationality, and advocated the use of reason to restore humoral equilibrium. The late early modern period saw old and new "science" combining; empiricism and "reason" were not diametrically opposed to Hippocratic interpretations of plague.

As with doctors, French administrators combined Eurocentric Orientalist sensibilities, knowledge of Hippocratic science, and emergent rationalist approaches to prevent and contain disease. Convinced that plague spread through the foreign *levain pestilentiel* that corrupted air, royal and local administrators in Marseille and other ports strengthened plague prevention programs by reforming two existing institutions, the lazaretto, or quarantine hospital, and *bureaux de la santé,* which established regulations for travelers from the Levant. Meanwhile, the monarchy increasingly interfered in administering these institutions; upon opening Marseille to duty-free Levantine commerce, the Crown centralized both institutions, placing local health management under royal control and patronage. Led by Colbert, the monarchy imagined that it would protect the city and state from medical danger through royal regulation and streamlined administration. Civic leaders—the *échevins* and *intendants de la santé*—resisted, convinced that quarantine hospitals and bureaux in Marseille were civic institutions that required autonomy.

Like the "science" it was founded upon, plague prevention was thus a combination of old and new. It built on civic institutions that predated French commercial expansion. At the same time, an emergent power—a bureaucratized state—struggled to wrest away authority from local health intendants, who continued to believe that health in a municipality was a civic issue. Seeing commercial expansion and the developments that threatened it—pirates, foreign competition, and plague—as state, rather than local concerns, the monarchy sought to adopt local systems of administration under its patronage, asserting that it alone could assure the health of the public. Ultimately, however, the bureaucratic machine failed in 1720.

UNDERSTANDING PLAGUE IN EARLY MODERN FRANCE

What was plague? The plague's causes were not discovered until 1894, when Alexandre Yersin located a bacillus, later named *Yersinia pestis*, on dead rats and human plague victims. In 1898, scientists decoded the relationship between *Yersinia pestis*, fleas, and rats: fleas ingested bacilli from infected rats; they spread disease as they regurgitated bacilli on host bodies or defecated into the punctures created by their bites.[10] Until such epidemiological discoveries, medical experts only knew that plague was a terrible disease. Fever, chills, and delirium; the eruption of black carbuncles; the bubo, the large roselike inflammation on the groin or armpit that secreted pus and blood; the bile spilling from the mouth and bowels; a "prompt death"[11] after three days: these symptoms earned the disease its reputation as "the assemblage of all that is the most contrary to life," in Jean Pestalozzi's words.[12]

This disease that inflicted such violence on the body moved swiftly through Europe, Africa, and Asia. In Rennes in 1605, 20 percent of plague victims died within a day, 48 percent within two days, and 80 percent within five.[13] Between 1703 and 1716, plague devastated Europe every year: it left 18,000 dead in Kraków in 1706; 25,000 in Danzig and 21,000 in Stockholm in 1710; 215,000 in Brandenburg in 1715. An outbreak in 1713 killed a third of Prague's inhabitants and a tenth of Vienna's.[14] At its height in 1720, the plague claimed a thousand deaths a day in Marseille. Across the Mediterranean, in Constantinople alone, outbreaks claimed from 12 percent to 30 percent of the population. Similar numbers held true for Salonika, Smyrna, Alexandria, and Cairo into the nineteenth century.[15] During the eighteenth century, Constantinople was ravaged by plague 64 years out of 100; Anatolia, 57 years; Syria, 49 years; and Egypt, 44 years.[16]

Southern France, and Provence in particular, suffered numerous plague outbreaks between the Black Death of 1347 and the Plague of 1720, the last epidemic in the kingdom. Daniel Panzac counts thirty epidemics between 1347 and 1450; forty-three between 1451 and 1550; and twenty-nine between 1551 and 1650. While the region only saw four epidemics between 1651 and 1750, the threat of plague remained high.[17]

Early modern European observers turned to classical humoral theory to comprehend this violent disease. Introduced by the ancient Hippocratic school of medicine, the humoral theory developed under Galen and Byzantine and Persian physicians such as the renowned Avicenna (ca. 980–1037), before it was reintroduced in translation to European intellectuals in the Italian city-states and Islamic Al Andalus (Spain); Latin plague treatises on the Black Death drew on Arabic sources.[18] Humoralists divided the world into four elements—fire, water, air, and earth—corresponding to fluids in the body. Each element was associated with colors, temperaments, seasons, smells, tastes, and age. According to humoralists, plague spread due to miasmas, or disequilibrium in the air. Corruptions in the air upset the relationship between elements and corresponding humors inside the body. Following such Hippocratic teachings, early modern physicians maintained that the plague was bad air: "The plague being a very subtle vapor, it communicates itself easily from one to another subject," Pierre-Jean Fabre, the king's physician, wrote in 1652, "this vapor contains venom that is totally contrary to life, and it destroys it completely." While healthy bodies contained "natural heat," the plague was "a cold vapor deprived of all heat."[19]

From classical Greece to early modern Europe, physicians across the Mediterranean world assumed that "moderation" could counteract humoral corruptions. Arabic modifications on Galen included six principles of moderation: air-intake, food and drink, work and rest, wakefulness and slumber, evacuation and retention, and emotion.[20] During plague outbreaks, physicians restored equilibrium in three ways: bloodletting to reduce heat, excising boils to remove bile, and spreading clay over the skin to calm the humors. They relied on herbal and fruit concoctions for hydration. Above all, physicians stressed that good regimen and prudence could prevent and reverse bodily derangement, while, "the passions of the heart [and] movements of the spirit" could multiply disorder. According to one physician, such "passions" that stoked derangement included "movements of temper, of love, of sadness."[21]

Definitions of "moderation," "derangement," humoral balance, and disequilibrium were, however, open to interpretation. The Hippocratic vocabulary was highly elastic, allowing early modern writers to magnify the scope of plague by assigning various political, moral and social meanings to the term. Above all, early modern medical experts and administrators associated plague, the physical disease, with political derangement based on readings of classical plague texts written by chroniclers such as Thucydides, Procopius, and St. Cyprian that reinforced the relationship between medical, political, and moral catastrophes.

Thucydides' *History of the Peloponnesian War* was one of the primary accounts of plague in antiquity consulted by early moderns. Thucydides wrote how the second year of the war saw "a pestilence of such extent and mortality [that] was nowhere remembered." Plague for Thucydides symbolized the corruption of Athens and the destruction of the republic. Plague overwhelmed the physical body and stunned the sociopolitical body. The healthy abandoned their civic duties. Citizens succumbed to fatalism at the prospect of imminent death, abandoning public duties and pursuing personal pleasure: "men not knowing what would become of themselves became utterly careless of everything whether sacred or profane."[22] The heroism of Pericles that ruled Athens disappeared. Egotism prevailed.

Borrowing such interpretations from Thucydides, early modern French and Provençal intellectuals perceived plague as the destroyer of political order, as dangerous as political usurpers, anarchy, and tyranny. The physician François Chicoyneau, son-in-law of the first doctor to the Regent, used Thucydides' plague as a template to understand all subsequent outbreaks in Europe. Plague epidemics, "a malady as old as the world," he observed, had followed the same pattern though two millennia. As in Athens, war, political chaos and plague always appeared together.[23] Plague disrupted citizenship; consuls fled, immorality reigned, and inhabitants succumbed to self-interest. Patriots and traitors appeared in such moments in striking contrast, as did order and disorder, virtue and vice, health and sickness. Specifically in early eighteenth-century Marseille, physicians such as Jean-Baptiste Bertrand described how the city repeatedly suffered the combined catastrophes of war and plague: the city's oldest recorded plague devastated Massilia with Julius Caesar's army in 49 BC, while subsequent epidemics prompted political chaos, or vice versa. In 1580, he recounted, the epidemic spread as citizens and consuls fled the scene, while in 1630, political disorder brought plague to the city: "the divisions that reigned in the city led to the neglect of precautions that might have prevented [the plague]."[24] Other early modern plague writers associated plague with moral disorder. In *Histoire de la Ville d'Aix,* the physician Jean-Scholastique Pitton argued that while war and political instability "attracted the anger of the Lord,"[25] immorality also generated plague. Epidemics, he claimed, began when "women of debauchery" spread disease.[26]

By the eighteenth century, plague developed into a multilayered term involving physical, moral, and political imbalance. The article for *peste* in the first edition of the *Dictionnaire de l'Académie française* (1694) illustrates the term's broad scope. After defining *peste* as a "contagion, an epidemic malady that comes from a general corruption in the air and causes a great mortality," the author provided several figurative usages. As a noun, a *peste* was "a person with whom frequentation is dangerous." The dictionary specified that "a person of bad example" was a *peste* against "the public," and that a bad citizen in power was "a *peste* against the Republic."[27] "Lively and malicious young women" could also be *pestes*. Jean-François Féraud's prerevolutionary *Dictionnaire critique de la langue française* (Marseille, 1788) reinforced such metaphorical definitions, stating that "people and things capable of corrupting the spirit of the heart" were plagues. "Bad Princes are ordinarily taken by *pestes de Coeur* . . . Flatterers, *peste fatale*, destroy states more than the armies of enemies." The verb *pester* meant "to wage war."[28]

Plague signified more than bad people with bad intentions doing bad things. It was any extreme expression of evil and anarchy: *peste* was "all the bad things of this world."[29] If physicians in the Hippocratic tradition defined disease as humoral derangement, historians, administrators and doctors in the early modern period tended to regard plague as maximum derangement.

RATIONALIZING PLAGUE IN EIGHTEENTH-CENTURY FRANCE

Dictionaries aside, early modern French discussions of plague most often appeared in the form of plague treatises, usually published in Paris, Lyon, or Toulouse.[30] Often titled *Traité de la peste*, the classic treatise included a preface, a discussion of the disease's origins, signs—of its approach and symptoms—preservatives, and disinfection measures. These texts were hardly intended solely for physicians; rather, they were aimed at medical, religious, and municipal personnel in general.

While they adopted Hippocratic explanations of plague that connected disease to disorderly sociopolitical environments, early eighteenth-century epidemiologists introduced new interpretations that tended to shrink plague's dimensions. While preserving Hippocratic theories of miasmas, physicians assumed a rationalist tone that reduced the disease to its "simplest forms."[31] They configured plague, disharmony, and irrationality against experimental knowledge and rationality. The medical views of two renowned physicians who practiced and wrote during the plague of 1720, Jérôme-Jean Pestalozzi and François Chicoyneau, point to this transition.

Pestalozzi was professor of medicine in Lyon and a member of the Académie royale des sciences de Montpellier. Following Hippocratic teachings, he attributed the plague to yeasts activated by miasmas. His *Dissertation sur les causes et la nature de la Peste* and *Avis sur la Peste* described how air imbalances created yeast, which spread through commerce. This yeast, he explained, was foreign; "in certain climates," he described, "an assemblage of salts that compose a foreign and completely inassimilable yeast . . . puts everything in disorder." The yeast multiplied in the blood and deranged humoral balance; it sent bodies off kilter by introducing "a cold vapor."[32] It gained strength "in our climates," surviving "outside the [human] body without decomposing"; it survived for months in clothes, textiles, and merchandise.[33] Echoing classical discussions, Pestalozzi then argued that plague destroyed more than the physical body: as individual victims fell, political and social bodies collapsed. "If this particular malady in man deranges all the economy of his body, the general and contagious malady entirely reverses the political order and ruins civil society."[34]

Pestalozzi insisted, however, that plague was a simple disease. It destroyed many things, but it did so in the same way. Plague disrupted healthy relationships among humors in the body; likewise, it disturbed healthy relationships among inhabitants in society. In a word, plague deranged "economy," understood biologically as "a harmony between different parts and qualities of the physical body" and figuratively, "as the order by which the political body subsists."[35] Plague skewed relationships, but they could be righted through scientific observation.

Pestalozzi advocated a simplified scientific method of confronting the plague: observation of the disease's effects. He adopted an empirical method that "consist[ed] in knowing the malady by its effects, by its signs and accidents, of judging its different circumstances, of taking these indications and following the best paths, and finally of performing means known to medicine."[36] Rather than focusing on the myriad causes, he advised the physician to observe the symptoms to discern what had been deranged. Plague, he argued, had to be reduced to its simplest forms. The variations and "bizarre complications" that plague produced in different bodies suggested that it required "different methods" of treatment. He argued, however, that "everything depends on one principal . . . all the variations can only come from the modification of the same principle." Reduced to basics, plague could "be attacked by one method . . . by the same genre of remedies."[37]

Pestalozzi's scientific method was fraught with tensions. Though he had inherited the Hippocratic vocabulary, his investigative process leading from particular effects to general ideas made him a budding empiricist. While he subscribed to ideas about plague that linked physical derangement with political and social disorder, he attempted to strip it of metaphors and reduce it to biological dimensions to make it manageable and curable.

Meanwhile, Pestalozzi's contemporary and rival François Chicoyneau (b. 1672, the son of Michel Chicoyneau, chancellor of Montpellier University) also marshaled rationalist approaches to claim that plague did not exist. Chicoyneau received his medical degree in 1693. Following his mentor (and father-in-law) Pierre Chirac, doctor of the royal army and first doctor to the king, Chicoyneau achieved fame for refuting contagionist theories and for arguing that plague only existed in the imagination.

In *Notice sur les principales pestes qui ont ravagé le monde*, Chicoyneau, like Pestalozzi, characterized plague as an uncomplicated disease. Using the first recorded plague outbreak during the Peloponnesian War as the paradigm for all subsequent epidemics, he demonstrated that "the most terrible wars have destroyed fewer people in entire provinces than the plague." The plague, however, was predictable; it remained unchanged through centuries. "While wars have varied," he explained, "plague almost always has the same characteristics: the oldest plagues are like pictures of the new [ones]." In all outbreaks, "one sees the characteristics of all other plagues; the origin is the same; the complications resemble one another; the progress is equally rapid; what follows is equally terrible; they have inspired the same beliefs."[38] Following the Athenian outbreak described by Thucydides, all plagues appeared in the same political context. All victims suffered the same fate. Fear of and anxiety about plague threw bodies into disequilibrium, which then succumbed to fever, gangrene, inflammation, bile discharge, ulcers, and pustules. Sleeplessness and dehydration led to quick death.[39]

For Chicoyneau, it was not plague that killed, but rather fear. "The concept of fear," he detailed, produced "a conviction that one will be attacked; from this fear, a perpetual imbalance of the mind; from this imbalance, a quivering of the brain; from this quivering a vertigo and a strong belief that illness and death are not far off; from this belief a growth of terror; from this a stoppage of the blood and lymph or the blockage of fluids and solids; from this blockage, inflammations and gangrene; and finally the plague and death."[40] This hypothesis downgraded the plague "to psychosomatic dimensions," Daniel Gordon writes.[41] According to Chicoyneau, plague did not exist. Fractured minds produced fractured bodies. A scientific mind, devoid of apprehensive imaginings, would eliminate plague.

Chicoyneau's refusal of plague was radical. Nonetheless, he was ultimately a traditionalist who employed conventional remedies to restore humoral balance, bodily and mental equilibrium. Attributing the disease to fear and "unwholesome food," Chicoyneau recommended better bread and, during the Plague of 1720, counseled musicians to play "violins, drums, and fifes . . . and lively airs, . . . to drive away melancholy" and "superstition."[42]

Early eighteenth-century epidemiologists brought together Hippocratic medicine, classical historical interpretations, and emergent notions of empirical rationalism to understand plague. Attributing disharmony to bad air and foreign yeasts, physicians preserved the remnants of traditional humoral theory. They also began limiting, if not discarding, the wide metaphors of plague to uphold what would become an Enlightenment reading of disease; they introduced the idea that reason and experimental science could control and ultimately abolish biological and natural disasters. Early modern readings of plague, therefore, oscillated between pessimistic visions of an apocalyptic medical catastrophe that rendered humans powerless, and optimistic assumptions that the human mind could control nature.

PLAGUE PREVENTION AND THE BUREAU DE LA SANTÉ: A PREMODERN OR MODERN INSTITUTION?

While plague writers argued whether plague existed or not, administrators in European cities along the Mediterranean coast developed preventative measures to shield the continent from a medical catastrophe that they assumed was foreign and "Asiatic." In this regard, they were motivated not only by Orientalist impulses; by the sixteenth century, it was a known fact that plague did not originate in Europe. During the classical and medieval periods, plague epidemics broke out indiscriminately in Europe, Asia, or Africa. By the seventeenth century, however, climatic changes and rodent depopulation had reduced plague's "permanent foci" to the Near East, Africa, and Asia. Seventeenth-century Europeans agreed that the Ottoman Empire was the center of plague activity, with Constantinople, Smyrna, and Alexandria forming the triangle where the yeast to which they ascribed plague developed. The convergence of Orientalist views and biological realities supported European administrators' polarized and distorted understanding that the Turkish Empire was the inverse of a properly functioning order.

Plague-prevention initiatives in early modern Europe consisted of several defining characteristics. First, as commerce was transnational in character, so too were the programs created to protect it. Like commerce, health maintenance transcended local and national boundaries. Bureaux of health, health intendants, and quarantine hospitals established from the sixteenth through eighteenth centuries throughout Euro-Mediterranean cities, republics, and states mutually communicated intelligence to minimize the outbreak of plague; they worked with the premise that standardized rules and international collaboration would lead to the perfection of human health. The eighteenth-century *mémoires* of the Marseille Bureau de la santé revealed the universalist message: "The health bureaux that are established in all the ports of the Mediterranean exist within the jurisdiction of each government and its principal administration. Even in time of war, they continue to correspond with one another to convey mutual advice for all who can contribute to the conservation of health in the universal society of mankind [*société universelle des hommes*]."[43] Correspondence among bureaux testifies to this collaborative aspect of health maintenance. The Marseille bureau sent or received approximately 250 letters regarding plague annually. The majority of its correspondence involved Spanish and Italian health bureaux; 72 percent of the letters were from or went to Genoa, Livorno, or Venice. Correspondence surged during plagues. The Archivio di Stato of Venice has conserved 5,653 letters received or sent between 27 June 1720 and 4 February 1724 during Marseille's plague of 1720. Each bureau specialized in news of plague outbreaks in the Ottoman Empire; collaborative efforts among European bureaux to publicize reports to other bureaux played a critical role in preventing and containing plague in Europe.[44]

The health bureaux therefore had several identities. As institutions established in a particular municipality and run by health intendants chosen by civic administrators, they were committed to serving the interests of local communities. Located in major port cities that served as gateways into the larger state, these bureaux were also corporate bodies beholden to the monarch. Finally, as part of a loosely organized Euro-Mediterranean-wide health organization, they were committed to safeguarding Europe from "foreign," "Turkish" disease. These layers of commitments often resulted in much tension over authority and proper protocol.

Another distinguishing feature of plague-prevention initiatives was their combination of premodern and modern systems of health management. Unaware of the biological causes of plague, administrators and physicians employed by European health bureaux used Hippocratic medicine to define and diagnose disease, and to treat and disinfect people and merchandise suspected of contamination. At the same time, the bureaucratic machinery was rather modern and unprecedented. In France, it was the product of Colbert's desire to centralize commercial administration; as the controller-general associated plague prevention with securing commercial activity, he insisted that the Crown control health management in Marseille. Much before the establishment of a democratic welfare state, the French monarchy began claiming authority to govern subjects' bodies—something previously limited to local and religious authorities. Furthermore, the systematized procedures for the quarantining of mariners and merchants conformed to "modern" standards of disciplinary management rather than premodern methods. Michel Foucault, after all, located the physical model for Jeremy Bentham's panopticon in the plague-containment practices established in the lazaretto: "immobilized by the functioning of an extensive power that bears in a distinct way over all individual bodies—this is the utopia of the perfectly governed city. The plague . . . is the trial in the course of which one may define ideally the exercise of disciplinary power. . . . traversed throughout with hierarchy, surveillance, observation, writing. . . . Bentham's Panopticon is the architectural figure of this composition."[45] The quarantine system instituted by early modern health bureaux can be analyzed as an early attempt at the detached scientific objectification that Foucault would find perfected in nineteenth-century detention centers.

Early modern European plague prevention was founded on a simple and logical premise: disease could be minimized by limiting contact with travelers. European countries shielded themselves from plague by first restricting the points of contact between the Levant, Barbary, and Europe. That Marseille became the only port in France authorized to receive vessels directly from the Levant had as much to do with limiting exposure to contagious disease as with increasing profits in trade through monopoly.[46]

Second, European states updated their lazarettos, making health surveillance a mandatory requirement for international traffic and travel. The completion of Marseille's new lazaretto, the Nouvelles Infirmeries, in 1668, in time for Colbert's edict of 1669, was no coincidence. The Crown could not risk the appearance of plague in France; a plague outbreak would shut down the port and disrupt the country's international trade. Plague meant not only physical deaths but the disruption of commerce. This royal attention to pestilential outbreaks appeared clearly in the edict of 1669, which made quarantines compulsory. Building a new lazaretto at Marseille would prevent "the ruin of commerce and the exposure of the whole kingdom to the communication of the contagious malady."[47] Though a "communal institution," the lazaretto was "national property." Louis XIV reached into his own coffers to create it, providing 62,000 *livres* "for the acquisition of lands and the construction of the Nouvelles Infirmeries," which would be "a great advantage and utility for the public."[48] By 1669, the city's Bureau de la santé regularly held quarantines at the completed Nouvelles Infirmeries.

The lazaretto system was confined neither to Marseille nor to the late seventeenth century. The lazaretto was a legacy of the medieval leprosaria; as the incidence of leprosy decreased, leper asylums were converted into confinement centers for mendicants, the insane, and those with infectious diseases.[49] Quarantining the "suspected sick" began in the fifteenth century in the Italian city-states, whose trading links with the Levant led them to implement measures for plague protection. In 1423, Venice constructed the first lazaretto on the island of Santa Maria di Nazaret to contain and prevent pestilential epidemics. Following Venice, Livorno established a permanent health administration, and expanded its existing lazaretto in 1590. Naples, Genoa, Trieste, and Split (Dalmatia) built or expanded their lazarettos by the eighteenth century. This wave of expansion projects coincided with the rise in international trade. As Françoise Hildesheimer has demonstrated, the renovated lazaretto became "the establishment most immediately representative of [modern] health administration."[50]

Far from serving as mere sites for quarantine, the architectural design of lazarettos served a symbolic purpose. They signified power. Visually, they "became vast establishments whose dimensions reflected the importance of the ports that depended on them."[51] A hierarchy of ports developed, reflected in the size of the quarantine centers. The expansion of a lazaretto promoted a port from a local commercial center to an international trading hub. As Daniel Panzac has argued, "the founding of a lazaretto was an act of political will that preceded future economic activity."[52] The reconstruction of the Livorno lazaretto (expanded from 10,750 m^2 to 12,700 m^2 in 1722 and 33,000 m^2 by 1781) coincided with the expansion of the city's Levantine commerce.[53] By its last expansion, the lazaretto had its own port. Similarly, the commercial powerhouses of Venice and Spezia expanded their lazarettos. The new Venetian lazaretto was three stories high, with imposing towers. The plans for the Spezia lazaretto were more spectacular: encased in high walls, two massive rectangular structures led to the main body of the lazaretto, built as a square supported by rows of arches.

Consistent with such expressions of commercial power, Marseille's lazaretto on the Île de Pomegues, according to eighteenth-century British traveler John Howard, was "very spacious, and its situation rendered it very convenient for the immense commerce that the French conducted with the Levant."[54] Iron fencing separated an open gallery from twenty-four holding rooms on the first floor. Disinfection halls extended from the gallery; rectangular stone counters for textile disinfection extended along the halls. The lazaretto's two other wings involved the same layout of halls and counters. The outer walls had apartment barracks for officers and ship captains, and warehouses for merchandise.

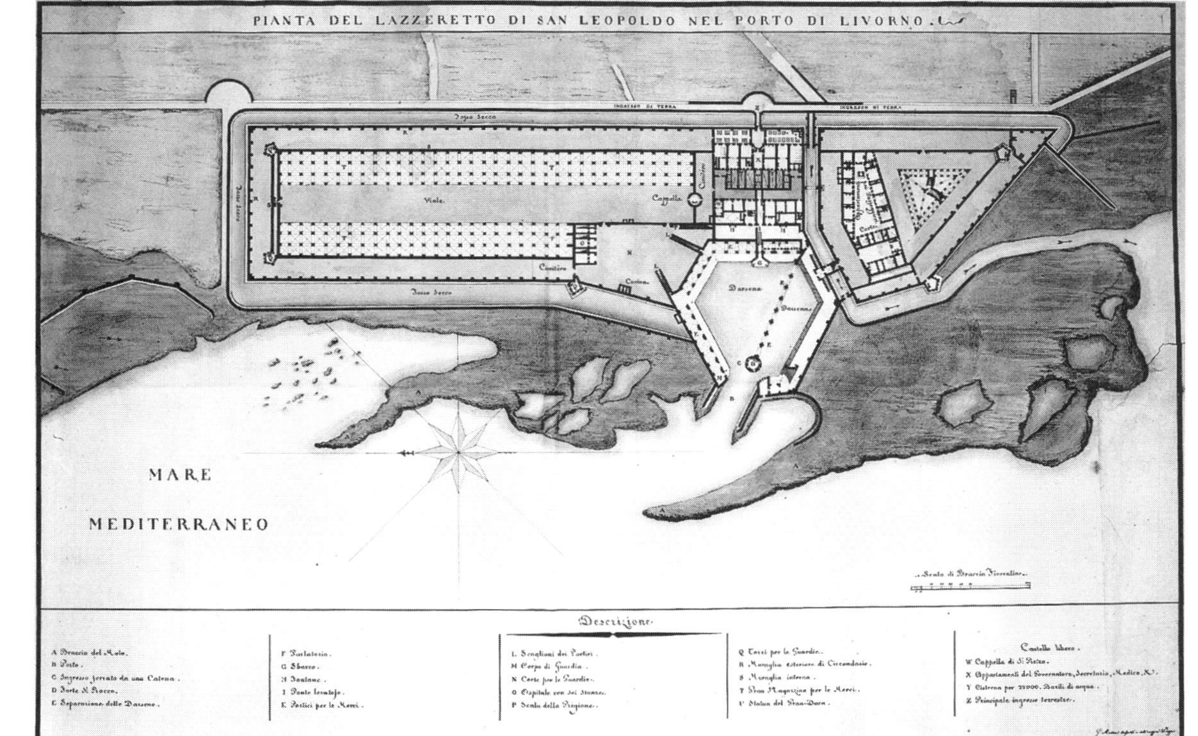

The Lazaretto at Livorno. *Courtesy Archivio di Stato, Venezia (653.A).*

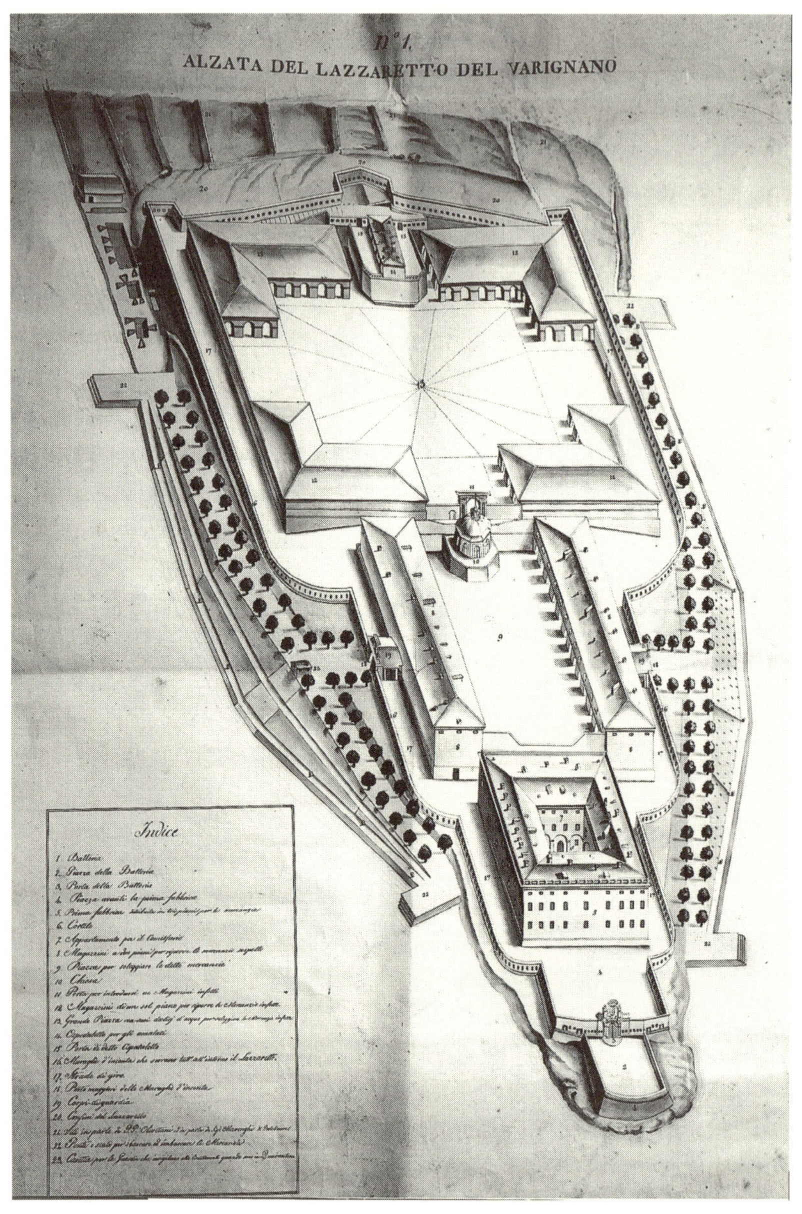

The Lazaretto at Spezia. *Courtesy Archivio di Stato, Venezia (653.B).*

Besides the power of the port, the lazaretto also demonstrated the power of surveillance. The structure stood at the entry to European ports, confronting travelers as they arrived by sea. The lazaretto purified bodies and made them fit for "civilization." The lazaretto projected the power of this transformative process by drawing attention to contrasts: its immense size versus its isolated quarantine chambers; its reception hall for dirty travelers versus its aerated barracks for the purged; spacious hallways for the health intendants versus the prisonlike spaces for the unclean. In Marseille, iron bars separated the observer from the observed. Iron fencing caged in travelers while intendants "observed the quarantine"[55] and "superintend[ed] the observance of every regulation established for the preservation of public health."[56] The lazaretto underscored binaries and hierarchies: clean versus contaminated, disordered versus organized, detained versus the disinfected. A fortresslike structure that separated the European city from the Mediterranean Sea, the lazaretto by its very architectural plan drew attention to the notion that he who ran it—the sovereign ruler, whether king, doge, or prince—was a force to be feared.

An anonymous author in the eighteenth-century French *Encyclopédie* confirmed that a lazaretto indeed operated much like an incarceration center. It was "a public building in the form of a hospital" that imposed a "kind of exile or imprisonment so unpleasant to bear."[57] In his *Confessions*, Jean-Jacques Rousseau commented on the uncomfortable experience of being quarantined in one:

> I was . . . conducted to a large building of two stories, quite empty, in which I found neither window, bed, table, nor chair, not so much as even a joint-stool or bundle of straw . . . My dinners were served with no small degree of pomp; they were escorted by two grenadiers with bayonets fixed; the staircase was my dining-room, the landing-place my table, and the steps served me for a seat; and as soon as my dinner was served up a little bell was rung to inform me I might sit down to table.[58]

A century later, the living conditions in lazarettos seem to have improved but little. A Parisian architect, Marchebeus, complained that the intendants of the lazaretto in Malta where he was detained forced upon him, "sixteen days of deadly boredom," in addition to "ridiculous inspections" and outrageous fees that were "double the cost of the best hotels in the city." The lazaretto, he concluded, was a "horrible prison."[59]

Simultaneously "a prison for containment and a hospital establishment for contagion,"[60] the lazaretto was intended for both internment and disinfection. The staff at the Marseille lazaretto confined "suspects" behind bars in separate apartments with "absence of physical communication." Detained travelers communicated only with the captain, the chief health official, who issued three types of certificates or bills of health *(patentes):* the *patente nette,* signifying "that in the place of departure, there was no suspicion of plague," the *patente soupçonnée,* for those from places rumored with plague, and the *patente brute,* for those from places ravaged by plague.[61] These bills of health determined the length of quarantines: sixteen, thirty, and forty days respectively.[62] Repeated inspections and disinfections would transform voyagers and merchandise from the Levant and make them eligible for entry into France.

MARSEILLE'S BUREAU DE LA SANTÉ

Who administered and determined operations at quarantine centers? The Marseille lazaretto was run by the city's Bureau de la santé, which originated around 1640 and was restructured by royal command after the 1666 *agrandissement* into an agency "composed of sixteen incorruptible men, who without complacence would order quarantines, disinfect everything received from suspect places . . . and severely punish those who transgress orders."[63] These intendants, who were "chosen from among the principal merchants of the city," rotated in annually.[64] The *échevins* served as the top two intendants. The other fourteen were *négociants.*[65] The 1730 *Mémoire sur le Bureau de la santé de Marseille et sur les règles qu'on y observe* stipulated that they were to be selected from "among the city's principal merchants, who have resided many years in the Levant."[66]

The men chosen to direct plague prevention for city and state in Marseille were thus not doctors specializing in disease control, but merchants. The individuals elected to the Bureau de la santé came from the same pool of *négociants* as those elected to other political and administrative municipal offices. When Louis XIV issued his municipal constitution restricting municipal administration to the merchant class following the conquest of 1660, he extended the privilege of leading health management to *négociants* as well. This royal decision underscored the association between commerce and plague prevention. The Crown accepted that plague spread through commercial exchange. It assumed that experienced merchants in the Levant trade who had spent their careers trading in the Ottoman Empire were most familiar with plague and how to prevent it. Furthermore, it determined that it was in the interests of commerce and commercial individuals that a major trading center remained plague-free; no one wanted to see plague arrive on Marseille's shores, and least of all merchants, who would see commerce halted during epidemics.

Objections that profit-driven merchants might not ensure impartial quarantines did not materialize, given the hegemonic power these *négociants* gained in 1660. Controlled by municipal leaders and connected with the Chamber of Commerce, the Bureau de la santé's political and commercial associations did occasionally overshadow its identity as a department for public health. Nonetheless, given the political and commercial monopoly Marseillais *négociants* enjoyed in administration, complaints that interests of the market and health might diverge remained unaddressed or muffled. Established elite merchant clans, such as the Roux, Borelly, or Remuzat families, dominated civic administration and were perceived as "rare and respectable citizens" of the *patrie*.[67] Their leadership in health management went unquestioned for decades.

The Crown's decision to entrust health administration to Marseillais merchant elites was also motivated by pragmatic motivations. By placing plague prevention in the hands of merchants who were also members of the *échevinage* and the Chamber of Commerce, the Crown limited control to a select few, streamlining its lines of communication with the city. By not cluttering different departments—commerce, health, and politics—with redundant personnel, it restricted the size of Marseille's city government, thus benefiting the monarchy's centralization efforts. The late seventeenth and early eighteenth centuries saw responsibility for "the protection of populations" gradually transferred from local authorities to the central state. This transformation can be tracked through an analysis of legislative material concerning the Bureau de la santé in Marseille from 1660 to 1720. Initially led by Colbert, the Crown endeavored to establish "a sense of precision, rationalization and uniformity" in health regulation.[68]

After ordering the construction of the new lazaretto and the restructuring of Marseille's health bureau in 1666, the Crown immediately began interfering in health administration there. It directed the *échevins* and health intendants to report on pestilential developments through correspondence with the parlement and the royal intendant in Aix and outlined the strategies it deemed necessary to protect Marseille and France from contagion. Deeming its "*règlements* . . . necessary to the control of the franchise of the port [Marseille]," the Crown ordered health ordinances to be followed with "exactitude and fidelity." From one edict to another, it ordered seafarers to present bills of health for those on board their ships, and laid down rules for those arriving from places suspected of contagion. Clear from these edicts was the understanding that plague would result in "the total ruin of commerce."[69]

The monarchy remained particularly attentive to plague in the Levant and Barbary, and it stepped up regulations to minimize contacts between Levantine and non-Levantine traffic. By 1689, the Crown forbade French ships to approach vessels of Levantine provenance "without the presence of one of the intendants of health, or by his written consent."[70] A year later, the royal intendant Pierre-Cardin Lebret made quarantines mandatory for all French vessels arriving from the Levant, Greek islands, Candia (Iráklion in Crete), the Morea (the Peloponnesus), and Barbary.[71] In 1709, the Crown ruled that quarantine and passport inspection evasions would incur corporal punishment, confiscation of vessels, and a fine of 3,000 *livres* from each of the vessels' shareholders.[72] Following 1718, regulations became increasingly rigid. The Crown reserved a specific area within the harbor for merchant ships coming from the Levant. Other vessels were ordered to navigate around these waters.[73]

Although initially, the Marseille Bureau de la santé's *intendants* ran it as an autonomous municipal office and were "charged . . . to act following their knowledge,"[74] Crown control increased steadily in the eighteenth century. Intrusive royal intervention started as early as in 1694 with demands for information regarding administration and finances. The Crown requested that there be a paper trail and forbade the Marseille health intendants to sequester financial records at the end of each year.[75] By 1726, the royal intendant ordered the bureau to inform the Crown "of all news from the sea reported by the captains and shipowners who come from the Levant.[76] By 1751, the health intendants would send weekly reports of activities in the lazaretto to the intendant; in times of heightened security, they would send reports every two days. Meanwhile, a new directive stipulated that the bureau could only execute decisions regarding "important deliberations" after "Versailles' approval."[77] In addition to merely requesting information, "the king exercised direct rule . . . despite the officially formulated principle [of autonomy]."[78]

Constant royal interference led to frequent sparring over control of health regulation between the monarchy and the Marseille Bureau de la santé. The escalation in 1698 of a century-long quarrel between the bureau and the tobacco-trading Compagnie d'Occident, illustrates how royal pressure intensified the efforts of the bureau and the Marseille Chamber of Commerce to preserve their autonomy. The Compagnie d'Occident insisted on its merchants' rights to visit their ships and cargo prior to quarantine. The Bureau de la santé deemed such visitations hazardous. The company responded by hiring its own inspectors to ensure security and prevent smuggling, which they deemed sufficient to avert pestilential disease. The Crown intervened by issuing an *arrêt* allowing the company what it wanted, agents both inside the bureau's lazaretto and on board ships. The bureau remonstrated, maintaining that surveillance was only effective when managed at a single location—the lazaretto. The Crown tried to end the fiasco by placing an embargo on tobacco. The bureau protested again, arguing that given the high demand for tobacco, an embargo would increase smuggling and amplify the risk of plague, and that furthermore such an embargo encroached on Marseille's status as a free port.

The Bureau de la santé underlined tobacco's risk to public health, then emphasized the need for both surveillance and open commerce. It stressed that tobacco was "susceptible and always presents risks" to public health because, like any other merchandise, it could carry plague, and its pestilential vapors would be released into the air when lit. The disease would spread further when smokers carelessly emptied their pipes of ashes "without sterilizing them in linens." Tobacco smuggling threatened to set this deadly chain of events into motion. The bureau therefore argued that the solution was to leave Marseille a free port, and to charge the bureau alone with all surveillance rights. "Marseille is known as a free port, and if not completely free, it is not at all . . . ; it is necessary for trade to be left entirely free in Marseille, where all sorts of merchandise enter freely by sea without duties or regulations."[79] The bureau cited the very priorities that Colbert had emphasized in the 1660s—commercial liberty and public health—to resist encroachments on its power. It interpreted commercial liberty as municipal offices' autonomy and Marseillais merchants' freedom to trade in any Levantine commodity.

THE FAILURE OF CENTRALIZATION: THE GREAT PLAGUE OF MARSEILLE, 1720–1723

The Great Plague of 1720 marked a *potential* high point for centralization in health management; medical catastrophe provided the Crown with a legitimate reason to diffuse any calls for autonomy and decentralized rule. In this sense, the plague offered the monarchy an unusual opportunity—a state of emergency—to maximize its control and surveillance over afflicted provinces. The absence of civic order would seem the ideal moment for a Crown bent on amplifying centralization. With international trade suspended and the municipal administration wounded by rising mortality rates and social and political disorder, the city, it would seem, would succumb to French systems of power, administration, and knowledge exported from the center.

While transnational contacts between Marseille's Bureau de la santé and similar bureaux all around the Mediterranean became strained, the monarchy initially responded to plague in Marseille with more surveillance and police, attempting to convert all France into a gigantic lazaretto. It established new bureaux of health that operated under a royal Conseil de la santé, and issued quarantines in all afflicted municipalities. The Crown assumed that a sufficiently strengthened centralized administration would contain the disease. Ultimately, however, the expanded bureaucratic machinery failed to contain the epidemic, and centralization in health management reached a crisis point in France.

Plague arrived in Marseille in May 1720, as delayed quarantining of the plague-ridden merchant ship *Grand Saint-Antoine* and clandestine hauling of the *premier échevin*'s merchandise from the vessel to the city's warehouses brought pestilence-carrying fleas and rats into the Vieux Port. While the appearance of the infamous carbuncles and buboes on the bodies of the sick and dying suggested that bubonic plague was beginning its ravages, doctors and administrators chose to deny it.[80] Concerned that rumors of plague would decimate French and Marseillais commerce, the *échevins* and Bureau de la santé distributed letters to the Regent and "all the *officiers conservateurs* of health in all the European ports" in July 1720 declaring that the "contagion" had been contained.[81] Later the same month, when Marseillais *échevins* agreed to discuss "the nature of the disease and measures to be pursued to prevent its spread," with physicians, the royal intendant, and the *premier consul* of Aix-en-Provence and *procureur du pays de Provence,* Joseph de Clapiers, seigneur de Vauvenargues, the city's administrators insisted that the disease was a malignant fever.[82] Doctors echoed such claims. When the Regent sent Montpellier's renowned anti-contagionist François Chicoyneau with his associates to Marseille to offer their diagnoses, Chicoyneau concluded that "this sort of plague" was nothing more than a common malady. Plague in his mind, after all, did not exist.

Even as they ultimately admitted that the "contagious malady" in Marseille was indeed plague, civic administrators and the Bureau de la santé continued fearing for Marseille's reputation, as well as their own. Sending weekly reports on the situation in Provence and urging public health authorities all over Europe to maintain or strengthen quarantines, Marseille's bureau insisted that it never acted in self-interest: it remained "interested in preventing such a scourge" in neighboring territories. Showering praise on other health intendants and governors, claiming that "the esteem that Your Excellencies have acquired through Europe by your great foresight and prudent measures to preserve your most serene state from the scourge of contagion has made us regard correspondence as the most precious advantage,"[83] the health intendants pleaded a continuance of "reciprocal" cooperation.[84] They assured their counterparts that Marseille's bureau concealed nothing: "Your Excellencies can count on the fidelity of the news that we communicate to you." The health intendants sent letters to their sister agencies detailing specific news on the increase or decrease in deaths, the methods used in disinfecting goods and peoples, the systems in place for separating the suspected, the accidents that occurred, and the exact number of sick in the communities throughout Provence, as well as copies of mandates and edicts by the Regent, military commandants, and *échevins*.[85] Pressured by foreign health bureaux to contain the plague, shunned by countries and states that embargoed French trade, the civic administrators of Marseille—at once merchants, health intendants, and political leaders of their city—found themselves in a precarious position.

While surrounding states stopped trading with Marseille, the French Crown increased its communication with the city's administrators. As the epidemic continued to spread from the poorest section of the city to the port and neighboring towns, "for the first time in France, the fight against the plague took on a national dimension."[86] The Regent's minister of war, Claude Le Blanc, ordered six line battalions and militia to Provence to prevent the epidemic from moving north. Meanwhile, the Crown established a new Conseil de la santé at Versailles, emphasizing the need to concentrate disease containment under the Crown's authority to prevent conflicting regulations.[87] To prevent possible conflicts of jurisdiction, Versailles issued a comprehensive *arrêt* restricting travel to and from plague-stricken provinces, established military cordons, forbade traffic in and out of Provence, and issued directions for quarantines. It required *certificats de santé* issued by municipal officers for anyone traveling to and from Marseille, and restricted traffic to one gate.[88] The Crown established more *bureaux de la santé* in Provence, which would be run jointly by the royal intendant, the military, and municipal administrators.

The Crown subordinated the health bureaux in Provence to a new Conseil de la santé, headed by the minister of war, the controller-general of finance, and Parisian medical experts.[89] The Conseil would protect the kingdom by "containing everybody in one rule." Standardizing information communication, it instructed each bureau to submit a monthly register to the royal intendant. These registers contained information regarding the number and quality of hospital and religious personnel; the staff employed at hospitals to dispose of the dead; the number and quality of beds, sheets, drugs, aromatics, and provisions at each hospital; updated mortality rates and numbers of the sick and convalescent; the number and quality of the administrative staff in each institution; and a memorandum of supplies requested.[90] The Crown ordered the royal intendant of

Provence "to compose from the particular accounts [of each bureau] a general picture" to send to the controller-general.[91]

Additionally, the Conseil mobilized a micromanaged centralized organization to administer food and relief, totaling three million *livres* from the royal treasury.[92] It ordered 600,000 *livres* to be given immediately to Provence to buy grain.[93] Grain was transported down the Saône or the Rhône to Provence; distribution involved "equality and proportion," "good order and intelligence." The Conseil employed five individuals to "establish not only the exactitude of service, but also order and rule."[94] It guaranteed accuracy through registers containing "exactly all that is received and dispensed to the last cent." Daily notations were "to clearly inform . . . by whom the grain has been purchased, the name and the residence of the vendors, at what measure, and the weight of the measure, the price, the place of delivery . . . whether at a granary or if the vendor rendered his delivery on board ship."[95] Warning that "breaches of trust" would be punished severely, the Conseil ordered recounts of all supplies before embarkation and disembarkation. It issued mandatory passports to all vendors and buyers, which were to be "copied not only in the Bureau des fermes du Roi, but also in the Bureau des péages [Bureau of Tollgates]."[96]

The Crown, therefore, spread its tentacles of power over the plague-infested provinces. It assumed that transparent, organized, and rationalized administration would contain and ultimately end the epidemic. But neither its hierarchically organized ladder of communication nor centralized disaster assistance systems could stop the disease from spreading. By mid-August of 1720, 300 on average died daily; at the Hôpital Saint Jacques de Galice in Marseille, 30 to 40 orphans succumbed each day.[97] Contagion spread to Aix, St. Rémy, Cassis, Toulon, and other towns north of Marseille. Despite all efforts, plague continued until 1723. By the time it disappeared, half of the population of Marseille was dead. And the massive centralized apparatus created by royal statecraft to contain it seemed to have all but collapsed.

THE IMPORTANCE OF THE GREAT PLAGUE

The significance of the Great Plague of Marseille lay in the fact that both traditional and rationalist medical knowledge had been unable to cope with it. Neither Hippocratic explanations of imbalance nor more "modern" ideas that rejected the existence of plague as mere irrational fantasy reduced mortality. Meanwhile, as was evident from the rise in looting and pillaging, and the exodus of terrified inhabitants, centralized governance had failed to establish order. Finally, the temporary suspension of international and domestic commerce in Marseille, in addition to rumors that the negligence of the city's *négociant* elite had exacerbated the calamity, suggested that commerce and merchants did not contribute as much to the general good as had once been thought.

The plague temporarily disrupted many of the local and national programs of Louis XIV and Colbert. Beginning in the 1660s, Colbert had introduced several policies to control and strengthen French commercial activity. His plans regarding the regulation of commerce (Chapter 1), the Crown's ultimately exclusionary policies toward Levantine immigrants and traders (Chapter 3), and its micromanaging of plague prevention and containment (Chapter 4) all rested on the king's distrust of his subjects and complete reliance on royal guidance. As Colbert's many letters reveal, he worked under the assumption that in a kingdom composed of different particular bodies, the Crown alone could manage diverse interests in a way that sustained the public good.

Simultaneously, however, the Crown had extended commercial activity in Marseille and beyond by embracing a contrary position toward elite merchants founded on trust. As demonstrated in earlier chapters, it advocated a new commercial civic spirit that portrayed *négociants* and *le négoce* as essential to civic and state communities. In 1720, however, a medical catastrophe of epic proportions put extreme pressure on the system of administrative centralization and royal regulation and on the notion that elite merchants were trustworthy, honorable citizens and subjects. Jacques Savary's hypothetical *parfait négociant* had not materialized; rather, Jean Eon's foreigners, *imparfait négociants* and a greedy *échevin,* it seemed, had introduced an "Asian" disorder into Marseille. The plague suggested that Marseille's commercial elites had made the wrong choice in opting for the Crown's method of commercial expansion and centralization. It suggested that such elites and their commerce were threats—not foundations—for stable society, politics, and morality.

Given the simultaneous crises in medical knowledge, administrative centralization, state-building, and commercial civic spirit, what alternative methods of social, political, and moral organization could civic and royal administrators cobble together to restore the city to health? Finding answers to these questions became all the more urgent for royal observers and local administrative elites, as the very systems established to keep plague-stricken Marseille connected to the kingdom ended up isolating the city. The Crown attempted to contain plague to Marseille and protect its plague-free provinces with standardized administration and police. Such measures intended to wrap France under one uniform system of surveillance separated Marseille and the plague-stricken provinces from the rest of the kingdom. Even as centralization intensified the Crown's surveillance of all its provinces, the creation of cordons, physical boundaries, and limitations on travel and commerce detached Marseille from France in unprecedented ways. Cut off from the Mediterranean and Levant through trade embargoes, walled off from the rest of France by cordons and *arrêts* forbidding physical contact, plague-stricken Marseille lost the two lifelines that kept it a functioning city—its transnational marketplace and its connections to the kingdom. If French officials had "othered" plague as a Turkish disease before 1720, plague "othered" Marseille in 1720.

In this state of emergency, Marseillais *échevins*, citizens, and royal commandants turned to the old tradition of civic republicanism to formulate their responses to plague and social fragmentation. They mobilized, above all, the notion of political virtue—of citizens renouncing their personal interests to save a republic in crisis—to guide policies, emergency laws, and civic order during medical catastrophe. The concept of republican virtue strengthened particularly because it could overlap with Hippocratic medical notions of moderation and time-honored religious ideas of civic charity and morality. Furthermore, this collection of medical, political, and religious vocabularies that emphasized virtue served the needs of administrators and citizens interested in critically re-evaluating merchants and commercial activity in Marseille. Reactivating local republican political traditions, they rediscovered Marseille's identity as a non-commercial republic. The next chapter, therefore, investigates virtue without commerce in the plague-stricken city.

CHAPTER FIVE

Virtue Without Commerce

Civic Spirit During the Plague, 1720–1723

Plague disrupted the activities that made a community a community. No commerce, no city. The physician Jean-Baptiste Bertrand, one of the few doctors who remained in Marseille through the epidemic, observed that the plague "dissolved society," "severed all ties of blood and friendship, and halted trade." "The churches, the exchange, and all public places were shut up," he wrote; "the courts of justice ceased to function; neighbors and even relations stopped visiting each other."[1] Deserted boulevards—particularly the famous Cours—became emblematic of social disintegration as spaces used for commerce transformed into hemorrhaging avenues filled with garbage and rotting corpses.[2] The discontinuance of social activity carried political implications. According to Bertrand, it bred amour propre and annihilated the spirit of civic service: plague "dissolve[d] society, interdict[ed] the communication of mutual assistance. . . . Each individual, attentive to his own preservation, consider[ed] himself as released from giving his neighbor that assistance we naturally owe to each other."[3] Plague, Bertrand explained, reduced a city to a collection of isolated individuals concerned exclusively with self-preservation.

How could a community remain a collective body when robbed of the things that made it a community: commerce and collective sociability? What were the principles of cohesion when commercial exchange no longer bound citizens together? How could the civic spirit be reanimated? This chapter argues that Marseille's *échevins,* military commandants, and civic volunteers experienced and responded to plague through lenses tinted in civic republicanism. Diverse texts pertaining to previous epidemics, ranging from published histories to *règlements* and *ordres*, provided Marseillais administrators guides to fashion their responses to plague in 1720. Historical accounts by various authors, such as Thucydides from classical Greece, Giovanni Boccaccio in fourteenth-century Florence, and Daniel Defoe in early modern London, provided them with the moral and political vocabulary to formulate their understanding of medical crisis; these collectively mobilized a polarizing language that pitted selfish inhabitants who preferred personal safety and pleasure against charismatic leaders and citizens who saved their community.

Such emphasis on civic commitment drew on early modern *règlements* and *ordres*, which stressed how citizens needed to align their private interests with the public good to restore their community. These *règlements* and *ordres* expanded the authority of municipal officials by relegating to them emergency powers to punish—often with death—inhabitants who failed to comply with their orders. Meanwhile, they established emergency police and surveillance systems by mobilizing citizens as guards, spies, and trial witnesses to combat social and political disorder. Such systems that extended the power of municipal leaders and civic volunteers predated the expansion of France's monarchical regime; in Provence, they were established in 1501 and relied on coordination between municipal administrators and the parlement in Aix.

Traditional responses to plague epidemics, which polarized public against private interests, and virtue against immorality, were particularly suited for a city like Marseille that continued to toy with its republican identity. In 1720, Marseillais administrators resurrected the rhetoric of the republic in crisis, understanding their medical emergency as a moment where mythical Massilia stood in the balance between life and death, between corruption and republican virtue. Using the historical script of the corrupting republic of Massilia to comprehend medical catastrophe, they comfortably adopted traditional moralized definitions of, and responses to, plague.

The unprecedented strength of traditional civic methods in plague containment in 1720 derived, however, from their intersection with newer models of enforcing order provided by the French monarchy. The monarchy played a pivotal role in reactivating aspects of Marseille's republican traditions by introducing administrative innovations. Royal centralized administration led by its Conseil de la santé failed to defeat plague, but Versailles followed up by deploying military commandants to Marseille, dispensing absolute sovereignty to municipal leaders, and imposing martial law. Together with municipal officers, royal commandants reactivated a republican rhetoric of warfare and civic crisis, and equated the struggle to cleanse bodies of plague yeasts with one to purify citizens. Commandants, *échevins,* and the *marechaussée* ordered summary trials and executions, banished individuals who expressed interests contrary to public order and health and, according to critics, led brutal reigns of terror. Steeped in municipal traditions but unprecedented in their association with royal power, Marseille's emergency systems established an austere municipal order that administrators and citizens understood as the source and product of civic virtue.

This rhetoric of restoring virtue was, above all, critical of commerce. Behind the idea of the commercial republic that had taken hold from the conquest of 1660 were deeper traces of ambivalence about the market, which were reactivated. During the plague, commandants and civic volunteers in Marseille rejected commercial civic spirit and criticized the *négociants* who had led the Bureau de la santé. They argued that these had betrayed the public good and placed their financial interests over public health. While post-conquest urban expansion and international trade stimulated new ideas that reconciled commerce with civic engagement, plague pressured this association and prompted a reconsideration of the market as a source of political and moral disintegration. As the social and political climate soured, those most closely associated with the exchange and trafficking of goods were targeted as criminals and wrongdoers. These included merchants, contraband traffickers, looters, and prostitutes.

During the epidemic, therefore, a city that was suddenly stripped of its international market saw royal military leaders and citizens craft a new order for Marseille centered on its republican history and noncommercial version of civic virtue. In this context, the French Crown emerged as a triumphant ally that helped Marseillais citizens redefine their civic community. The model of centralization based on streamlined bureaucratization and rational approaches to disease control took a backseat to a more nuanced form of royal intervention. Royal commandants donned their republican hats, reactivated a civic political vocabulary of virtue, and helped save Marseille from ruin. As in 1660, a disruptive event saw the king's men enter the city gates and emerge republican heroes.

MORALIZING PLAGUE: PRECEDENTS BEFORE 1720

Eyewitnesses of past plagues, from Giovanni Boccaccio in fourteenth-century Florence to Daniel Defoe in seventeenth-century London, expounded on the disappearance of civic activity during medical crisis. In the *Decameron*, Boccaccio described how survivors "abandoned their rightful city, their rightful homes."[4] Communal bonds disintegrated as citizens deserted their families; "brother forsook brother, uncle nephew . . . wife, husband . . . fathers and mothers refused to tend their very children."[5] Defoe witnessed similar processes in London; during the plague, his "strangely altered" city became lifeless, with "streets . . . usually thronged, now grown desolate."[6]

Writers from previous epidemics agreed that plague destroyed communities by cultivating two extremes: by discontinuing healthy relationships and amplifying perverted ones. Plague generated hedonism, an activity destructive of civic normalcy. Boccaccio wrote that "the executors of the laws were either dead or ill like everyone else, or were left with so few officials that they were unable to do their duties; as a result, everyone was free to do whatever they pleased." People disregarded prohibitions against congregating in public, drinking, and carrying on sexual activity in public spaces, surrounded by the corpses, such as they assumed they would soon become. Plague signified and induced immorality.

Jean-Baptiste Bertrand's comments in Marseille, with which this chapter opened, closely echo the observations of social decay and civic negligence documented by Boccaccio and Defoe, indicating the longevity of this moral discourse on plague. Doctors and administrators shared such attention to the disappearance of civic cohesion and morality, as evidenced in *règlements* and *ordres* issued during early modern epidemics. Emergency laws relegated absolute power to magistrates to contain social and political disorder, while outlining methods for volunteerism to guide inhabitants to prioritize general welfare over personal interests. A mid-seventeenth-century plague author urged magistrates, "true physicians of the people," to "use draconian methods through the law they established for the preservation of the state . . . to maintain the whole body, and to prefer the general interests to the particular."[7]

Treatises like the *Ordres à observer pour empescher que la peste ne se communique hors les lieux infectez*, printed in Paris in 1668, released to municipal magistrates, the authority to act with "complete severity" and "punish by death" infractions against general order.[8] They advocated the use of surveillance, witness denunciations, and purges to contain the epidemic and maintain political and social stability. Surveillance systems organized by magistrates counted on civic mobilization. Citizens formed the core of the emergency Bureau de la santé, an office "composed of the chief justice, the mayor or *échevins*, and a health intendant in each quarter chosen from the most honest of men . . . that had all authority in health and police."[9] The bureau provided health intendants in each quarter with citizen-syndics. Each syndic supervised citizen-sentinels chosen "for their probity." They prepared lists of inhabitants and keys to all houses. The syndics led citywide quarantines, took roll and received medical reports from the sick. If a licensed surgeon suspected plague, guards and carters called "crows" (*cor-*

beaux) escorted the patient and his or her housemates to one of three infirmaries: for those sick with plague, those suspected of being ill, and those in convalescence. Meanwhile, citizen-militias guarded the Hôtel de Ville and the city's quarters, "to render prompt obedience of the people, the most absolute authority of the magistrates, and to survey all disorders and robberies."[10] Additionally, emergency health bureaus also counted on civic volunteers—men and women—to serve as spies and denouncers to facilitate surveillance. No military or police experience was required; "all artisans and peasants were capable" of participating.[11] They turned in those who concealed their sick or sicknesses. They rounded up vagrants and those who evaded quarantines. Health intendants patrolled their subordinates, "to know if the syndics carried out [their duties], to receive the claims of the inhabitants, and to survey their actions."[12]

Though plague manuals called for the joint efforts of magistrates and citizen-volunteers, surveillance systems often remained an unrealized ideal. Volunteers fled or fell victim to plague; replacements were difficult to find. "Thousands of people die, as much from the absence of the principal and best bourgeois of the city who retire to the country to save their lives," François Ranchin wrote, noting that those who fled the city in this way included doctors, the *prévôt de marchands* (i.e., the de facto mayor), and the *échevins*. "During times of precaution," he continued, "one can find numerous volunteers to serve the city; but when the need arrives to serve the city in times of plague, one finds few, because each wants to avoid peril."[13] The recurrence of such complaints suggests that the methods outlined in plague *ordres* were often unrealized rather than followed in their entirety.

Given the discrepancy between ideal and actual situations, medical and ecclesiastic personnel reinforced administrative elites' calls for civic service. An example of the crossover between political-administrative and religious writing, the ecclesiastic Maurice de Toulon's *Le Capucin charitable* (1662), a much-reprinted book in the seventeenth century, discussed how to maintain public order. In its preface, the author prided himself on his own efforts for the public good: "I cannot offer [my readers] simple speculations, like the philosophers, who by their beautiful thoughts have built a republic of paper [*république de papier*] that never had substance. I only write of what I have practiced myself in several cities in France and Italy [for] over twenty-five years in service of the plague-stricken." Packed with religious imagery and biblical allusions, the *Capucin charitable* laid out "the political order that messieurs the magistrates must establish in cities afflicted by plague," and stressed how magistrates and inhabitants had to serve "the common good of the public."[14] Maurice de Toulon specified that administrative leaders and citizen-volunteers had to possess "disinterestedness and . . . have nothing other than the public interest."[15] The desire for personal gain or power was not a legitimate reason. "I have seen men eager to become health inspectors, not out of motives of service, but to serve their own interests."

Plague texts denounced all forms of egotism and frowned on professions or behaviors linked with personal profit or pleasure. In this regard, municipal authorities and medical and ecclesiastic leaders came down hard on "depraved concupiscence" by merchants, "vagabonds, public whores, and other useless and scandalous people,"[16] exacting severe punishments for those who contravened quarantine measures, hid infected people and merchandise, or failed to report for curfews. The physician Nicolas de Valeriolle wrote during the outbreak in 1630 that man, an animal "with virile force, vital spirits, and natural heat," fell prey to instincts when the plague's "vaporous humidity" tinkered with their "spirits, desires, and imagination."[17] Combined with "a generous [dose] of wine," such emotions led to "the depravation of mores, bad habits, and all that ruins man, [they] led to disorder of generations . . . and in all cases, imbecility." Magistrates issued punishments for promiscuous activity, charging that it spread immorality, plague, and "hereditary diseases" like leprosy, epilepsy, gout, and stones.

Plague writers justified authoritarian rule by arguing that self-interest was a public hazard that had to be punished severely. François Ranchin (1630) wrote that "justice must be rigorous against plague victims who communicate with the healthy, and even more severe against those who insist on communicating or spreading plague among the people."[18] In his *Le prosélite charitable* (1666), Pierre Gabriel argued that if administrators used "draconian methods through the law they established for the preservation of the state, they did so to maintain the whole body, and to prefer the general interest to the particular."[19] Prisoners and the poor recruited to dispose of bodies bore the brunt of these laws. "The extraordinary means, when the superiors are constrained to force these poor people in this exercise, seems cruel and pitiable, and against the laws of justice and of charity, but nevertheless, where necessity reigns, laws can lose their authority."[20] Civic administrators agreed that the establishment of health and order justified ruthless methods.

ADOPTING AND REJECTING PRECEDENTS: PARLEMENT, MARSEILLE, AND PLAGUE, 1501–1720

What were the established local modes of plague containment in Provence and Marseille, and how were these systems put into play and updated in 1720? The parlement in Aix traditionally collaborated with plague-stricken cities in Provence to organize emergency communal mobilization. Sixteenth- and seventeenth-century *mémoires instructifs, règlements,* and *ordres contre la peste* show parlement and municipal governments working together since the sixteenth century. The parlement issued directions for cordons, quarantines, and disinfections, while the municipalities mobilized citizens to carry out these initiatives. "Première cour de justice souveraine,"[21] the parlement had wielded supreme power over criminal justice during medical crises since its creation in 1501.[22]

The *Arrêt et règlement général fait par la chambre ordonnée en temps de vacations du parlement de Provence pour la conservation de la santé publique* (1629) illustrates the typical rules the parlement generated for plagued communities. Its hundred and thirty-five articles ordered the consuls of plague-stricken cities to post all bulletins announcing epidemics, to establish bureaux de la santé, and to organize guards to interdict travel.[23] It ordered closure of public events, markets, cabarets, and public houses, and the hospitalization of those suspected of being sick. Officers would have to slaughter cats and dogs and disinfect streets and homes with "laurel, rosemary, juniper, lavender, storax, and other herbs." In no fewer than twenty articles, the *Arrêt* outlined rules for disinfecting people, carriages, merchandise, and textiles.[24]

The parlement and Marseille followed precedents when plague broke out in 1720. The parlement's decrees focused on quarantine, barricades and food distribution. They ordered the municipal leaders to register the sick, burn suspected merchandise, and establish *corps-de-garde* and *certificats de santé.*[25] They allocated grain, fixed prices, and ordered markets opened in Marseille's healthy zones on Mondays, Wednesdays, and Fridays.[26] They forbade smuggling. The parlement required doctors to offer service; abandoning the city would result in the confiscation of their titles.[27] It stressed that disobedience would result in galley sentences, whippings for women, and occasionally, death.

Meanwhile, Marseille's *échevins* mobilized the civic militia and volunteers. City captains heading fifty-man companies, the citizen militia, and five Brigades du privilège du vin took turns escorting the municipal leaders during their city tours. On 3 August 1720, the *échevins* established 150 *commissaires* in the city's five parishes.[28] Volunteer captains and subcommissioners spread out through the neighborhoods to look after "the needs of the poor, distribute bread and other provisions at the expense of the community, and work toward everything prescribed for the public good and health." Neighborhoods were nonetheless abandoned as volunteers died or fled. Concern that officials would abandon the city ran rampant. The Bureau de la santé therefore recruited informants within its organization, ordering that "all negligence will be reported, [as will] conniving by intendants, to the court, which will judge appropriately; . . . prevaricators will suffer painful severity, and denouncers will be compensated."[29] Meanwhile, the *échevins* recruited ecclesiastics, knighted *négociants,* and galley slaves to collect bodies for burial.[30] Desertion was punishable by death.

By the third month of the plague, however, traditional collaborative links between Marseille's *échevins* and the parlement withered when the Aixois magistrates relocated to Saint-Rémy-de-Provence and ultimately dispersed as a result of the plague's appearance in Aix. On 4 August 1720, the *échevins* petitioned the king for a transfer of judicial authority, normally held by parlementary magistrates. Citing "the disorders that arrive in times of contagion, and the need that exists for a swift power to reprimand and make examples to contain malefactors," the *échevins* "wrote to the *prémier président* to obtain from His Majesty similar letters patent." This request for extraordinary judicial power was not unprecedented: the *échevins* reminded the royal intendant that whenever the city has been afflicted by the plague, as in 1580, 1630, 1649, and 1650, kings had always granted letters of patent to their predecessors giving them the power to judge all crimes.[31]

The Crown acquiesced. It designated the *échevins* as substitute judges and ordered them to keep parlement informed of all sentences. It specified three processes for different kinds of crimes and sentences. "In ordinary cases," it ordered, "criminal processes will be judged by ordinary judges who reside in the city or, in their absence, by at least three consuls and lawyers." Lesser crimes and sentences "that carry no corporal punishment and that only impose pecuniary fines of 100 *livres* or less will be dealt with as provided for notwithstanding appeal." For crimes and sentences that "carry the penalties of death, torture, the galleys, or other corporal punishment," the "consuls" or *échevins* of Marseille would "oversee the execution of said sentences; the records of these criminal processes would be [transcribed], soaked in vinegar [for disinfection] and provided to the clerk of our court."[32] Marseille's *échevins* thus enjoyed total legal, judicial, and executive power. The monarchy approved "all procedures, ordinances, sentences, and judgments in criminal cases" of the police in Marseille. The *échevins* and police commissioners enjoyed "a power that was absolute."[33]

View of the port of Marseille from the Hôtel de Ville. *Courtesy Archives municipales de la ville de Marseille, 11Fi41.*

The Cours of Marseille during the plague. *Courtesy Archives municipales de la ville de Marseille, 11Fi27.*

The Crown then buttressed the *échevins'* powers by implementing martial law. On 12 September 1720, the king appointed Charles de Langeron, *Chef d'escadre des galères et maréchal des camps et armées du Roy* as commandant of Marseille.[34] Independent from parlement, the military commandants through Provence became direct liaisons between municipal leaders and the Crown. They became, with the *échevins,* chief executors of martial law, with sovereign power in municipal administration and police. Langeron continued the *échevins'* appeal to Marseillais to establish volunteer corps to police, quarantine, and disinfect inhabitants and their belongings. He and the *échevins* directed cases against suspects who jeopardized physical and moral order, calling citizens as witnesses. Most important, he mobilized the civic rhetoric of virtue, encouraging Marseillais to follow the examples of dedicated citizens whom he likened to republican heroes from the classical past.

REPUBLICAN VIRTUE AND A ROYAL COMMANDANT

While early modern French plague *ordres* and *règlements* repeated calls for civic commitment, moral altruism, and authoritarian severity, it was particularly in

Provence that such calls were couched in republican language. During epidemics, local writers revived classical metaphors, plotted their own medical catastrophe into the historical narratives of ancient Provençal republics, and applied the script of a republic in crisis to represent the actions of their administrative elites and citizens who displayed exemplary civic behavior. In 1629, for example, plague writers celebrated "the virtuous actions, extensively practiced during the plague in the city of Arles, the sixth Roman colony." Praising the consuls' civic dedication during epidemics, Nicolas de Valeriolle claimed that in Arles, Roman virtue had "continued [to exist] from father to son until our own century." He traced the city's consular government to the ancient Arlesian republic and claimed that "the wise council" of said government "served as the impenetrable bastion" against the plague. These leaders were "true *pères de la patrie*," who "imitated Achilles,"[35] and other Greek heroes. Whether in Arles, Aix, Marseille, Saint-Rémy or in other Provençal villages, writers, poets, and artists reanimated the image of consuls and citizens resuscitating the virtues of ancient Greece and Rome.

In 1720, the royal commandant Charles de Langeron strengthened civic moralized responses to medical disaster and rekindled the rhetoric of republican virtue. One of the most telling reactions to Langeron's arrival in Marseille emerges in the published journal of the royal prosecutor, Pichatty de Croissante. Croissante saw in Langeron a charismatic consul comparable to Pericles and the Roman republican Marius Caius: "[Langeron] inspired . . . in all citizens, those healthy as well as the sick, in all people in general, as much joy, pleasure, and happiness as confidence, strength, and courage; one can no longer believe that one can die under such a dignified commandant."[36] Croissante observed that "the Roman consuls filled themselves with *l'amour de leur patrie*; but they never steadfastly pushed their zeal this far." In his view, Langeron and the *échevins* earned "the just title of *pères de la patrie*, by the ardor with which they have exposed their lives." Always disposed to the community, "Langeron was on his horse from morning until night . . . scornful of danger, to remedy drawbacks that seemed insurmountable, forcing others to do the same by his example."[37] Local historians and poets echoed Croissante's sentiments. Jean-Baptiste Bertrand exclaimed, "History boasts of the courage and valor of the ancient Roman consuls in their military expeditions, but is not a greater fortitude requisite to brave the dangers of contagion than those of war?"[38] Martial imagery abounded, with references to Mars, Alexander the Great, Ulysses, and Nestor, as well as to Julius Caesar's conquest of Massilia.[39]

Contemporary Marseillais employed mythical and republican allusions to honor their own native volunteers as well. One of these was Charles Roze (1671–1733), a Marseillais chevalier of the Order of Saint Lazarus, knighted by Louis

The plague in the city of Marseille in 1720 (1723). *Courtesy Archives municipales de la ville de Marseille, 11Fi12.*

XIV for his military services against Spain. Roze returned to Marseille during the plague, and recruited galley slaves to dispose of corpses around the Vieux Port. Authors described how he dismounted from his horse, collected bodies, distributed food and disinfectants, and organized hospital care. "Monsieur Roze, commander of the Order of Saint Lazarus," the caption to a celebrated engraving by J. B. de Troy read, "endangered himself for the health of his *patrie* during the height of morbidity, collecting in one day countless plague cadavers piled at the Place de la Tourette, where the fumes carried death everywhere, and by the success of such a dangerous enterprise, saved all his fellow citizens."[40] Even a century later, a writer lauded the "noble virtues" of this "generous citizen," who "only seemed to exist for others."[41]

These descriptions of Langeron and Roze did more than activate allusions to classical Greece, Rome, and Provençal antiquity; they revived local classical republican consciousness. Poems and histories written during the plague glorified the ancient republics of Massilia, Arles, and Avignon, depicted commercial luxury as inviting corruption, and celebrated the heroes who had appeared to save the republics. Marseille, one poet began, had "many citizens and great men / Honored long ago for its great warriors / . . . Famous for its port that supplied the opulent merchant and the brave soldier." Of Arles, the same poet wrote, "This city [was] once equal to Rome." After revitalizing the utopian myth of such classical republics, poets and historians lamented how once-perfect republics fell into decay. "A formerly formidable people became, in a few days, deplorable." "Avarice corrupts interest," and "theft, killings, arrogance . . . and the tyranny that virtue detests" took over the community. Only the "heroism" of Langeron and other *pères de la patrie* had restored peace and order for "the common good."[42]

This narrative of perfect republics, their fall, and their restoration embodied a set of behavior patterns, models, and metaphors that Marseillais administrators deployed in 1720 in response to the plague. Their "script" valued martial steadfastness, self-sacrifice, and devotion to the common good; it condemned self-interest, tyranny, and cowardice. It rested on polar oppositions: virtue versus vice, and republic versus anarchy. Once put into play, it provided a template for the royal commandant and his *échevin* allies to shape their administrative policies during the epidemic.

VIRTUE MEETS EMERGENCY MILITARY JUSTICE

The administrative association between the royal military and Marseille's *échevins* was a peculiar and unlikely one. Langeron expressed his distaste for merchants during his tenure in Marseille. Moreover, he did not have any particular attachment to the city to which the Crown had appointed him. The *échevins* were *négociants* and Marseillais citizens, men who had made their fortunes and established their reputations in international trade with the Ottoman Empire. How could these two groups, military personnel and elite *négociant*-administrators, join forces to police the plague-stricken city?

The plague provided both with an extraordinary amount of power. The *échevins* found their administrative and judicial authority expanded with the absence of parlement and the temporary closure of the Chamber of Commerce and other commercial institutions. It was in their interests, therefore, to remain on good terms with the royal military, which provided the arms necessary to preserve such authority. This alliance remained stable so long as the *échevins* relinquished their identity as merchants and focused on maintaining social and political order. By the epidemic's end, they began donning their merchants' hats once more, and the question of who, the *échevins* or the royal commandants, had the interests of the community more in mind would lead to struggles between them.

But in the early months of the plague, Langeron and the *échevins* worked in lockstep. The *échevins* complied when Langeron decreed *ordonnances par le Roy* mandating civic cooperation. They ordered citizen-guards to mark stores, apartments, warehouses, and markets for surveillance.[43] They ordered guards to submit inventories of belongings found in vacant homes to the Hôtel de Ville. They generated a list of forbidden acts that would elicit punishment. These included disregard for curfews, concealment and hoarding of possessions suspected of contamination, and spreading the plague either by association with the sick or by careless actions.

The Crown's proviso of extraordinary emergency powers allowed the commandant and *échevins* to arrange emergency courts against malefactors modeled on military procedures. Criminals were judged by a chamber of police presided by the commandant. This tribunal of *échevins* and *commissaires* of police "had become sovereign."[44] Once discovered, the offender was imprisoned at the Conciergerie du Palais Royal. Interrogations run by a *commissaire* followed. The defendant was ordered to state his name, age, and domicile and to answer leading questions that called for responses in the affirmative or negative. Meanwhile, the plaintiffs provided a description of the offense in a private audience with the same *commissaire* who had interrogated the defendant. The police collected witnesses or spies evaluated by the *commissaire* or the commandant. Subsequently, the chamber, consisting of the commandant, *échevins,* and *commissaires,* presided over a confrontation between the witnesses and defendant. A confrontation between the plaintiff and defendant, and sentencing, followed. Finally, the royal prosecutor Pichatty de Croissante summarized the affair and verdict, providing a copy for police records.[45]

The commonest crime throughout the outbreak was burgling abandoned buildings, for which the standard punishment was imprisonment for life in the galleys. In a trial involving "burglary of goods suspected of contagion," the ringleader and his collaborator were sentenced to life and nine years in the galleys, respectively, while their two female partners were banished from Marseille.[46] Escape or return to the city would be on "pain of death." Another crime, the carrying of arms, also resulted in a harsh penalty. Laurens Audrie, "taken by surprise with prohibited arms in the street at night by officers and soldiers," was sentenced to nine years in the galleys, and death if caught attempting escape.[47]

While processes regarding theft and possession of arms remained consistent through the plague, the tribunal increasingly focused on other forms of corruption once parlement adjourned in November 1720. Believing that the plague led to the "depravity of morals" and "enormous crimes," it intensified efforts to rein in sexual activity. Langeron observed how inhabitants satisfied their pleasures while disregarding civic service; widows and widowers were "marrying again immediately," while prostitutes jeopardized public order. He ordered a curfew, shutting down taverns and "houses of pleasure."[48] "Women of excess . . . and their accomplices" faced "summary processes."[49] Spies located where "prostitution . . . perpetuated the *mal contagieux*."[50] According to Jean-Baptiste Bertrand, Langeron searched "the city and country for all suspected persons," and "frequent executions repressed the licentiousness of the people . . . many persons were condemned to death, to the galleys, and to other punishments; and all civil affairs were referred to [the tribunal's] jurisdiction."[51] Indeed, sexual crimes met the most severe punishments during the plague. While burglary resulted in galley sentences and banishments, "rape" trials habitually resulted in executions.

Why did the emergency tribunal focus on sex crimes during plague? What does this obsession with curtailing sexual recklessness reveal about how Langeron and the *échevins* understood virtue and its relevance to civic order during medical catastrophe? Judging from available trial dossiers of "rape" cases in plague-stricken Marseille, one of the main sexual activities that the tribunal tried to curtail was prostitution. Prostitution while plague raged was particularly reprehensible, because it was "commerce with men,"[52] according to one trial record, and "commerce was prohibited in times of contagion."[53] Prostitution symbolized the worst excesses of commercial trafficking, including self-interest and disregard for public health and order. Religious condemnations of sexual excess directed from the pulpit, meanwhile, helped entrench this link between commercial depravity and sexual excess even further. Marseille's bishop, Henri Xavier de Belsunce in particular issued numerous *mandements* during the epidemic relating commercial luxury to sexual overdrive and characterizing the city as a whore who sold herself for the riches of the Levant. He condemned the sexual indecency of her inhabitants, which he claimed had brought the city to its ruin: "O you, you libertines of the century!" he thundered; "you women and worldly girls forever shamelessly showing yourselves without waistbands, disrobed indecently and immodestly!"[54]

An analysis of proceedings against prostitutes and "rapists" during the plague demonstrates how municipal leaders departed from customary procedures and proved more ruthless in the context of medical crisis. Records from 1710 to 1720 show that municipal administrators followed an established practice to confront prostitution prior to the plague. The practice conformed to the law of

23 February 1688 and Louis XIV's letters patent dating to 1691. The *échevins*, whom the king appointed magistrates in this respect, were to confine women certified by the Bureau de la Maison des filles et femmes pénitentes to contribute to "public debauchery" in the Maison du refuge, rather than prison.[55] Over three to five years in the Maison du refuge, the wayward women would be rehabilitated through a religious program that included prayers, Mass, catechism, and meals consisting of bread, water, and soup. The director and the mother superior would help reform these women, dispensing rewards of "meat or some fruits . . . if the girls regretted their disorders."[56] Those who failed to improve behavior would find their daily portion of soup withdrawn. This program rested on the assumption that sexual deviance could be corrected through penitence.

During epidemics, emergency laws regarding sexual activity trumped customary ones. Procedures against prostitution fell under the jurisdiction of Langeron and the *échevins*, rather than the superintendent of the Maison des filles et femmes pénitentes. The sentences became increasingly more severe than the customary penalty for prostitution during the ten years prior to the plague (which had remained consistent at three to five years in the Maison de refuge). The sentencing of prostitutes to public whipping, banishment, and even death suggests that authorities steered away from the idea that prostitutes could be reformed. Rather than trying to "fix" prostitutes, the tribunal led "summary processes" that ended at times with capital punishment. When the prostitute was placed in the Maison de refuge, it was for a much longer period of five to ten years, and she was taken there only after being publicly whipped.[57]

The case against the Marseillaise Pelisson sisters, Elisabeth and Catherine, demonstrates the typical procedures taken against prostitutes during the plague. The women had invited men into their home to sell themselves and another girl, Mariane Granier. After committing "a thousand disorders that scandalized their neighbors," these women were incarcerated for two months. While awaiting trial, they were suspected of "being contaminated" and transferred to the Maison de santé for "observation." Mariane attempted escape, but she was caught. Such "continuous debauchery" and "public havoc" warranted "exemplary punishment," because "copulation with persons suspected [of being infected] . . . is very dangerous."[58]

Once Commissioner of Police Dominique Alexis Estienne had taken the women into custody, he gathered witnesses. According to testimonies, commissioners, guards, and neighbors attested to the women's "indecent postures" and "public havoc"; it was alleged that they sang raunchy songs and had loud sex in the afternoon. One witness claimed that he had observed seven men and three women in the house committing "grave disorders." Meanwhile, Estienne questioned the women at the Hôtel de Ville, and informed them that they would be judged summarily, with no chance of appeal. Mariane Granier admitted that she had indeed slept with men. The Pelisson sisters, however, denied all allegations of prostitution.

The royal prosecutor, Pichatty de Croissante, recommended that Mariane Granier ought to suffer the harshest penalty for her crime of "evading quarantine . . . and prostituting herself to men for money during these times of contagion." He "condemned her to be taken to an intersection near the city walls, where at its foot, she will be shot and beheaded." As punishment of Elisabeth and Catherine Pelisson for their crime of "prostitution during the plague," he called for double public whippings at all the public intersections of the city, after which they were to be banished from the city in perpetuity. Any attempt to return would be punishable with death.[59] At the last minute, the commandant overruled capital punishment: he sentenced them to public whippings followed by incarceration for nine and five years respectively.

Prostitutes were not the only ones condemned for sex crimes during the plague. Langeron and the municipal leaders were particularly sensitive to the problem of sexuality in the context of a medical catastrophe that placed the family in crisis. Pestilence robbed mothers of their children, husbands of their wives, brothers of their siblings. Anxiety emerges in several accounts that emphasize the breakdown of the family and the confusion of sexual boundaries. The royal prosecutor Pichatty de Croissante described "the infinite number of sick of both sexes and all ages, states, and conditions that are found sleeping in the streets and in public places . . . on the pavement and avenues."[60] In a *Discours sur ce qui s'est passé à Marseille pendant la Contagion*, a Monsieur Terran wrote how "avarice brought families to their ruin in the widow and the orphan." The healthy "abandoned their parents" in streets strewn with "completely naked cadavers of both sexes in every kind of condition."[61] The anarchic collection of nude, dismembered, rotting corpses in the streets symbolized the utter disorder of bodies that the plague generated. Boundaries crumbled between home and street, the interior and the exterior, the family and the stranger. "Incestuous marriages and adulteries . . . the violence of our passions" reflected the "violence of the terrible plague."[62] The obsession over sexual order can be analyzed as an expression of the ambivalence toward bodily chaos, which in turn, was equated with civic and communal chaos. Emergency commissioners and judges maintained that families had to be rehabilitated and prescribed gender roles had to be reestablished to restore order to the community.

From the winter of 1720 on, Marseille experienced a rapid escalation of "rape" (*rapt, viol*) trials.[63] Trials concerning the violation of prescribed gender roles rather than the violation of the victim's body, these cases attempted to reconstruct and protect the virtuous family. That the sexual man was a menace to family emerges in the dossier of Honoré Taneron, who was obsessed with a woman.[64] At Easter 1719, the twenty-seven-year-old cloth merchant, originally from Cotignac, laid eyes on Dorothée Gouffre, the twenty-five-year-old daughter of a well-to-do Marseillais *négociant,* Joseph Gouffre. Taneron solicited Gouffre for eight months "with the intention of wedding her in legitimate marriage," but she "dismissed" him. The stalker "fluttered about the street of [her] house." He followed her repeatedly to Mass, where he "reproached her for the injustices she had committed in dismissing him." She answered that she could only consent "when circumstances were ready for the consummation of their marriage."

One day in March 1720, circumstances seemed ready to Taneron. "Her mother and father having left for certain affairs," Taneron found Gouffre alone at home. He repeated his proposals and she replied "there were certain difficulties that prevented her from agreeing." Then he "enjoyed her carnally notwithstanding all the resistance that she made to avoid what occurred again seven or eight more times on different days when the mother and father were away from the house." After repeated visits, Gouffre discovered she was pregnant.

On July 20, 1720, Taneron departed for his native Cotignac, promising to marry Gouffre upon his return. The plague, however, impeded him; he was detained in his hometown for months. Meanwhile, Gouffre gave birth to a son, Honoré Marc Antoine, "to the great chagrin of her father and mother, from whom she had hidden her pregnancy." Gouffre desired to legitimate her bastard child and called on Taneron to marry her. When Taneron ignored "the plaintiff perhaps on account of the pregnancy," Gouffre turned him in to the police on 30 June 1721.

The police clerk recorded the order to arrest Taneron on 2 July.[65] Taneron's day in court followed four days later. Questioned about his pursuit of Gouffre, his sexual relations with her, his fathering of the child, and Gouffre's request for marriage, Taneron answered in the affirmative. He was reticent at his confrontation with witnesses—all female neighbors of Gouffre's—who claimed that they had seen Taneron on several occasions. In his second interrogation, Taneron expressed his fear of plague and his enduring desire to marry Gouffre. He commented that "he wished to be freed from the prison where he remained with great fear due to the contagion." When asked of his intentions regarding Gouffre, he responded that he wished to marry her, both "to honor her and honor the love that he had forever for her, as well as to legitimate the boy to whom she had given birth."[66]

Langeron, however, called for the death penalty. Taneron had dishonored one of Marseille's most notable families. He had violated sacrosanct familial relationships—between daughter and parents, husband and wife. "Because only our justice . . . can repair the honor that has been stolen from the petitioner and . . . from a harmonious family of honest people of the city," Langeron called for swift judgment. Despite the plaintiff's father's request that the court "provide a true father for the innocent [child]," the tribunal sentenced Taneron to death by hanging and strangulation.[67]

VIRTUE AND THE MARKET: QUESTIONING COMMERCIAL CIVIC SPIRIT

While the commandant, *échevins,* and *commissaires* worked together to prosecute petty criminals, thieves, and prostitutes, one issue put pressure on their collaborative efforts to rule Marseille during the plague: what to do with the domestic and international merchandise locked in warehouses and storage. The question of whether such valuables ought to be disinfected, confiscated, or saved for future trade hinged on conflicting notions of whether *négociants* and commerce benefited or harmed the state and local community. At stake in these discussions, therefore, were the honor and virtue of *négociants,* as well as the viability of commercial civic spirit.

Until the plague, Marseillais criticism of commerce most often materialized from the religious angle; as articulated by Bishop Belsunce, this critique held that merchants were individually sinful for pursuing material wealth, while they were socially guilty for spreading luxury and covetousness. Langeron's attacks against the city's leading merchants launched secular denunciations of commerce. By restoring the traditional equation that pitted civic spirit and citizenship against commercial activity, he reactivated the kind of mistrust of local merchants that Jean-Baptiste Colbert had revealed decades before. Could merchants think beyond their personal interests? Could merchants be good citizens? The well-known facts that a merchant ship had carried plague to the city and that *négociant*-intendants of the Bureau de la santé had failed to prevent the catastrophe seemed to provide negative responses to these questions. Langeron condemned the *négociants,* charging that power and avarice corrupted them.

Langeron's attacks against commercial civic spirit intensified in the context of administrative discussions over disinfection. In the winter of 1720, he organized the city's first general disinfection, a process whereby citizen volunteers fumigated buildings, furniture, clothes, textiles, and papers with various herbs, oils, and vinegar. In August and September of 1722, after noting a rise in mortality, Langeron ordered another general disinfection, decreeing that this was necessary "for the security of the entire kingdom."[68]

Not all citizens were willing to comply with these complicated processes that involved registering, cleaning, and confiscating merchandise. *Négociants* in particular vocalized their resistance, insisting that such procedures violated their commercial freedom. An assembly of several Marseillais *négociants* drafted a memo justifying the uselessness of disinfection. While praising the commandant, they stressed redundancy: "Monsieur de Langeron's caution has been so great through the plague that it would not be possible to add anything to the order that he has already established," they began, "all houses, stores, boutiques, mills, ateliers, religious houses, communities and the merchandise, furniture, and clothes that they contain have been purged, aerated, and perfumed several times, the timbering and frameworks washed with vinegar and the walls bleached."[69] Claiming "mission accomplished," they stressed that no plague-stricken community—whether in England, Spain, Germany, Italy, or France—had enforced successive disinfections.

The *négociants* reluctantly suggested an alternative: they could each submit inventories confirming that their merchandise was clean of plague. The *négociants*, however, claimed that this too was an "inconvenience." Citing the need for absolute discretion in commerce, they insisted that inventories could jeopardize their credibility and status in the market. "It is an uncontestable fact that secrecy is the soul of business, and is particularly so in commerce," the memo read, "Each *négociant* has his credit . . . which he would be obliged to abandon, were he to confess his resources." "Many have nothing in their funds, others have no merchandise, some have neither," it continued, "but as the merchant's goal is to buy and sell, and to give oneself in blind confidence founded on secrecy and in good faith with which one works in commerce, it would completely ruin and send an infinite number of honest men into disorder, if obliged to make public the state of their affairs."

The merchants insisted that disclosure of each merchant's possessions would not only ruin the merchant's business but would destroy French commerce in general. If information in these inventories spilled into foreign hands, they would be alerted to France's financial secrets and profit at the kingdom's expense. Foreigners who "consume a great amount of Marseillais merchandise . . . will be informed of the quantities of merchandise, and they will adjust their designs to [them . . .] they will manage their commissions to match the quantity that has been disclosed to them, in order to drive down our prices," the Marseillais *négociants* protested. This would spell disaster for city and state: "they will achieve the ruin of the *place de Marseille*, so that our *négociants* will be able to maintain neither their credit nor their reputation." "This is of obvious interest to the state," the *négociants* concluded; "[commerce] provides the means to support its charges, cultivate arts and industry, and procure immense revenues for the king."[70] The Marseillais *négociants* mobilized the language of commercial civic spirit that predated the plague to frame their protests against disinfection. They assumed that commerce and the *négociant* benefited the state. They maintained that *négociants'* interests and Marseille's commercial strengths converged with those of the kingdom.

In 1722, however, the widely known facts about the plague's origins rendered such arguments by merchants suspect. That Captain Chataud had introduced the plague into Marseille, whether through his own treachery or through the "complacence and inconsistency" of the merchant-run Bureau de la santé tarnished the notion that the *parfait négociant* was a good citizen of the virtuous marketplace. Two dominant stories regarding culpability had emerged; that the greedy merchant, Chataud, had manipulated his way into Marseille's port, and, that self-interested *négociant* health intendants had rendered such treachery possible. While such rumors circulated around France, the governor of Provence, Marquis de Pilles, imprisoned Chataud "for contraventions to the ordinances of health, false declarations, having entered merchandise before purgation and for having favored the escape of a man on board during the quarantine."[71] Meanwhile, the captain and admiral of the royal navy in Marseille and Toulon discussed the culpability of the *premier échevin*: "This sordid interest has appeared completely criminal to His Highness, he has ordered me . . . that you inform yourselves exactly of the interests of Sieur Estelle."[72] Unlike Chataud, the *échevin* had patrons, the royal governor, Marquis de Pilles, and royal intendant Lebret who allowed him to escape official condemnation. Nonetheless, such rumors helped associate commercial activity with plague. They tarnished commercial activity with the stain of self-interest.

This critique of commerce and elite merchants was not limited to Marseille. The inflationary crisis that culminated throughout France from 1720 to 1722 as a result of the crash of John Law's financial system weakened commercial civic spirit. Law, the Scottish financier-turned-controller-general who had persuaded French subjects to trade in paper money, had sparked an economic bubble that ended disastrously by 1720. Initially, Law's misfortune in Paris did not directly seem to affect Marseille. Early in the outbreak, the *échevins* received news that Law was sending them a contribution of 100,000 *livres*.[73] The donation, however, was an empty one. Law ordered a deposit in his own banknotes, which had become worthless after the French market crash of May 1720.[74] The flustered *échevins* wrote to Law: "We gave the 100,000 in cash . . . to the Hôtel de la monnaye to change the banknotes," but "they refused to convert them."[75] The money never materialized; John Law fled France for Belgium.

From the fall of Controller-General Law to the incarceration of Captain Chataud, from rumors about Estelle's role in corrupting quarantines to the Marseillais *négociants*' unwillingness to comply with disinfection, the activities of financiers and elite merchants seemed contrary to public welfare. Langeron's unsympathetic stance toward Marseille's *négociants* emerged out of a general shift in thinking about the market prompted by three years of medical and financial catastrophe. In his *Mémoire au sujet d'une désinfection générale,* he pointed out that "if there has never been [complete disinfection] in the lazaretto of Marseille, it is the particular interest of the *négociants,* who have always composed the principal part of the Intendance de la santé, which decided that over the [interests] of public security." The "particular interests of the *négociants,*" Langeron asserted, "must give way to those of public security."[76]

The anonymous *Mémoire sur les infirmaries* and *Mémoire sur quelques abus qui se commettent dans les villes de Marseille et de Toulon à l'égard des quarantaines et de la santé* repeated Langeron's condemnation of commercial interests. Indicting the *négociants* of the lazaretto for complacency, the authors targeted commercial interests as the corrupting force that had led to the "tranquilization" of vigilance. "Because these intendants are for the most part *négociants,*" the first *Mémoire* claimed, "they find themselves always interested for themselves, their parents, or their friends."[77] They turned a blind eye to contraband. "Indulgence" and "the avarice of the captains [of the *infirmaries*]" jeopardized Marseille and the kingdom as a whole.[78] The *Mémoires* maintained that only "prompt punishment" and "discipline" could remedy corruption and "reconcile the conservation of health with the interests of the *négociants.*" One suggested that the Bureau de la santé be reformed by installing troops in French quarantine centers. The author proposed that women be forbidden visitation. He suggested that lawyers remain in the lazaretto to "balance the authority of the *négociants,* who have taken possession of the entire city, under the pretext of favoring commerce, while they destroy it [commerce] themselves by their particular interests, which operate often and completely against the public interest."[79] The second *Mémoire* was not so optimistic. Distrustful of the *échevins* who "were at the same time the judges and the parties [judged]," the author argued that quarantines could not be led by merchants. He argued that the Crown ought to install spies to curb corruption within the Bureau de la santé. He proposed that the king name the captain of the infirmaries and employ "denouncers" to report "negligence or the conniving of the health intendants."[80] In short, he called for more centralization.

Although the Bureau de la santé never realized the reforms proposed in these *Mémoires,* Langeron successfully passed his *Acte déclaratif de l'état présent de la santé de la ville de Marseille et de la désinfection générale que y a été faite par ordre du Roy*. Facing opposition by the *échevins* and merchants, he pressed the Crown for his second disinfection, which it ordered in December 1722 and bypassed the *échevins,* calling on Marseillais to "perfect the state of health in the city."[81] He installed new commissioners chosen from among "the most zealous inhabitants" to ransack all warehouses, and stores of elite merchants. Langeron determined to see Marseille the civic community triumph over Marseille the commercial city.

The commandant continued his efforts even after the Crown announced the end of the epidemic in January 1723. Months after the Te Deum of Deliverance, Langeron issued another ordinance in August 1723. Asserting that "the public good that is our principal attention" required the "same zeal" "for virtue" that had "marked the times of our last calamity," he solicited citizens to volunteer as spies to "denounce to us the places of prostitution and debauchery, prohibited games, the vagabonds and disreputable men, women of bad reputation, malefactors, blasphemers, soothsayers, those who in the day or at night carry prohibited arms, and those who carry swords illegally." They would ensure "that nothing will pass that can trouble public tranquility, and will report to us to avert illicit assemblies, tumults, emotions, and all disorders and violence." Langeron repeated the theme of virtue that he emphasized throughout the epidemic: "Citizens . . . without any other view than that of being useful to the *patrie*" would keep Marseille a city of "good order" and "mores."[82] Langeron remained a man of absolute oppositions: virtue versus corruption, self-interest versus the public good, earned him the title of *père de la patrie.*

THE PARLEMENT'S LAST STAND: TRADITION VERSUS INNOVATION

Langeron was determined to restore Marseille to order and virtue, but the parlement upon returning to Aix-en-Provence doubted that his efforts were as well-intentioned as he depicted. From the start, the new collaboration between the monarchy and municipal leaders had aggravated the parlementary magistrates, who believed that the Crown had diminished their judicial authority by granting municipal officials and royal commandants despotic power during crisis. The noble magistrates, therefore, remonstrated with the king, complaining that the innovations in administering justice and police through military commandants had generated chaos and tyrannical rule. The magistrates depicted Langeron and his subordinates as irrational, unjust, corrupt, and excessive. The commandant and his men had provoked "universal derangement," they claimed. "They elected themselves sovereigns of the province . . . made laws . . . appointed sub-commandants, condemned [people] to death without the approval of [His] Majesty . . . revoked *arrêts* of parlement, and judged both civil and criminal cases in matters not concerning contagion."[83] Appealing to tradition, reason, and citizenship, the parlement insisted that the institutionalization of martial law in the plague-stricken provinces of Provence had made a travesty of justice for three years.

The magistrates saw justice in parlementary tradition and arbitrary despotism in innovation. "Abuse [comes] from a system that is new and artificial," they claimed. They invoked the parlement's two-centuries-long experience in policing plague to assert that they alone had the accrued wisdom needed to run a lawful police force. "Legitimate jurisdiction," they insisted, was "perpetuated by tradition from father to son," and could never be trusted to "innovations." Skeptical of the new, they insisted that "ancient authority" had to be reestablished to ensure "good rules and healthy discipline."[84] The use of commandants, "a system as new as it is artificial," was founded on "neither law nor legitimate usages." It had introduced a "despotic" and "arbitrary sovereign power."[85]

The magistrates attributed this despotism to the commandants' lack of citizenship and civility. Parlementary magistrates, they asserted, "are judges but at the same time citizens of the province." They stressed that citizens possessed property and shared a sense of kinship with fellow citizens who likewise held property and goods in the province. Commandants and soldiers, they argued, were not citizens. As itinerant soldiers, they imported their mercenary discipline into civil affairs, regarding Provence as their "conquered land." They introduced the "examples of barbaric nations" into civilized society, "killing men without subscribing to any sort of formality, without understanding the accused, follow[ing] in their judgments no other rule that that of caprice and their own interest." They disregarded the fundamental "law of the state" that required parlementary process for crimes involving corporal punishment. The commandants armed themselves against the inhabitants, "burned, pillaged, drove up taxes and duties," and sentenced innocent citizens to death. "This abuse of the public," parlement stressed, was "an example of lèse-majesté." The commandants and their troops were bloodthirsty men of war with no understanding of civic duties or virtues. They were "enemies of the nation."[86]

Such noncitizens, the magistrates continued, understood no law but that of passion, self-interest, and avarice. The commandants' military discipline, they charged, rested on "popular emotions" and were "always arranged by interested parties." The magistrates accused Langeron and the many commandants installed in Provence of taking advantage of royal letters patent and the parlement's absence to extend their powers illegally, trade in contraband, and raise duties for their own profit. Langeron in particular, the magistrates argued, plainly demonstrated his excesses; he presided over trials relating to "rape and all other ordinary misdemeanors," he annulled parlementary *arrêts,* fixed currency rates, and imposed taxes without the Crown's consent.[87] Finally, the commandant had shown his "despotic authority" in his unnecessary general disinfection that disregarded the principle of "liberty of commerce."

In all these actions, the magistrates charged, the commandants acted for their own interests to the detriment of the public. The aristocratic magistrates offered a conservative judicial critique of royal martial law, exposing Langeron and his subordinates' virtue as a charade; these military personnel had packaged their personal interests as a passion for the general good. The magistrates pleaded for a return to orthodoxy. Seeing the nobility as guardians of citizenship, the parlement looked for stability in the past.

The plague and its aftermath saw various parties—commandants, *échevins,* and parlement—offer competing definitions of citizenship and various ways of discerning the public good. Plague disrupted the belief that commercial pursuits were virtuous, the merchant was an exemplary citizen, and the marketplace was the laboratory of virtue. Once plague destabilized this commercial civic spirit, Marseillais *échevins* and police *commissaires,* parlementary magistrates, and royal commandants redefined ways of organizing and ruling over citizens and subjects. The commandant and *échevins* used the language of civic participation and virtue to sustain their severe laws that they believed were the only foolproof method to revive civic spirit. Later, the *échevins* and *négociants* broke their alliance with Langeron, protesting his disinfections by making claims on behalf of commerce, merchants, and their concern for the state's public good. Finally, the parlement saw noble virtue and citizenship as fundamentally opposed to the commandants' versions of civic spirit. It was attempting to restore a municipal order founded on tradition, social hierarchy, and property.

The Crown sided, ultimately, with Commandant Langeron. Parlement never recovered its policing privileges during epidemics. But plague never reappeared in France.

BEYOND PROVENCE: PLAGUE AND MODERN STRUCTURES OF POWER

Severe, authoritarian responses to plague instituted by Commandant Langeron and the Marseillais *échevins* were limited neither to Provence nor to France; indeed, the strengthening of royal and municipal authority during time of plague has attracted the attention of historians who have observed in such developments the emergence of modern systems of discipline and governance. These argue that the early modern period saw secular administrators assume more power in controlling the bodies of their subjects.[88] Examples of growing secular authoritarianism can be found, for example, in England, where the Plague Act of 1604 allowed penal sanctions to be used for quarantining the sick. The same law gave watchmen power to implement quarantines. "Anyone found wandering with a plague sore could be hanged," Mark Harrison states.[89]

Meanwhile, other historians have compared plague administration to mechanisms of terror and revolutionary government; René Baehrel has written that "France under the Terror only revived what each community knew in times of contagion."[90] The rounding up of suspects, summary executions, and the collective mentality against self-interested individuals were, for Baehrel, common to both diseased and revolutionary spaces. He and Foucault characterize early modern responses to plague as a fundamentally modern one. They show that administrative control assumed a new utopian vision that sought to maximize authority, transparency, and repression, albeit under republican or democratic regimes. For such historians, this could only happen in a modern state that had developed enough networks to support total surveillance.

My study has attempted to show that such emergency systems were not solely indicative of the development of modern systems of surveillance and repression; rather, old and new systems competed and interacted. In plague-stricken Marseille, a city forced to suspend commerce during medical crisis, administrative elites and citizens had several traditional tools to formulate responses to plague and to forge alternative principles of civic organization *sans commerce*. The repertoire of austere political plague metaphors that pitted corruption against virtue, the historical sources that emphasized the polarity between healthy and sick republics, and the *ordres* that outlined how to conduct police formed a collection of civic rituals and institutions that predated monarchical power. While Marseillais administrators reactivated these traditions, the Crown provided them with new options, new tools and collaborators, and new choices. This royal intervention strengthened some traditional apparatuses while weakening others. Most notably, it undermined parlementary cooperation with the city. However, it allowed Marseillais *échevins* to achieve an unprecedented level of authority and power. While old plague-containment sources outlined utopian goals of absolute virtue and health, the combination of municipal traditions with the Crown's new systems of governance provided the energy to realize these objectives. Old goals were realized with new agents of power, while their accomplishments were understood through old languages of civic republicanism.

In this sense, modern centralization did not triumph during the plague, but the modernizing French state helped realize traditional civic ideals. This intersection of seemingly incompatible options—between tradition and innovation, Marseille's republican past and royalist future—was precisely the phenomenon that allowed Marseillais administrators repeatedly to reformulate viable civic identities for their city in the context of French royal state-building and amplified foreign pressures. From the conquest of 1660, Marseillais elites—*échevins, négociants,* and robe nobility—saw the monarchy repeatedly interfering in "the old way of doing things," from changing rules for administration and commercial activities to developing new mechanisms of health surveillance. While the Marseille born out of Colbert's mercantilist designs differed vastly from the Marseille of 1720 that temporarily renounced commercial activities, one thing remained rather consistent: the Marseillais administrators' abilities to adapt to new royal strategies of governance without relinquishing old civic habits and practices. Thus, both in 1660 and in 1720, civic leaders credited the Crown with having restored ancient Marseille: Louis XIV breathed commercial vigor into Massilia, and the Regent reestablished its virtue.

CHAPTER SIX

Civic Religiosity and Religious Citizenship in Plague-Stricken Marseille

While civic leaders and physicians attributed plague to foreign yeasts and antisocial acts of self-indulgence, another group of elites—religious personnel—reactivated a traditional plague discourse of divine punishment. They preached that God was unhappy with Marseille, that Jansenist heresy within the Church and immorality among the wider population had provoked God's anger. According to Bishop Henri de Belsunce of Marseille, "the voice of the priest—that of the holy Church herself, and her formidable censures, were spurned with contempt by rebel sons, who dared to elect themselves judges and arbiters of the faith."[1] God, the bishop of Arles echoed, was punishing Provençals for "our spirit of revolt."[2] Agreeing that Jansenists' "multiplied sacrileges" were "the principal cause"[3] of "the plague of error," the bishops insisted that excommunication of heretics would restore the Catholic community to health.[4]

Such interpretations of and reactions to plague are hardly a surprise, given the ease with which medical, religious, and moral definitions of "contagion" could intersect in early modern Europe.[5] One need only browse through the 1694 edition of the *Dictionnaire de l'Académie française* to see how medical catastrophe could prompt religious commentators to cry spiritual decadence. Of the seven definitions provided for "contagion," only two were of a medical sort. While plague was the worst form of "communication of a malign malady," "contagion" was also a figurative disease that included "vice," "heresy," "wicked mores," and "evil things communicated by frequentation or example."[6]

If ecclesiastics had associated spiritual corruption with plague for centuries, what was particular about how these utterances materialized in 1720? How did they interact with secular calls for civic engagement? How did commerce factor into this religious response? Did religious reactions to plague strengthen civic republican traditions in southern France?

During the plague of 1720, traditional religious responses, including rhetorical and physical attacks on Jews, non-Christians, non-Frenchmen, and non-indigenous inhabitants, remained muffled. Rather, the loudest religious reactions to the epidemic developed out of doctrinal arguments within the Catholic community that predated the medical catastrophe. These discussions belonged to a broader religious conversation in late seventeenth and early eighteenth-century France regarding Church governance and the proper limits to papal authority. Before the plague, Jansenists—Augustinian Catholics in France protesting ultramontanist claims—began invoking Gallican traditions to argue that the Church, represented by a general council, was superior to the pope.[7] Comparing the council's responsibility to restrain papal authoritarianism to citizens' rights to oppose tyranny, Provençal Jansenists and their supporters in the parlement in Aix idealized civic participation. The Church, they argued, should be governed like a republic. The orthodox establishment responded by condemning all forms of "immorality," including Gallican heresy, sexual corruption, and commercial luxury. When plague arrived in 1720, Jansenists and orthodox Catholics interpreted it as God's punishment for religious decadence and perceived plague-stricken Marseille as a divinely chosen locus for a showdown between heterodoxy or orthodoxy.

In this context, questions of religious devotion and civic spirit converged in several ways. Three kinds of civic practices that emerged in plague-stricken Marseille—collective baroque ritual, charitable service, and public discussion—demonstrate that as with the republicanism discussed in chapter 5, religious responses to epidemic brought together old practices with new vocabularies. First, the religious establishment, led by Belsunce, consecrated Marseille to the Sacred Heart of Jesus. By organizing a collective and public ritual of atonement to re-Catholicize the city, Belsunce integrated Marseille's civic space into his project for religious renewal. Public spaces once used for commercial exchange became sites for communion with God. Meanwhile, discussions over serving dying plague victims fused religious charity to acts of civic spirit. Jansenists and orthodox Catholics competed over civic service, accusing each other of unchristian neglect and self-interest. They appealed to a new species of abstract arbiter, a literary and participatory "public tribunal," to decide who demonstrated proper religious civic behavior.

Although historians like Michel Vovelle and Dale Van Kley have analyzed *longue durée* processes of secularization and connections between revolutionary politics and religious controversies in early modern France, convergences between religiosity and civic spirit remain surprisingly unexplored. The role religious discussions played in shaping civic practices and the ways civic concerns strengthened religiosity during the Enlightenment have received limited attention, perhaps owing to the assumption that the age of Newton, Voltaire, and the *Encyclopédie* saw religious activity retreat behind developments in secularism and deism. This chapter tests such assumptions with three main claims. First, it demonstrates that Jansenist ideas of participatory Church administration borrowed from and strengthened the secular ideal of civic service and republican governance, across France as much as in Marseille. Second, it shows that in plague-stricken Marseille, ecclesiastical and municipal leaders who saw religious decadence in terms of sociopolitical decay, and vice versa, moved comfortably between the ideas of a republic in crisis and a Church in crisis. Third, this chapter shows how despite trends in secularism, the eighteenth century saw the development of a religious and civic tradition—the Cult of the Sacred Heart—that would ultimately grow into an enduring alternative to secular republicanism after the end of the Old Regime.[8]

Additionally, this chapter contributes to the historical analysis of "public opinion."[9] French historians generally agree that administrators, intellectuals, and writers began employing the rhetorical construct of "public opinion" in political discussions in the latter half of the eighteenth century.[10] This chapter argues that while politics may have emerged out of its absolutist casing in the 1750s, the rhetorical practice of invoking the "public" as an abstract arbiter of rational justice predated the mid eighteenth century.[11] Hardly confined to state politics, the "public tribunal" was vested with absolute authority in the context of debates between Jansenists and the Catholic establishment during the plague of 1720. The appeal to this "public tribunal" led ecclesiastics and laypersons into a discursive field where the Catholic community could hope to restore religious order. This space served as a fertile training ground for enlightened rational discussion and contestation against illegitimate power in the decades that followed. The discursive space of religious debate, and Marseille's once-commercial physical spaces—the port, the galley Arsenal, and the boulevards—emerged as major sites where ecclesiastic leaders toyed with seemingly incompatible ideas of baroque religiosity, Enlightenment rationalism, and republican governance.

DEPARTING FROM PRECEDENT: WHAT ABOUT ANTI-SEMITISM?

One of the most commonly held notions regarding religious responses to plague is that they involved the unleashing of verbal and physical attacks against Jews. Although this is true of the fourteenth and fifteenth centuries, such attacks were infrequent by the eighteenth. Somewhat surprisingly, given the intensity of the debates on the acceptability of Armenians and Jews as trading partners, citizens, and subjects in France (Chapter 3), there were very few attacks on Jews and non-Christians during the plague of Marseille in 1720.

Collections of primary sources demonstrate how Jews were murdered for allegedly conspiring to exterminate European communities by poisoning wells in the fourteenth and fifteenth centuries.[12] Jean-Noël Biraben, a French authority on medieval and early modern plagues, has shown that during the Black Death, lepers and Jews were tortured and burned alive in Tours, Périgueux, and Salignac and massacred by the populace in Toulon. Attempts by popes, princes, and authorities to curb vigilante violence failed in Provence. From Avignon, Pope Clement VI issued a bull stating that God did not distinguish between Christians and non-Christians during plague, while Queen Jeanne compensated the Jews by reducing their taxes and sending her army to curb popular violence. The inhabitants, however, continued their massacres.[13]

By the sixteenth century, such attacks on Jews had waned. Historians studying the London plague of 1665–1666 have failed to uncover evidence of anti-Semitic outbursts.[14] Other "target groups" replaced Jews as victims of attacks of mass hysteria. William Naphy has shown how the fifteenth and sixteenth centuries continued to see some "economically motivated anti-Semitism," but that streetwalkers, travelers, and lower-class plague workers were targeted in growing frequency in the western Alps. This transition, he notes, was connected to rising fears of witchcraft. Those tortured, executed, and massacred were wanderers, widows, or poor travelers from neighboring states and towns: people whose combination of gender and poverty placed them at the edges of communal life.[15] Plague epidemics, therefore, did not prompt a consistent form of anti-Semitic xenophobia in the early modern period.

Still the question remains: what happened to the population of religious others, non-naturalized and naturalized inhabitants of Marseille during the plague of 1720? The answer remains a mystery. Neither eyewitness accounts, plague histories, nor diaries point to large-scale criminalization of, or discrimination against, naturalized and foreign non-Christian immigrants. The only references to xenophobic policy come from Marseille's Hôtel de Ville and the parlement de Provence in the first weeks of the plague. On 31 July 1720, after parlement suspended commerce between Marseille and other Provençal cities, the Hôtel de Ville expelled the Jews, non-naturalized foreigners, vagabonds, mendicants, and individuals of "disreputable character" from Marseille, "on pain of death." This order, however, was never followed up, since the parlement forbade travel.[16] The "foreigners" were trapped in Marseille. Meanwhile, a royal *arrêt* in October freed the galley slaves, ordering them to dispose of the corpses in Marseille's streets. This latter order suggests that non-Marseillais and non-French galley slaves had continued living in the city once ships were grounded. If they survived, the Crown guaranteed them freedom after the plague. The assumption is that the majority of them died, along with half of the population of Marseille.

While administrative policies from 1720 did not focus on targeting Jews and non-Christians, religious responders to plague—bishops, priests, and other ecclesiastics—also refrained from implicating non-Christians as vectors of disease or provokers of divine anger. Rather, as the following discussion demonstrates, they remained chiefly concerned with the state of Catholicism in Marseille, and sought, in different ways, to restore a religious order to the city consistent with their theological leanings.

CONCILIARISM AND JANSENISM IN FRANCE AND PROVENCE

Calls for participation in Church governance predated the 1720 plague by centuries. Medieval proponents of conciliarism introduced the idea that only a "general council" could effectively reform the Church.[17] These argued that an ecclesiastical council wielded more legitimate authority than the papacy. In early modern France, the monarchy merged conciliar arguments with Gallicanism, a tradition that "upheld the temporal independence of the monarchy and the spiritual independence of the Gallican Church in their respective relations with the papacy."[18]

While French monarchs used Gallicanism to augment their power by limiting papal authority in France, it proved to be a problematic strategy. The principle of royal temporal independence undercut papal sovereignty, but the "republican implications of conciliar Gallicanism" threatened all sovereign rulers. As Pope Innocent XI remarked, "if councils were superior to the popes whose power comes from God, then the Estates General would have leave to press the same claim against kings."[19] Favoring rule by many over rule by one, conciliar arguments could—and did—fuel the constitutional theory of "limited monarchy."[20] The French Crown therefore stepped up efforts against conciliarism, particularly after the Abbey of Port-Royal-des-Champs became a Jansenist stronghold in the 1630s.

Seventeenth-century Jansenists called for a particular kind of Gallicanism and Catholic reform that followed the teachings of Cornelius Jansen (1585–1638), bishop of Ypres. Led by Antoine Arnauld, Antoine Le Maître de Sacy, and Blaise Pascal, among others, French Jansenists called for a return to Augustinian traditions. Jansenists maintained that Adam's original sin had enslaved man in his passions; only God's incomprehensible grace could guarantee salvation.[21] Emphasizing predestination, Jansenists rejected secular and ecclesiastical hierarchies. Le Maître translated the Bible, Mass, and Divine Office into French to increase lay participation in doctrinal discussions. Pasquier Quesnel's *Réflexions morales sur le Nouveau Testament* (1692) argued that man admitted sins to God alone, not to bishops, cardinals, and popes; the Church was "composed of the angels, the just, the predestined, not recognizing any leader than the invisible Head."[22]

Such denial of hierarchy and human will steered Jansenism close to Calvinist Protestantism, outlawed in France with the Edict of Fontainebleau. Anti-Jansenists claimed that such Protestant-like arguments "transformed Christ's 'Monarchical' church into a 'Republic'" and endangered spiritual and secular order.[23] Intent on realizing "the political principle . . . *cujus regio, ejus religio*: no confessional pluralism in the same territory,"[24] Louis XIV crusaded against Jansenist Port-Royal and Pierre de Bérulle's Oratory, "a congregation of secular priests that was devoted to the restoration of the priests' sacerdotal dignity against regulars." He razed Port-Royal in 1711 and solicited the papacy's help against heresy. The papacy issued its Apostolic Constitution *Unigenitus* in 1713.[25]

Unigenitus denounced the Jansenists' doctrine of efficacious grace and calls for an anti-hierarchical Church. It rejected the Jansenist emphasis on lay participation in doctrinal affairs: Jansenist teachings that "all sorts of persons, [ought] to study the Scriptures, to know its spirit, piety and mysteries" were pronounced heretical. *Unigenitus* condemned the claim that "to peacefully suffer excommunication and unjust anathema, rather than betray the truth, is to imitate St. Paul."[26] The episcopal establishment took aim at Jansenism's most Calvinist-seeming teachings by denouncing ideas that valued the elect and predestined over the ecclesiastical hierarchy.

Unigenitus, however, proved unsuccessful and divisive. Louis XIV ordered the parlement of Paris to register the bull as law. The archbishop of Paris, Cardinal de Noailles, in addition to several bishops and the faculty at the Sorbonne, however, rejected it and demanded that Rome provide explications justifying the bull. Though the parlement of Paris succumbed to royal pressure and registered *Unigenitus* as law in 1714, "several individuals refused to adhere to its mandates. Insubordinate ecclesiastics were imprisoned; others were obliged to flee."[27] When the king died in 1715, the crisis over *Unigenitus* remained unresolved. Louis XIV's successor, the Regent Philippe, duc d'Orléans, experimented with new strategies to contain religious turmoil, but as royal edicts and papal bulls continued to repress religious dissent, Jansenists in Provence began unleashing their most stringent attacks against papal tyranny and the Church hierarchy.[28] Marseille became a hotbed of religious discussion in the years just before the plague.

Marseille's Oratory College and Notre-Dame des Anges, "a Provençal Port-Royal," educated and housed a large number of Jansenists. While only a handful of priests in southern France admitted to being appellants, so called because they appealed to a "future general council" of the Church to reject *Unigenitus*, Provençal Jansenists increasingly vocalized their contempt of the Church hierarchy.[29] In the years between *Unigenitus* and the plague, Provençal Jansenists articulated three major points. They reiterated the ideals of Gallican liberty; they used political metaphors in religious discussions; and they mobilized the republican language of political will to describe and solve religious crises. These developments in Provence reflected a trend throughout France as Jansenists politicized their rhetoric against papal sovereignty. In Provence, these claims crescendoed after Pope Clement XI excommunicated appellants with the bull *Pastoralis Officii* in 1718. The ultramontane position of Marseille's Bishop Belsunce helped kindle Jansenist reactions.

La politique des Jesuites demasquée et l'appel justifié par les principes des libertés de l'Eglise gallicane, an anonymous pamphlet dating from 1719, illustrates the politicization of Jansenist rhetoric in Provence. The author compared papal power to despotism and the sovereign Church to a republic. He began with the Gallican claim that Church sovereignty rested in its body of believers, not in the pope: "the throne of Peter is not the center where truth resides forever stable and immobile." Rejecting papal infallibility, he argued that "truth lies in the Church; infallibility is only given to her." Popes and bishops only held the right "of representation and juridical declaration" as administrators. "The faith," he wrote, "forms the public law of the Holy Nation (*nation Sainte*); nothing is clearer in a nation than public law; nothing is less subject to change than these laws." Just as a kingdom continued to exist despite the deaths of monarchs, so too the Church was immortal despite the death of mortal rulers.[30]

The author specifically compared the Church to a republic: "It is principally to the Christian Church that one can apply what Aristotle once said, that a republic is a society of free people: *civitas est societas liberum*."[31] As first ruler of this republic, Christ established "a government of complete humility and charity; if he forbade the rebellion of inferiors and the tyranny of superiors, he wanted the pastors to command according to the laws. . . . and the faithful to obey the same laws. This is the essential liberty." Guaranteed such freedoms, the lay population had the right to distinguish between just and unjust submission. The author accepted "legitimate submission of inferiors to a governor who bans independence and libertinage for just subordination." Citizens had the right, however, to refuse unjust submission to any "despotic" or "tyrannical domination" that produced "slavery."[32]

The metaphor of citizens fighting against despotism appeared in countless Jansenist treatises in Provence. The *Lettre à Monseigneur l'évêque de Marseille,* for example, described illegitimate extensions of paper power in Rome. The anonymous author discussed how the pope had acquired "a taste for the idol of infallibility" and usurped "prerogatives that he never received from either Jesus Christ or the Church." Papal rule turned into "a despotic government." Worse, this despotism of "the court of Rome [was] contagious."[33] Meanwhile, the distinguished Jansenist Vivien de La Borde, author of *Principes sur l'essence, la distinction et les limites des deux puissances, spirituelle et temporelle* and *Du témoignage de la vérité* (1716), introduced a more radical argument.[34] While he echoed Jansenist condemnations of papal despotism, he took the language of political will further to encourage a revolution in religious organization. He urged virtuous citizens in the Church community to testify to the truth and to topple the ecclesiastical hierarchy.

La Borde distinguished how pope and prince ruled over spiritual and temporal domains respectively, and that the extension of one authority into the other resulted in "confusion and disorder."[35] The spiritual community, or Church, he wrote, was a nation; as with "all nations of the world," it had "its laws, its rights, its police, its government, its primary and secondary magistrates, etc."[36] Extending this analogy further, he likened ecclesiastical leaders to "France's parlement of Paris."[37] These magistrates enjoyed infallibility only when it expressed the infallible "voice of the state":

> The holy order of Church magistrates is established as a public symbol, to turn away nonbelievers while the faithful citizens must find in their ministry the consolation, instruction, exhortation, and correction they need. Because all is divine

> in the Holy Nation, the magistracy is divine and cannot die . . . It is through the magistrates that the state speaks. The voice of the state is divine, and is consequently infallible. The voice of its magistrates is therefore [infallible]. But is this so in all circumstances? Does each magistrate enjoy the privilege of infallibility? In sum, the magistracy of the Church is divinely infallible only in circumstances where in all other nations the magistracy is humanly infallible.[38]

The pope and his ultramontane bishops, La Borde claimed, transgressed these boundaries of magistracy and limited infallibility. *Unigenitus*, he continued, introduced a new era of "oppression" as Church leaders "obscured" the "voice of the state."[39]

La Borde advocated a radical overhaul of the Church constitution. He suggested that the monarchical Church be reconstituted as a republic, "where each deputy, without prejudice of rank and preeminence that place one under the other, raises his voice for all bodies of the nation." In such a republic, La Borde imagined witnesses replacing judges and magistrates. The greatest authority, La Borde argued, resided not in "the authority of judgment," but in the "authority of testimony." Elect citizens, distinguished by their rejection of amour propre, "concupiscence" "interest, passions and all the intrigues that oblige the mouth to contradict the heart" would rescue truth and liberate the Church.[40]

La Borde conceded, however, that such citizens were hard to come by. During unstable "times of violence," such as his own, witnesses became "suspect," testimony was "obscured, and contempt progressively spread [as] Satan transform[ed] into the Angel of Light."[41] La Borde's Church was a republic in crisis. After overthrowing despotic magistrates, a handful of virtuous citizens faced the challenge of restoring "truth," by provisionally ruling "in the name of the great number." Unless mankind was "restored to the state of innocence," the community as a whole would never see the truth.

La Borde's worldview was a pessimistic one; republics hung precariously between corruption and extinction. His dark musings seemed to be transformed into reality when, a few years after he described this religious crisis, plague broke out in 1720.[42]

ORTHODOXY AGAINST JANSENISM IN PROVENCE, 1703–1719

While Jansenists called for a reform of the Church from below, Orthodox Catholics advocated reform from above. Both Jansenists and their opponents insisted on the need to restore virtue to the religious community. Jansenists saw virtue as a prerequisite for legitimate representation and participation in doctrinal decisions. The virtuous elect would overthrow despotism and restore the "voice of the church-state." In contrast, the establishment saw virtue as an end rather than as a means; restoring virtue involved crushing heresy and the sexual and commercial depravity that threatened the Church from below.

Papal supporters stepped up their condemnation of Jansenism upon the assumption of power by the Regent, Philippe, duc d'Orléans, who they believed had instituted a dangerous policy that empowered Jansenists. While Louis XIV had attempted to root out heresy, the Regent ordered "complete silence" on doctrinal disputes. This strategy, "despite its tendency to favor nobody, was favorable to the Jansenists, who were left in their desired positions."[43] Furthermore, because the Regent owed his position to the parlement of Paris, he had restored the noble magistrates' privilege of remonstration. Parlements began exercising their authority by entertaining "appeals by priests interdicted for opposing *Unigenitus*." Parlements thus became shelters for the religiously dissident.

Led by the pope, the orthodox attacked Jansenism by mobilizing the metaphor of contagion. *Unigenitus* depicted Jansenism as plague. "The contagion of its pernicious maxims has passed along. . . . from nation to nation, kingdom to kingdom," it asserted. "We recognize that the dangerous progress it has made, which increases daily, comes principally from the *venom* of this book [Quesnel's *Testament*], which is concealed, like an *abscess*, whose corruption is not visible until one makes . . . incisions."[44] Provençal archbishops and bishops stood behind the pope. In Marseille, Bishop Henri de Belsunce began campaigning against heresy upon his arrival in the city in 1709. He was joined by Joseph-Ignace de Foresta, bishop of Apt, one of the first in France to openly protest Quesnel's *Testament* (15 October 1703), Jacques de Forbin de Janson, archbishop of Arles, and Monsigneur de La Tour du Pin-Montauban, bishop of Toulon.[45]

Shortly after *Unigenitus*, Belsunce described to a colleague how he crusaded against Jansenism: "I burned, on the Eve of Saint John, more than a thousand Quesnels, and I shall have the pleasure of burning another two thousand tomorrow on the Eve of Saint Peter's!"[46] In addition to book-burning, Belsunce threatened appellants with excommunication.[47] Meanwhile, Bishop de Foresta wrote of how the duc d'Orléans showed an "excess of clemency" to heretics. He likened the Sorbonne and the parlements to the Pharisees: "A spirit of vertigo and error filled the majority of the Jews: the priests, the doctors and the interpreters of the law, by their enlightenment and their piety, concealed their general corruption."[48]

The parlement de Provence in Aix responded to Belsunce and Foresta by citing the Regent's desire to hush religious chatter.[49] Insisting that Belsunce encouraged religious disorder, it issued two *arrêts* (7 December 1718 and 4 January 1719) against him. In addition to forbidding Belsunce and his subordinates from harassing the Oratory, the parlement suspended the bishop's revenues for five installments."[50]

Belsunce appealed to the Regent to annul the parlement's orders, claiming that Marseille's Fathers of the Oratory refused to "submit to the Church or the bishop" and spread Lutheran doctrines.[51] Belsunce reminded the Regent that no secular entity enjoyed authority over doctrine; neither "the king nor his parlements had the ability to decide whether *Unigenitus* would become the judgment of the Church, because this question directly concerned faith." He furnished royal ordinances dating back two centuries that conceded authority regarding matters of faith to the ecclesiastical establishment. This authority, he described, was jeopardized by secular bodies that elected themselves experts in doctrinal affairs; "The Sorbonne and parlements have become the judges of doctrine, and *voilà*, schism and Presbyterianism is established."[52] This spirit of revolt, he claimed, was nothing short of treason.[53]

On 15 June 1719, the Regent again ordered "absolute silence" on religious matters. Belsunce solicited papal aid.[54] Proclaiming that the time for "patience, silence, and slowness . . . has passed,"[55] Clement XI thereupon issued his bull *Pastoralis Officii*, excommunicating appellants. The Aixois magistrates sided with the appellants.[56] In the midst of this religious uproar, the plague appeared in Marseille.

BELSUNCE AND THE COMMERCIAL CITY: BATTLING HERETICS AND LIBERTINES

The plague of 1720 not only gave bishops in the Provençal dioceses an opportunity to sharpen their attacks on Jansenists, it provided Belsunce with a platform to condemn sexual depravity and luxury, which he saw as particularly rife in his urban diocese in Marseille, a bustling commercial metropolis of 100,000.

The *Statuts synodaux du diocese de Marseille* he published in 1712 reveal Belsunce's anxiety about spiritual fragility in Marseille prior to the plague. The bishop intended the *Statuts* to help ecclesiastics in the diocese of Marseille "maintain a holy life."[57] Bombarded with the luxuries and "vanities of the century," they faced a serious challenge, he stressed. Belsunce directed his brothers in Christ to avert their eyes from the temptations that flooded Marseille.[58] He ordered churches to be washed at least once a year, swept every week, and purified of "anything indecent." He provided his ecclesiastics with a list of places and sights to avoid in Marseille. In addition to forbidding smoking, opera, billiards, palm readings, card games, and bowling, he particularly prohibited activities associated with sexuality. "The frequentation of cabarets being an infallible mark of the derangement of mores . . . we forbid all ecclesiastics, clerks, religious, and hermits of our diocese, and all secular priests and regulars, under pain of suspension for a month . . . to eat and drink in the cabarets or other places where one can buy alcohol in quantity." He forbade male religious from employing "women under the age of fifty years, or whose reputation has been ambiguous at a less advanced age." "Mothers, sisters, aunts, or nieces" of male ecclesiastics were prohibited from visiting religious houses.[59]

Belsunce equated women with sexuality. He described women in the streets dressed "in simple cornets with their hair down, breasts exposed."[60] He recounted to Pope Clement XI how ecclesiastics at the famous abbey of Saint Victor opened their doors "to women curiously attired; they invite them in . . . introduce them into their private rooms and offer them things to eat." Religious celebrations, he continued, were not immune to female sexual depravity. In addition to Ascension, Pentecost, and the Nativity, the Marseillais Catholic calendar boasted no fewer than twenty-five feasts a year. On such occasions, he wrote, "the sanctity of our temples is profaned in the worst manner with immodesties and scandalous irreverence we can no longer tolerate in this city and diocese."[61] Belsunce's dread of female sexuality led him to impose physical barriers against women in religious spaces: "we order that confessionals from now on have small rails; they are to take place in the open, and never in obscure locations; we forbid confessors to take the confessions of girls and women in their rooms, [or] in sacristies and closed areas, under pain of suspension ipso facto."[62]

Belsunce's campaign against sexuality to perfect holiness among his ecclesiastics can be attributed to his Jesuit education and his baroque-inspired episcopacy. The second son of aristocratic Protestant parents who made pragmatic concessions by educating him at the Jesuit Louis-le-Grand *lycée* in Paris, Belsunce compensated for his Huguenot origins by fervently embracing the Catholic religion. He continued his studies at the Collège de Clermont in Paris and entered the Society of Jesus. Battling multiple illnesses, he left the Society in 1699 and became vicar-general of Agen, where he completed a biography of his saintly aunt, Suzanne de Foix.[63] He arrived in Marseille in 1709.

The Jesuit program stressed "external observances, collective rituals, and some of what Protestants would consider magical superstition," Lynn Martin writes. Adoration of saints, veneration of images, festive processions, and extravagant sermonizing were the chief elements of Jesuit religiosity. Belsunce's ministry followed this model of baroque piety; he organized pastoral visits to religious orders, restructured Marseille's lay confraternities to fall directly under his supervision, and promoted a collective, "publicly demonstrative" Catholicism characterized by externally manifest devotion.[64] He emphasized the power of images to strengthen or disrupt religious devotion; holy images and holy sites strengthened devotion, while corrupt images led the soul astray. What goes on "in the interior, man can ordinarily judge by what appears in the eyes," he warned. The image of the sexual woman became, for him, the symbol of impiety.[65]

Belsunce regularly used the symbol of the depraved woman in his attacks on immorality during the plague. He subsumed the evils of religious heresy and commercial luxury in the figurative symbol of the debauched female. He depicted commercial Marseille as a prostitute, describing in his most famous mandate delivered during the plague: "Marseille . . . which you delighted to show, to excite the admiration of strangers; her beauty . . . her magnificence . . . [and] commerce that extended from one end of the world to another . . . she is destitute." "This city," he continued, "whose crowded streets we could scarcely pass through—with their affluence, their industry and their commerce, is now delivered up to solitude, to silence, to indigence, to desolation to death!"[66] The commercial city had become a nesting ground for vice: "luxury reigned without moderation in all estates . . . There was fraud in commerce, wrangling in the bars, and blasphemy in the sanctuary."[67] God, therefore, responded with plague: "It is by the excess of our crimes that we merit this severe judgment. Impiety, irreligion, bad faith, usury, impurity, and luxury were at the height among you!"[68] Heresy, sexuality, and luxury mutually reinforced one another in the commercial city.

Though he criticized Marseille for its sins, Belsunce claimed that God had specially designated the city to carry out his divine mission. Marseille, in other words, was destined for an exceptional role in Church history. If God had targeted the city for destruction because of its bad example, the plague offered Marseille an opportunity to emerge as the best example of spiritual renewal. Like Jerusalem, or Savonarola's Florence, Marseille was divinely selected for Christian regeneration; "After the siege of Jerusalem," Belsunce insisted, "I think what which we experience is the most dreadful there ever was."[69] According to the bishop, the Great Plague of Marseille was a historical watershed in ecclesiastical history. The epidemic would usher in a new age for Catholicism. The city hung in the balance between "total ruin" and "deliverance."[70]

While distinct from the secular responses to plague generated by Commandant Langeron and Marseille's *échevins*, the religious reaction to plague that Belsunce developed reinforced some similar concepts. Implicating women, sexuality, and commercial luxury, he focused on the same moral and social corrupters that the secular elites targeted. Additionally, secular and religious elites alike mobilized various metaphors of crisis—of a community strung between life and death, salvation and damnation, virtue and corruption. Plague-stricken Marseille, in other words, could be symbolized either as a republic in crisis or as a religious community in crisis, and arguments for the recovery of political and religious virtue could spill over and meet.

CIVIC RELIGIOSITY: COMMERCE, HERESY, AND THE SACRÉ-COEUR

During the plague, Belsunce fashioned a new civic religiosity for his diocese by consecrating the city to the Sacred Heart of Jesus. Motivated by his struggle against heresy, sexuality, and commercial luxury, the Festival of the Sacred Heart redefined Marseille as a God-chosen community, distinct from the rest of France. What emerged in the festival was a contradiction; a bishop who denounced commercial luxury used the city's commercial public spaces as a unifying source to deepen the diocese's sense of cohesion, to strengthen spiritual life among the lay population, and to marginalize religious outsiders.

Devotion to the Sacred Heart predated Belsunce's career as bishop. Ecclesiastical authorities during the Counter-Reformation stressed Christ's compassion, charity, and love in their reaction against Calvinism. In this context, the Sacred Heart emerged as a powerful icon following the founding of the Visitationalist order (1610) by Jeanne de Chantal and François de Sales. This order emphasized an intimate spirituality based on "an inspired union with the heart of Jesus." In the late seventeenth century, Marguerite-Marie Alacoque, a Visitationalist nun at the convent at Paray-le-Monial, began reporting visions, ecstatic reveries, and divine voices. From 1680 on, she described how Jesus had commanded her to promote devotion to the Sacred Heart.[71] Insisting that the Sacred Heart "demanded recognition from the Sun King," she claimed that it would strengthen Louis XIV against heretics and political dissidents.[72] It remains unknown whether the king learned of these demands; in any case, he never acted on them. Nonetheless, Alacoque received support from a powerful ally: the Jesuits. In Aix-en-Provence and Marseille, Jesuits energized devotion to the Sacred Heart.[73] Aix celebrated a Sacred Heart festival in 1693, and devotion to the Sacred Heart appeared in Marseille among Visitationalist convents in 1695.

The Visitationalist Anne-Magdelaine Rémuzat (b. 1696) and Belsunce coordinated efforts in the early eighteenth century to establish Marseille as the center of the cult. When eight years old, Rémuzet had "asked her parents for permission to renounce the world and consecrate herself to God in the Monastery of Saint Claire."[74] At sixteen, she took her Visitationalist vows. Soon after, she reported reveries like those of Marguerite-Marie Alacoque. Jesus, she claimed, removed her heart from her body in exchange for his.[75] She sported a blemish that remained on her chest until her death.[76] Faith for Rémuzat consisted of internal devotion and external manifestation. Outward bodily signs of faith like the stigmata and bloody wounds indicated devotion within. This type of faith was consistent with Belsunce's appetite for spectacular public ceremonies and outward signs of devotional purity. Faith, for Rémuzat and Belsunce alike, involved visual presentation. The Cult and Festival of the Sacred Heart of Jesus in Marseille was born out of their predilection for an image-driven faith.

Belsunce, who had encountered devotion to the Sacred Heart at Louis-le-Grand, supported Rémuzat and authorized her to do "whatever was consistent with the wishes of the Heart of Jesus." In 1718, Rémuzet and Belsunce won papal support to establish the Association de l'Adoration perpétuelle du Sacré-Coeur de Notre Seigneur Jésus-Christ (Association of the Sacred Heart). As head of this association, Rémuzat called on nuns to give "their hearts to Jesus Christ, to make themselves victims who can repair by their adoration and by their homage the indignities that He received in the adorable Eucharist." Consecrating themselves "wives of Jesus Christ" these Visitationalists stressed love, adoration, and devotion in their commitment to the Sacred Heart.[77]

During the plague, in October 1720, Rémuzat told Belsunce of a message she had received from the Sacred Heart. God, she said, "wants to purge the Church of Marseille of its errors. . . . He demands a solemn festival on the day that he himself has chosen, the day following that of the Holy Sacrament, to honor his Sacred Heart."[78] Belsunce responded with his Mandate of 22 October 1720, consecrating Marseille to the Sacred Heart and establishing the festival in the city's ecclesiastical calendar. He announced that the consecration, a demonstration of the city's collective contrition, would help end the epidemic:

> To appease the anger of God; to end the formidable scourge that desolates the flock that we hold dear; to honor Christ in the Holy Sacrament; to repair the outrages committed by vile and sacrilegious communions [i.e., by the Jansenist appellants], and the irreverence that He suffers in His mysterious love for man; to make him love all the faithful committed to our bosom; finally in reparation for all the crimes that have attracted the vengeance of Heaven; we have established in the diocese the Festival of the Sacred Heart of Jesus, which will be celebrated every year, on the Friday immediately following the octave of the Most Holy Sacrament.[79]

The inaugural Sacred Heart festival was a communal event designed to cleanse Marseille of heresy, immorality, and commercial decadence. The festival combined spiritual sentimentality with visual theatrics that only a metropolitan city could sustain. The accounts of the event written by Belsunce and the royal prosecutor, Pichatty de Croissante, captured the dramatic appeal to God:

> The first of November, the festival of All Saints (1720). Monsieur the Bishop left his palace in procession . . . and wanting to appear as a scapegoat charged with the sins of his people, as if he were the destined victim of their expiation, he marched barefoot with a rope around his neck, the Cross in his arms, to the end of the Cours on the side of the Gate of Aix where he celebrated a public Mass at an altar that he had dressed, and after a beautiful exhortation that he made to the public, he led them to penitence to quell God's anger and to obtain the deliverance from this cruel plague. He consecrated the city to the Sacred Heart of Jesus, for whose honor [the Devotion] was already established, a festival holiday for all time, by his last mandate . . . ; the tears that fell from his eyes during this holy ceremony and the extremity of his words excited repentance in every heart, even those of the least sensitive; each struck with profound pain requested the Mercy of the Lord.

The procession and consecration took place in the new Marseille of the 1666 *agrandissement*, not in the narrow streets of the Vieille Ville. It began at the Bishop's Palace and stretched through the city. At "eight in the morning, [Belsunce] ordered rung all the city bells and dressed an altar at the summit of the Cours, which is one of the most remarkable places in this city." Cannon from royal galleys blasted, and dramatic effect was added by "the impetuous wind that we call the mistral." The procession continued for three hours, "the most magnificent there ever was, to the infinite noise of the cannon of the citadels, the galleys, and vessels that were in the port that lasted continuously for over a half-hour." The procession wound through the center of the port, where the bishop gave the benediction and celebrated Mass.[80]

Although he condemned the city for its luxury, Belsunce embraced the symbols of Marseille's commercial identity and French naval supremacy—the Cours, the port, and the royal galleys—to take back the city from evil. Marseille was no mere backdrop for his supernatural drama; it participated as the protagonist. The city's public spaces were crucial to the inhabitants' reconciliation with the divine. "[S]taged in the *cours*, a center of the city's former splendor . . . the festival for its participants was probably more intense due to the participants' awareness that the appeal to the Beyond was coming out of the city's monument to itself," Daniel Gordon writes.[81] The boulevards, created as the main arteries for

Belsunce at the foot of the Cours of Marseille. *Courtesy Archives municipales de la ville de Marseille, 11Fi32.*

commerce, became a means to reconnect with God. Marseille's act of contrition simultaneously served as the city's homage to itself.

By reasserting the entrenched hierarchies of the Catholic community that they opposed, the festival processions to the Sacred Heart in November 1720 and on 20 June 1721 also helped marginalize the Jansenists. Members of Marseille's religious confraternities, distinguished by their colors and distinctive costumes, processed behind the religious and secular elite through the city, visually demonstrating the ecclesiastical chain of being. Moreover, the sentimentality and the visual theatrics of the festival's public appeal to the divine flew in the face of Jansenist theology. The Jansenists "reproached . . . the partisans of the Sacred Heart for having introduced sentiment in prayer." Perceiving sentiment as synonymous with human pleasure and sin, Jansenists opted for a theology void of love, charity, emotion, and ostentatious displays of devotion.[82] If the Sacred Heart was a cult of the city, theirs was a theology of the remote and private. Heretics and Protestants who refused participation in such festivities could be culturally marginalized. The bishop's consecration of Marseille to the Sacred Heart, therefore, reserved the city for its orthodox establishment. Marseille the commercial city became Marseille the city of the Sacred Heart.

THE JANSENIST REBUTTAL: APPEALING TO THE PUBLIC TRIBUNAL

The Festival of the Sacred Heart did not, however, signal an end to conflicts between Marseille's ecclesiastical establishment and the Jansenist appellants. The religious struggle, now linked to issues of civic engagement, escalated over arguments regarding service to the sick and dying. Both parties stressed the importance of charitable works and each accused the other of failing in its civic duties. Whereas Belsunce initially blamed the appellants for inviting plague to Marseille, the latter months of the epidemic saw him accusing them of betraying the community in a time of need. Religious traitors proved to be civic traitors as well.

Service was essential to Belsunce's theology; Jesuit humanism, as Dale van Kley has remarked, was more civic than contemplative.[83] Embracing the principles of charity outlined in hagiographic texts, Belsunce lauded the examples of Charles Borromeo and François de Sales, who stressed that "charity was the 'proper virtue' of bishops, understood both in the manner of compassionate love for God and neighbor and in the sense of a bishop's organized aid to the needy."[84] Belsunce insisted that caring for the sick, distributing Sacraments, and organizing aid were critical acts of civic service during medical crisis. He interpreted the alleged invisibility of the Jansenists in the streets as a sign of their lack of civic responsibility.

Belsunce and his subordinates made themselves visible through Marseille, allying themselves with the *pères de la patrie:* "the illustrious commandant," "zealous *échevins,*" and all "who a thousand times courageously exposed their lives for the public good."[85] A witness described the bishop's commitment: "The prelate has acquired an immortal glory, before God and man, he goes everyday through the streets discovering where the sick lie . . . he visits their bedsides, consoles them, encourages them, confesses them, and makes them well, both spiritually and secularly."[86] "His acts of piety are most heroic . . . This holy prelate remains with an unshakable firmness resolved to give his life for the health of his sheep," Pichatty de Croissante echoed. "His charity is active," he continued, "he is in the streets in all the quarters of the city to visit all the sick in the most high and most somber apartments of the houses; in the streets through the cadavers, at the public places, at the Port, the Cours."[87] Again, as in his account of the festival, the city and its monuments figured prominently in Croissante's narrative of religious civic spirit. He also praised Belsunce's subordinates who had died serving the sick.[88]

Belsunce found such civic service lacking in his appellant adversaries. "Our appellants and Jansenists have looked out for their own safety," he charged. "Those who are of the *morale sévère* [Jansenists] misjudge their duties and devoted themselves to saving their own lives, and those who are called the *morale relâchée* [the orthodox] sacrifice their lives . . . to aid their brothers."[89] Belsunce employed informants to declare the absence of Jansenist civic activity.[90] "Authentic witnesses to the truth" furnished certificates containing versions of the affirmation that "we attest that since the beginning of the plague in Marseille, we have never found in the streets of this city one Father of the Oratory; that we do not know if there has been any plague-stricken house that has received succor or aid from them."[91] Belsunce accumulated over forty testimonies from Capuchins, Trinitarians, Carmelites, Jesuits, Observationalists, confessors, canons, vicars, and superiors of religious houses, who testified that Jansenists preferred to save themselves rather than help their neighbors in need.

Provençal Jansenists refuted the bishop's charges. Some insisted that it was the bishop who had failed in his duties: "He was shut in his palace with his Jesuit."[92] They defended the Oratorians' civic activity with letters of support from *Echevin* Dieude that described how the Oratory was the first religious house to fall victim to the plague.[93]

Ultimately, Provençal Jansenists developed a new strategy to challenge the ecclesiastical authorities. While the bishop made a public appeal to God in the Festival of the Sacred Heart, the appellants appealed to another abstract power, the "public" to support their arguments against the bishop. Historians have noted how an appeal to such an abstract authority emerged in religious and political discussions between 1750 and the start of the French Revolution. The "public" was not, however, a novel invention of the latter half of the eighteenth century. Jansenists mobilized this alternative authority in their criticisms of papal and royal power at the dawn of the century. Far from restricted to the religious world, the "public" was also imagined as a universal and impartial judge in literary movements as early as the end of the seventeenth century.[94] The same year the plague broke in Marseille, the baron de Montesquieu invoked the "public" in his famous anonymously published *Lettres persanes*. "I have offered these letters to try the taste of the public," he wrote in the book's opening pages; the "public" would decide whether it was good or bad. Such an abstract authority could, and would, compete with formal institutions of power for the remainder of the century.

In his anonymous *Justification des PP. de l'Oratoire de Marseille, contre les accusations de l'évêque de cette ville* (June 1721), a Jansenist called on this "public tribunal" to judge the validity of Bishop Belsunce's accusations against the Oratory. "So that the entire world informed of the truth . . . can judge if the Fathers of the Oratory are truly guilty, . . . it is for the public that I write, [the public] that I recognize as the judge."[95] He entrusted this public "to prove the innocence of the Fathers of the Oratory of Marseille . . . for the whole kingdom."

The *Justification* opens with the question: "Why the public for a judge?"[96] There were, after all, established tribunals capable of judging accused parties. The "public tribunal," the author insisted, surpassed all others:

> The public is the sole judge where jurisdiction is not confined to the limits of a province or a state: it is the only judge that can draw the knowledge of causes that other tribunals cannot or do not want to know. It is the only judge that, not being constrained by judicial forms that do not permit accusations or defenses outside what human laws have determined, considers in the affairs brought to its tribunal only the truth of the facts, the soundness of proofs, and the force of demonstrations: it is the only judge that, having a true interest in knowing the character of those that compose the body of civil society, always and forever listens with pleasure to the denunciation of the guilty and the justification of the innocent.[97]

The "public tribunal," the author concluded, was "a natural judge." It was the only authority that enjoyed total impartiality and rationality. "The public tribunal, only being interested in knowing the truth, always listens with pleasure to accusations and to defenses, without examining the persons who speak, but rather solely the accuracy of facts."[98] That made this abstract body superior to existing forms of magistracy.

The author then described the makeup of this "public tribunal." Following Gallican principles, he claimed that it would be comprised of citizens. "It is the duty of a good citizen," he insisted, "to defend a congregation distinguished by its piety, by its erudition, by its inviolable attachment to the rights of our kings, to the liberties of the Church, and to the maxims of the kingdom that for a hundred years have not ceased . . . to equally instruct both people and scholars."[99]

Mobilizing concepts of liberty, rationality, and equality against Belsunce, whom he characterized as self-interested, irrational, and arbitrary, the author depicted the bishop's authority as illegitimate, diametrically opposed to the legitimacy embodied in the "public." He dismantled each of Belsunce's allegations against the Oratory by discrediting him and his witnesses. Belsunce "was a priest filled with ultramontane principles" who rejected the "liberties" of the Gallican church. This "fanatic" had "seduced" the public and defended himself with counterfeit evidence.[100] Other Jansenists echoed the author's skepticism. Vivien de La Borde asked: "The letters of Belsunce, are they the work of reason? Haven't such proceedings been inspired by sentiments, tricks, inductions . . . mad falsities?" The bishop, these Jansenists argued, depended on testimonies from subordinates who supported him to secure their own positions within the ecclesiastical hierarchy. Because the Jesuits, Capuchins, Recolets, Trinitarians, Observationalists, Dominicans, Augustinians, Antonians, Carmelites, and Minimites who testified against the Oratory were under the bishop's aegis, the Jansenists disqualified their testimonies: "Interested in the affair, declared enemies of the Oratory," they were "very suspect."[101]

The author contrasted the Oratory's piety, humility, and honesty with an orthodox establishment characterized by irrationality and self-interest. While the bishop made a show of his civic activity, the Fathers of the Oratory served in silence and refused to flaunt their civic service. Despite having been disgraced by the bishop, they opened their home and visited the sick. The Superior of the Oratory, Père Gautier, and his priests "assembled at the Hôtel de Ville to offer the *échevins* their persons, their goods, and their lives."[102] Gautier even concocted and distributed his own preservatives to the municipal leaders. Finally, the authors argued, the testimony of genuine witnesses secured the Oratory's innocence. *Echevins* Dieude and Audimar, joined by *Commissaire* Bonnefoy and Doctor Bouthillier from Montpellier, lauded the fathers for their service, saying that "they lacked neither zeal nor charity."[103] Given the choice between legitimate testimony and self-interested deceit, the public tribunal's decision, these authors claimed, would prove an easy one.

God was not happy with Marseille. On this, Jansenists and orthodox Catholics could agree as they competed to reconcile the ecclesiastical community with God. Despite their doctrinal differences, they were in common preoccupied with the problem of restoring virtue to a religious world in crisis. For both Jansenists and orthodox Catholics, appearances deceived. Vivien de La Borde suspected all potential witnesses to the truth in a universe where "Satan transformed into an angel of light." Henri de Belsunce scoured his churches, convinced that images of immodesty penetrated the holiest walls.

Both Jansenists and orthodox Catholics commonly assumed that the restoration of physical health and religious order hinged on the question of civic participation. While each sought to validate a different kind of religious order, one based on ecclesiastical hierarchy, the other based on Gallican liberty, they both strengthened republican traditions of civic engagement. Belsunce's alliance with Commandant Langeron, his emphasis on civic service, his religious condemnation of commerce, and his Manichean rhetoric of damnation versus deliverance intersected with Langeron's secular arguments for civic activism and moral severity to restore Massilia as a virtuous republic. Meanwhile, the Jansenists' comparisons of the Church to a republic animated the inclusive ideal of citizenship.

But it was the Jansenist author of the *Justification* who provided the most radical approach in overcoming spiritual corruption. Calling for a "public tribunal," he invited any truth-seeking individual, theoretically of any provenance or background, to participate as a "citizen" in open, rational public discourse. While Langeron's emergency courts wielded sovereign power, this writer appealed to an authority that would ultimately surpass that of the traditional royal and municipal courts. Abstract and universal, this source of legitimate judgment would, over the course of the Enlightenment, develop into a formidable authority residing in a political space separated from traditional entities of power: pope, Crown, parlements, and other official bodies. Such a "public tribunal" would ultimately become the chief sovereign authority to whom both subjects and the Crown would appeal, not only in religious discussions, but in political debates on the very nature of legitimate governance. In its infancy, this abstract tribunal found application in the limited space of religious confrontations in plague-stricken Marseille. It would develop into one of the central figures of revolutionary thought by the end of the century.

CHAPTER SEVEN

Postmortem

Virtue and Commerce Reconsidered

Following the plague, Marseille convalesced from the temporary suspension of commerce and commercial civic spirit. Once trading resumed, exports from the Levant rose to pre-1715 levels at 15 million *livres tournois*. By 1726, Marseille recovered its status as France's preeminent port for Levantine commerce. Trading stabilized until the mid 1730s, when a combination of famine and wars in the Persian Gulf rocked the Mediterranean market, and foreign competition (Venice) brought imports and exports between France and the Levant back to crisis levels.

Nonetheless, Marseillais and Franco-Levantine commerce strengthened for the remainder of the century. Despite setbacks during the War of Austrian Succession and the Seven Years War, France's position as the primary trading partner for the Ottoman Empire went virtually uncontested.[1] Franco-Ottoman trade value rose from 12 million to 16 million *livres tournois* between 1700 and 1726, and to 31 million by 1750. By 1776, French trade with the Ottomans accounted for 44.1 percent of Istanbul's trading activity, 49.9 percent of Smyrna's, and 59.4 percent of Salonika's. British trade with the Ottomans came in second, but paled in comparison to French numbers, totaling only in the 20 percent range for the same cities.[2] In the meantime, Marseillais merchants began looking westwards, supplementing their commercial activities in the Levant with new ventures in the West Indies, Africa, and the East Indies.[3] The famed artist Joseph Vernet captured this commercial *croissance* in his celebrated tableaus of the Vieux Port.[4]

Meanwhile, the demographic effects of the plague all but disappeared. High birth, migration, and immigration rates and low mortality allowed for quick repopulation. Even before the plague abated, Marseillais observed the influx of migrants. "*Les étrangers* crowd to repopulate Marseille," Père Giraud commented on 15 September 1721; "we receive *les étrangers* from villages in Provence and Languedoc, sometimes in the hundreds per day." An anonymous manuscript from 1723 stated "after the end of the plague, 10,000 souls have come to establish themselves in Marseille and its surrounding territory." While many of these were artisans, *négociants* and merchants numbered among them.[5]

"Catastrophe was quickly forgotten," writes Charles Carrière, one of the foremost historians of eighteenth-century Marseille. Indeed, the numbers would suggest so. But in terms of ideas and concepts, did Marseillais and French elites forget the plague? Did they easily readopt their commercial civic spirit, and eagerly accept that merchants were model citizens and subjects? Yes and no. Disease, depopulation, and decadence certainly remained on the minds of many, even as (and often because) commerce developed to unprecedented levels in the Enlightenment. In Marseille, plague became a useful and much-adopted reference point for many invested in questions of proper civic governance. The *noblesse d'epée* used it to support their claims that merchants were incapable of political leadership and model citizenship, and that their own inclusion in municipal governance was necessary for the preservation of their city and state. Other Marseillais elite referenced plague to help develop new institutions that they believed would foster citizenship; for example, intellectuals alluded to the Plague of 1720 in discussions that eventually led to the founding of the Académie de Marseille, which would disseminate ideas of civic duty and belonging.

Such conversations that stressed virtuous public spirit were not limited to Marseille. How does a society guard against luxury and self-interest while embracing commercial expansion? Is commerce useful or detrimental to society? Are merchants good subjects and citizens, or are they unable to align their personal interests with concern for the public good? The various answers that administrative elites and philosophers generated in Marseille and France after the plague demonstrate the potency of two branches of classical republican thought in the last century of the Bourbon monarchy. Those who mobilized the traditional variant of classical republicanism held that luxury produced by commercial society deteriorated virtue, liberty, and the body politic. They echoed the contention of François de Fénelon and Henri de Boulainvilliers that market society bred self-interest and warned against the social instability caused by the confusion of estates, hierarchies, and orders. They supported a state that privileged agricultural developments over urban commerce, and idealized the farmer as the virtuous citizen. These writers became the precursors of the future

Physiocrats. Those who adhered to commercial civic spirit held that commerce fostered social cohesion and strengthened virtue. Expansion of the marketplace, these claimed, led to progress, civilization, and the cultivation of the arts and sciences.

These authors in mid eighteenth-century France blurred the fault lines between traditional classical republican rhetoric and commercial civic spirit. They combined classical republican sensibilities, ideas of commercial civic spirit, and statist notions of utility and aristocratic discourses of honor while continuing to reveal deep-seated anxieties and mistrust of French subjects and merchants. Many agreed that commerce was useful and generated prosperity. They agreed that unregulated commerce would generate economic, moral, political, and medical catastrophe. Who then, could cultivate the virtue needed to safeguard commerce, state, and society from corruption? Some claimed that it was a virtuous prince, others, a virtuous and patriotic nobility, and yet others, a virtuous and patriotic merchant population. Regardless of their positions, writers mobilized the language of virtue against unregulated commercial expansion. While not all of these writers referenced 1720, the plague, or John Law's financial crash, they all discussed the importance of virtue for commercial society. Without being politically republican, they assumed that a stable political order rested on public spirit, patriotism, frugality, and the suppression of private interests. This study draws to a close by exploring how, between the plague and the mid eighteenth century, certain groups of French subjects—elite merchants, nobles, and administrators—became versed in the language of civic virtue well before France was constituted as a nation of citizens.

AFTER THE PLAGUE: VIRTUE AND COMMERCE IN MARSEILLE

The Marseillais intellectuals and royal administrators who founded the Académie de Marseille vividly remembered the plague of 1720. The Académie was a product of centralizing efforts aimed at exporting royal cultural standards to the provinces.[6] The Crown established it to encourage Marseille to embrace "Parisian norms, codes and values," promoting "a uniformity . . . that created a bond between Parisian and provincial administrations in the cultural sphere."[7] It thought this particularly necessary following the plague.[8] Observing the vast numbers of migrants from the countryside, Geneva, and the Italian states after the plague, a royal delegate wrote: "We are most exposed here . . . the foreign, allured by commerce, equally attacks civilities and the spirit of language." A popular saying among travelers, "Aix-en-Provence, Marseille-en-Turquie, Toulon-en-Barbarie,"[9] mocked the territory's foreignness. An academy would serve as a royal cultural stronghold. The Académie de Marseille, established in filial relationship with its parent institution in Paris, received its letters patent on 16 September 1726.

The Académie became a bastion for public spirit and local patriotism, however, and called attention to the city's ancient history. The Marseillais academicians "gave thanks to our new Mother" (the Académie des sciences et lettres in Paris)[10] for restoring the city's ancient Académie. It was "certifiably the most ancient of literary societies in the West," boasted one M. Olivier, an academician and lawyer. The ancient Académie of Massilia, he remarked, had "sweetened the mores of the barbarians and prepared them to become Romans." Having received the arts and sciences from Phocaea and Athens, Massilians developed knowledge that "contributed to commerce and the perfection of navigation."[11] While these academicians associated with royal correspondents to found the Académie, they established a civic institution, rather than a royal one.

The Académie's members—ecclesiastics, *échevins*, *négociants*, writers, lawyers, architects, painters and sculptors, doctors, and other members of the city's cultural elite—perceived themselves as model citizens who would recover Massilia's civic culture and virtue. "Our company will resurrect the phoenix from the ancient ashes," the Chevalier de Romieu, associate of the Académie, announced in 1727; "we constitute the healthiest part of the republic, [which] knows that ignorance is the source of all vice, and the sciences that of all virtue."[12]

The Académie's commitment to fostering virtue remained strong, it seems, to the end of the Old Regime, when under the directorship of Pierre-Augustin Guys, its members renewed discussions on how to strengthen commerce while resisting its corrosive effects on morality and public spirit. Born in 1721 during the epidemic, Guys was a *négociant* and prolific writer. Published letters from his voyages to Turkey and Greece and his reputation as an authority on ancient and modern Greece won him directorship of the Académie in 1755. As an academician and *négociant*, he studied "the utility of the sciences and letters for the great success [of commerce]."[13] Guys did not decry commerce. Convinced that it produced dangerous luxury, however, he urged his readers to reform public education to fashion virtuous citizen-merchants.

In his most famous publication, *Marseille ancienne et moderne*, Guys stressed how Marseille's Hellenic legacy rendered it superior as a commercial republic.[14] Commerce, however, was "Pandora's box." "The spirit of commerce, like the spirit of conquest, produces the greatest revolutions," Guys warned; "mores change, traditional simplicity flees, never to return; the poor nation enriches itself." Commerce introduced an excess of commodities and spread inequality. This tendency, he commented, was not new; commerce had corrupted ancient Massilia. Vices multiplied until "the sister of Rome could not preserve itself from contagious malady." Guys noted that plague had devastated both ancient Massilia and eighteenth-century Marseille. In each case the city paid dearly for its commerce.[15]

Guys nevertheless recognized that complete suspension of trade was hardly practical. Proper civic education, he suggested, could train merchants to remain good citizens. Guys proposed a "public education" that began with the family and that stressed the cultivation of relationships between citizens and the *patrie*, Marseillais' "common mother," who could "nourish and raise all her children." Guys urged women to imitate virtuous Roman mothers, who had taught their children to become "ornaments of the republic."[16] Once mothers provided children with a moral foundation, reformed *collèges* could instill French and Marseillais patriotism. Classes in languages, mathematics, rhetoric, logic, and metaphysics would train Marseillais boys for trade. Meanwhile, public exercises would "instruct citizens" as "subjects of the king, children of the *patrie*" and integrate the youth into the civic community. Guys urged *échevins* to stress how study divorced from civic duty was "useless and dangerous."[17] Unless public and civic education was implemented, the plague would return. Commercial extravagance could be neutralized only by "education in mores" and "mores in education."[18]

Guys was not the only Marseillais academician to articulate the dangers of commercial luxury. André Liquier, who won the Académie's essay contest in 1777, argued that trading with foreigners brought "derangement," "erased national characteristics, and introduced absurdity into laws and customs." Responding to the essay question, "Quelle a été dans tous les temps l'influence du commerce sur l'esprit et les moeurs des peuples?"(What has always been the influence of commerce on the spirit and mores of peoples?), he asserted that commerce was "incompatible with all great virtues." In a critique of progress echoing Jean-Jacques Rousseau's *Second Discourse*, he maintained that commerce was not essential to human society; man was not commercial by nature. Virtues and vices, he argued, had been unknown among natural man, who lived by hunting. As civilization progressed, citizens avoided corruption as long as they limited themselves to domestic trade. International commerce, colonization, and wholesale trading, however, led to "abuse of thought" and "corruption of taste." International trade, in particular, he insisted, destroyed citizenship; "one forgets one's country, one is there forgotten; if one returns, one is a stranger in one's own halls; father and children fail to recognize one another . . . women, that sex as dangerous as it is useful to mores, remain alone, free to pursue their needs and frivolity."[19] The international market, he concluded, had to be restricted.

Such academic utterances indicate that eighteenth-century Marseillais writers mobilized the ideas of traditional classical republicanism and commercial civic spirit together, supporting continued commercial activity while advocating caution. Like Jean-Baptiste Colbert and royal administrators years earlier, Marseillais academicians mistrusted unregulated commerce and unpoliced merchant activity. The memory of the plague heightened these concerns. However, unlike royalist observers who regarded the monarchy as the sole guarantor of order, law, and virtue, they placed their trust in civic education and in the virtuous citizen-merchant.

Marseille's sword aristocracy also invoked plague and the vocabulary of virtue to confront the problem of commercial corruption. The sword nobility, who had lost the privilege of holding public office in 1660, began regrouping shortly before the epidemic, submitting petitions to the Regent in 1716 to win back municipal political power. They explained that since its founding, Marseille had been a republic, then a protectorate under the comtes de Provence, then a free city under royal governance since 1481. The *noblesse d'epée* insisted that through these changes, Marseille had always been governed by three noble consuls and a legal *assesseur.* Louis XIV, they claimed, had broken with tradition in installing *négociants* as *échevins* in 1660, provoking a dangerous "revolution" and "derangement" in municipal leadership.

The aristocrats insisted that *négociants* made bad citizens. *Négociants,* they argued, were neither physically nor politically rooted in Marseille. "*Négociants* hardly own anything," these aristocrats asserted; "their fortunes consist entirely of money or movable property." The nobles connected the *négociants*' uprootedness to their self-interestedness. Subsequent petitions to the king claimed that the *négociants*' commercial priorities and cosmopolitan lives were not amenable to civic leadership, contending that "their transient habits rarely produce a patriotic spirit." The *négociants,* they charged, abused their authority in the Hôtel de Ville and Chamber of Commerce, where they exploited their administrative powers to monopolize business and raise the prices of commodities.

The petitioners insisted that the *noblesse d'epée* were best suited to govern the city. They "possessed less fragile, older links to society, and concerned themselves entirely with glory and prosperity."[20] They were grounded in Marseille, jointly owning over three-fourths of all property and liquid assets in the city. The sword nobles were patriots ready "to sacrifice their goods and their life for the service of the prince and their *patrie*."[21] If restored to power, they promised, they would put an end to financial corruption and reestablish "equality" (albeit from their privileged position in the Old Regime's hierarchical social order), as well as "wisdom" and "economy."

The nobles' arguments, framed in the rhetoric used against *négociants* during the epidemic, gained currency following the plague. "Everyone knows," they asserted, "that the plague was introduced in Marseille by the conniving of the officers who, against all rules, allowed infected merchandise be brought [into the city] for the *premier échevin*." Putting on their royalist hats, the nobility claimed that they were more faithful to the king than were merchants who had "abandoned the *patrie*." Merchants were distracted from civic duty by business, by associations with foreign merchants, and by financial troubles. They could not supply virtuous municipal leadership.[22]

Marseille's noble petitioners defined virtue as a long aristocratic heritage characterized by loyalty to the king, city and state patriotism, and exemplary public spirit based on "disinterestedness." The virtue they described was, moreover, synonymous with honor. This aristocratic quality was "indubitable" and guaranteed by the ancient constitution. Invoking precedent and history, the petitioners described how since time immemorial, "young and vigorous nobles assembled in the *corps d'armée*" had served their kings in the administration of justice, and held seats in royal councils.[23] Nobles possessed a masculine virtue that gave them the strength to "crush enterprises formed by the enemies of the state."[24] Insisting that the nobility still retained such virtues, the petitioners asked the Crown for the opportunity "to help their fellow citizens in their enlightenment, their zeal and their works for the public good."[25]

These nobles were well aware of the challenges in convincing the Crown that a commercial city would benefit from the leadership of nonmerchants. They admitted that as *noblesse non-commercante*, they were not versed in the particularities of trade. They were farmers. But they insisted that their agricultural pursuits supported commerce. Agriculture was "the most important activity to true citizens." Farmers grew the products essential for manufacturers. *Négociants* ignored the centrality of agriculture to commerce. The nobles used the example of Marseille's failing wine trade to articulate how agricultural labor went to waste under the current administration. "Wine," they pointed out, "is the sole product of Marseille's sterile, mountainous territory, and we only have the means of making the worst, most expensive [kind]." Farmers required protection and privileges to sustain their activities; *négociant administrateurs* overlooked them, however, in their rush to "enrich private individuals." Such neglect led to "a total ruin of commerce."[26] The sword nobles promised that if they resumed civic leadership, they would reconnect the interests of "the cultivator, the landlord, and the merchant." Proper attention to agriculture, increased production, better circulation of merchandise, and stabilized prices would allow for greater prosperity.[27]

The nobles converted their status as commercial outsiders into an asset, maintaining that a commercial city required the leadership of those who were least committed to making a profit. Nobles "were disinterested in commerce," while the *négociant administrateur* cared for nothing but personal gain. The *négociant administrateur,* in other words, "was incapable of understanding the true interests of commerce taken in the large sense." As *négociants,* they were "trained in the art of making their own fortunes and concerned only to preserve these." The noble who had no vested interests in business could govern various commercial bodies more judiciously. The nobles cited the *échevins'* early struggles against Colbert, particularly their resistance to the edict of 1669, as an example of their self-interests prevailing over concern for the public good.[28]

Finally, the nobles criticized the *négociant* administration by arguing that what seemed to be commercial expansion was in reality nothing but a mirage. On the surface, the eighteenth century might be a "golden age" of prosperity, but behind the façade, the civic government was "unfaithful" to the king, a "general confusion in all affairs" troubled the marketplace, debts accumulated, and revenues fell.[29] The nobles invoked Montesquieu to illustrate the festering problems afflicting a badly administered commercial society; "the author of the *Spirit of the Laws* has written, 'in countries where people are moved solely by the spirit of commerce, they sacrifice everything humane, all moral virtues.' "[30] Such a trade-off, they warned, was dangerous. It destabilized state and society. The empowerment of *négociants* to positions of civic authority exacerbated this social and moral derangement. "The kingdom is not made to become a republic of merchants," they warned, "[the state] is founded on arms . . . what will be the point of honor that renders our nobility invincible, if *négociants* become equal to them [in power]?" Such disorder—in morality, politics, society, and commerce—had become apparent in 1720, when plague devastated Marseille. "The plague," they explained "had access to Marseille only through the entry of merchandise coming from the Levant." The Bureau de la santé had failed to "moderate the cupidity of the *négociant,* to whom any delays [in quarantine] are onerous." The avoidance of future corruption and disaster required nobles to oversee the Hôtel de Ville, Chamber of Commerce, and institutions of health and police.[31]

The nobles concluded their appeals by maintaining that they, unlike merchants, were consistently motivated by their civic spirit, patriotism, honor, and virtue. Furthermore, they stressed that whereas "the republican character" was "always manifest" in the *négociant* administration, nobles were not inspired by quasi-*frondeur*-like republicanism. They were royalist subjects and model citizens who believed that "without the nobility, there is no monarchy, and without the monarchy, there is no nobility."[32]

The Marseillais *négociants* responded to these petitions by adopting the language of utility, virtue, patriotism, and public spirit, albeit differently from the nobility, to defend their positions of municipal power. In response to the most recent *Mémoire* of the *noblesse d'epée,* they declared that "the public voice of a maritime and commercial city is that of all *négociants.*" Rejecting the nobles' accusations that merchants were "self-interested," "vain," "ignorant," and "republican," the *négociants* argued that they made as many sacrifices for their country as did nobles on the battlefield for their king; "how many times have we put ourselves in danger to enrich [the state], to enhance its public image, to procure goods and merchandise for you?" The *négociants* insisted that nobles and merchants commonly served king and state, the former through their military conquests, the latter through their commerce; "we glory in our turn for being representatives of the nation," they described, "by making known our commercial freedom and the attachment we have to our prince." Commerce was useful to the state, moreover, and beneficial to the public good; "we render services that you know are useful, as *négociants,* as *échevins,* our markets are opened to the needs of the state, and when it is necessary to serve the *patrie;* although it may seem to you that we are entirely devoted to our commerce, we know how to sacrifice our time and our interests to the public cause." Finally, the *négociants* used their elite social standing to demonstrate how the Second Estate and the upper tier of the Third Estate were practically united: "we are your neighbors; our daughters are your wives."[33]

On 1 January 1767, the Crown issued a new, mixed civic constitution for Marseille that reestablished the sword nobility in civic governance. Marseille would be administered by a mayor, four *échevins,* an *assesseur* and a 36-member city council. The mayor could be a noble, *négociant,* or a non-*négociant.* The *premier échevin* was specified as a non-ennobled *négociant;* the second *échevin,* a bourgeois or merchant with assets amounting to a minimum of 20,000 livres. The *assesseur* would, as before, be a lawyer. Councilmen would hold three-year terms and cycle in twelve at a time: each cohort would consist of three nobles, three non-ennobled *négociants,* three bourgeois, two merchants, and a lawyer.[34]

Marseille's noble and non-noble elites mobilized vocabularies of virtue, citizenship, disinterestedness, moral responsibility, and patriotism in different ways to imagine a healthier, commercially prosperous and politically sound city and state. Both the sword nobility and elite merchants imagined that as administrators and academicians, they could inspire virtue in a commercial city. Yet, haunted by memories of medical and commercial catastrophe in 1720, these very people also conceded that commercial society tended to corrode such virtue.

It must be said that while these elites bound together different aspects of classical republican traditions, commercial civic spirit, and notions of utility and aristocratic honor, none—be they *négociant*, nobility or academician—would claim to be politically republican. "Revolution" and "republican" were pejorative terms that suggested instability, civil war, decline, and political unrest. Remaining royalist, they applied classical republican values to form their ideals of a model citizen and subject. In these formulations, the ideal royal subject looked more like an ideal citizen. Decades before the French Revolution of 1789 and the founding of the First French Republic, Marseillais elites cultivated moral values of public spirit without officially being rights-bearing citizens.

DARKNESS IN THE AGE OF ENLIGHTENMENT: CONTINUED FEARS OF COMMERCE

Beyond Marseille, French intellectuals and administrators participated in similar debates over commercial society. The writings of two prominent figures—Chevalier Andrew Ramsay and *commissaire de la marine* André-François Boureau-Deslandes—demonstrate how classical republican sensibilities permeated the intellectual landscape of Old Regime France in the mid eighteenth century. These men subscribed to a dark "republican historicism," understanding history as a cyclical story of continuous revolutions. Both accepted commerce as the basis for the arts, sciences, knowledge, culture, and proper sociability. But in their imaginations, commerce, the very motor of progress, threatened to destabilize state and society. They insisted that virtue was essential to prevent moral degeneration in commercial society.

One of the best-selling pieces of literature published after the plague on the subject of commercial society and the challenges of maintaining a sound political state was the Scottish-born Chevalier Andrew Ramsay's *A New Cyropaedia, or The Travels of Cyrus.* Ramsay spent the majority of his life in France, after meeting François Fénelon in 1710. His close friendship with Fénelon and his prolonged stays in Paris allowed him into the circles of Montesquieu, Bolingbroke,

Cardinal Fleury, and the duc de Sully. His *Travels of Cyrus* appeared in 1727; an English edition followed soon after.

The Travels is modeled on Fénelon's *Télémaque*. Ramsay describes the journeys of Cyrus, heir to the Persian throne, through Egypt, Greece, Tyre, and Babylon, during which Cyrus discovers various states and methods of rule. His political education begins with his departure from Persia, when he discovers that cities and states are prone to corruption. In neighboring Ecbatana, he finds that the spirit of conquest has generated luxury. Men have become "effeminate," "probity" and "honor" have disappeared, and people prefer "pleasure" and "idle passions" to the public good.[35]

This "fatal circle" materialized in all societies, in Ramsay's view, and was accelerated through unregulated commercial expansion. He therefore preferred agricultural societies to commercial ones, seeing in the former, the foundation for a sounder political and moral regime. In this regard, Ramsay's historical worldview was consistent with Fénelon's. He admired the ancient Egyptians, for instance. Governed by shepherd-kings, they contented themselves "in the simplicity of a country life," and made "agriculture, hunting and the liberal arts [their] choicest occupations." Conquest, commerce and luxury, however, turned the empire toward corruption, tyranny, rebellion, and anarchy. Cyrus learns that while in the past, "the Universe was in perfect harmony," human beings lurched toward their downfall. "The Empire of Opinion, that of Ambition, and that of Sensuality" destroyed ancient virtues, and people "became subject to diseases and death, the mind to error and to passions."[36]

According to Ramsay, republics, monarchies, and empires shared the same fate; Sparta, Athens, Corinth, and Egypt all fell after commercial excess introduced vast inequalities of wealth, the confusion of contradictory laws, and corrupted education.[37] Ramsay's *Travels of Cyrus* taught that "everything degenerates among men: wisdom and virtue have their vicissitudes in the body politic, as health and strength have in the natural." Monarchies tended to tyranny. Republican governments became prone to "factions, intrigues and cabals." No form of government was perfect; "the desire of unbound authority in Princes, and the love of independence in the People, expose all kingdoms to inevitable revolutions."[38]

Was there a way to hinder this degeneration? Ramsay insisted that the answer lay not in the forms of governments or contents of laws, but rather, in the virtue of rulers and of subjects and citizens. "All sorts of Governments are good," he claimed, when those who govern place public welfare above personal interests. Monarchies could be stabilized by virtuous princes; republics by virtuous citizens. While Ramsay argued that each political regime had laws best suited to it, he assumed that virtue was more or less the same among all men; it involved a preference for simplicity, an appreciation for just laws, heroism, "the generous forgetting of one's self," and distaste for luxury.[39]

State administrators shared with writers like Ramsay the notion that virtue was the panacea for declining commercial societies. André-François Boureau-Deslandes (1690–1757), *contrôleur* and *commissaire de la marine* at the port of Brest, discussed such concepts in his *Essai sur la marine et sur le commerce*, written for the comte de Maurepas in 1743, and his *Lettre sur le luxe* (1745). He wrote of commerce's utility to state, emphasizing how it served as a barometer for the state's stability and power. He stressed the importance of frugality, virtue, patriotism, and public spirit, urging Frenchmen to follow the examples of the Greeks and Romans and to realize their commitment to the state through participation in commercial ventures. Yet he clung to the notion that the French nobility, merchants, trading companies and monopolies, and general population failed to obey their monarch's regulating hand, and preferred to serve their private interests at the expense of the general good.[40]

Boureau-Deslandes began with a discussion of civilizations that distinguished themselves through naval and commercial activity. He credited the Phoenicians, Greeks, and Egyptians for their commerce and for the canals they engineered to transport commodities. Commerce improved politics; kings were merely "heroes" when they led wars; they became "sovereign" when they developed commerce. They established laws to govern commercial enterprises. Infrastructure improved. State and society, bolstered by fair trade laws and population increases, stabilized and strengthened.[41]

Virtue and commerce developed together in the early stages of progress. According to Boureau-Deslandes, commerce did not necessarily ruin states. He used the example of the ancient Romans to demonstrate how commerce softened the mores of the rugged and militaristic population. "Probity, disinterestedness and moderation," gave way to "new notions of virtue." In place of their "severity of manners," the Romans adopted *politesse*, elegance, and refined sociability. Such moral transformations manifested themselves in buildings, furniture, fashion, estates, and houseware.[42] Meanwhile, commerce in Alexandria allowed the Ptolemies to stabilize their government. The Hanseatic cites of the German north boasted a similar situation, as did Venice and Amsterdam later. These attracted foreign merchants and immigrants and became "magnificent," but the "private man" remained frugal. Farther afield in China, commerce and virtue also developed in tandem. The Chinese, Boureau-Deslandes wrote, were "active, frugal, and taken up entirely with the study of commerce . . . they avoid[ed] idleness and indolence." Their government was "the most perfect of any in the world, the wisest and least tyrannical, the most favorable to merit." Commerce made all these places cosmopolitan utopias.[43]

France, Boureau-Deslandes claimed, could have followed such examples. It was geographically well suited for naval and commercial activity. Led by Charlemagne in the Middle Ages, the Gauls established ports and created passageways linking the Atlantic to the Mediterranean. Religious pursuits, however, distracted them from commerce; first the Crusades, then the Wars of Religion disrupted trade. Frenchmen only rediscovered commerce under the guidance of the Bourbon monarchy. Boureau-Deslandes commended Cardinal Richelieu, Louis XIII, and Louis XIV for stimulating international commerce, encouraging foreign merchants to become naturalized in France, establishing trading companies and allowing the nobility to participate in commerce.[44]

French subjects, however, failed to follow the guidance of these latest monarchs. Boureau-Deslandes lamented how "private interest overbalances the love of public good." Patriotism, he claimed, did not exist in France. The most abominable group among the French population, he specified, was "the lazy nobility, who make the pursuit of pleasure their sole occupation." Effeminate and decadent, they forgot their "masculine and generous virtue" and clung to empty titles without demonstrating any personal merit. Meanwhile, egotism and avarice prevailed at all levels of society. French merchants ignored governmental regulations, imported more goods than the subjects could reasonably consume, and perpetuated fraudulent practices. In short, "the particular and private advantages . . . incline them, generally speaking, to sacrifice all concern for the public welfare, with respect to the nation."[45]

Boureau-Deslandes advocated education to rectify this lack of interest in the public good. An educational program that stressed commerce's importance to states would allow students to observe how the market could augment "the confidence of the public and the authority of the sovereign."[46] Boureau-Deslandes grew increasingly pessimistic, however, in his views on France's political and social stability. Two years following the publication of his *Essai*, his *Lettre sur le luxe*, written for the Académie royale des sciences de Paris and royal academies of St. Petersburg, London, Edinburgh, Bologna, Prussia, and Sweden, revealed his growing concerns that Frenchmen failed as subjects and citizens.

The *Lettre* begins: "Luxury is a pernicious thing in a state."[47] Boureau-Deslandes defined luxury as "an agreeable or brilliant superfluity, that adds to the indispensable needs of life: they are goods, advantages that one can absolutely do without, but that one procures for oneself out of vanity, due to an intemperance of taste, often because of a strong attachment to what is in style; finally, it is an excess where the price or value depends solely on imagination, and that has nothing in itself to do with reality." He distinguished between two kinds of luxury: *luxe de genie* and *luxe de moeurs*. The first was a positive luxury that allowed for the progress of culture, and the development of beauty and perfection; the other led to the corruption of taste and morality. Boureau-Deslandes lauded the "noblest" examples of art, painting, literature, philosophy, and science that attested to the "perfection" of culture and the "honor of the state." Such products contrasted against the *luxe de table, luxe d'habits, luxe de meubles* and "ridiculous" excesses that inundated the market. "France," he argued, "is now a country of decoration," where "simple mores conforming to nature are banished." Extravagance, he described, was most apparent in Paris, where trends in furniture and jewelry changed three times a year. Luxury, he continued, created disorder in the state by confounding orders and ranks. Clothes, fashion, and tastes tended toward uniformity until one failed to distinguish "those who by birth or by employment must necessarily be distinguished." Worse, useless commodities "ruined health" and "rendered men less strong, less courageous, less able to continue work." This *luxe*, Boureau-Deslandes warned, "prepared the liveliest nation for death."[48]

International commercial expansion in the mid eighteenth century was a source of anxiety to many French elites. From Marseillais academicians and sword nobility to state administrators, the constant influx of new commodities into urban centers raised fears that things and people were moving too fast. Marseille's duty-free trade with the Ottoman Empire, its rapidly shifting demographics, and the endless shuffling in and out of foreign and Marseillais merchants exacerbated these worries. Trends in fashion, furniture, and food came and went, Boureau-Deslandes wrote; merchants failed to establish roots in their native cities, let alone countries, Marseillais nobles observed. It did not take a misanthrope like Jean-Jacques Rousseau to notice these developments and the potential threat to political, moral, and cultural stability that they represented. Some who were quite supportive of Marseille's and France's commercial activities equally found the uprooting tendencies of the marketplace disturbing. While French subjects sipped Turkish coffee out of Chinese porcelain, adopted "eastern" sartorial styles, and embarked on physical and armchair travels to the Mediterranean, the Near East, the Far East, and the New World, observers questioned the moral effects of all this.

For observers like Boureau-Deslandes, the concepts of virtue and patriotism provided a means to reconnect and ground people: to reestablish their loyalty to the king, to connect them to their native cities, and to form a common interest for the community and public good. The classical tropes of civic virtue and *amour de la patrie* became useful to anchor a modernizing commercial state and society that were seen as fundamentally unstable. "[T]he French assertion of love of the *patrie* required a rethinking of the relationship between antiquity and modernity because patriotism's new appeal partly reflected a discomfort with certain features of the modern world—the increased role of money and finance, the growth of commerce, social mobility, egoism," Jay Smith writes. The ancient values that some administrators, philosophers and aristocrats idealized—of frugality, public spirit, and "disinterestedness"—united old classical republican traditions and established concepts of honor with a new patriotic sensibility.[49]

The adoption of ancient ideals to solve modern problems created an intellectual environment where the stabilization of commercial society could be understood both as restoration and reform. Restoration suggested a return to an ideal past, while reform involved creating an ideal new form of political and social existence. Those who understood stabilization as restoration attacked the problem of commercial society from politically conservative angles. These were the nobility, who saw themselves responsible for restoring their own order, the French people, and the state to a morally superior existence. They imagined the reestablishment of social hierarchies, the reinstallation of the nobility in their old positions of political power and privilege, and the curtailing of social mobility. Such were the Marseillais nobility who asked to be allowed to reenter the municipal administration, the Aixois parlementary magistrates who criticized Commandant Langeron's plague-time administration, and the Burgundian circle that sought to curtail the excesses of Louis Quatorzian self-aggrandizement. Those who understood the stabilization of commercial society as reform found comfort in a brighter future that emphasized equality; public education, meritocracy, and the creation of fair, judicious laws, they believed, would lead Frenchmen toward further progress, civilization, and enlightenment. In Marseille, academicians and merchants made up a large portion of this group.

Both approaches—restoration and reform—rested on potentially inclusive principles. In the last decades of the Old Regime, patriotism, honor, and virtue were ideals that were theoretically open to many. While Boureau-Deslandes, like the abbé Sièyes, accused the aristocracy of being the most corrupt group of Frenchmen, and while nobles charged *négociants* with moral deficiencies, various members of the political, intellectual, and administrative elites claimed that virtue, honor, and patriotism could be realized by French subjects regardless of estate or order. In other words, by appealing to such ideals like "disinterestedness," "probity," "honor," and "virtue" that were not limited to one particular order, French subjects implicitly challenged the importance of established hierarchies. Academicians claimed that they were the beacons of virtue and honor, as did *négociants*, ennobled royal administrators, and sword aristocrats. Members of all three estates made claims to virtue, honor, and patriotism, thereby threatening the rigid social hierarchies that had distinguished them for centuries.

Moreover, these discussions sometimes generated inclusive interpretations of "other" civilizations and populations outside of France. Eurocentric though they were, French writers noted that the ancient Greeks and Romans, Persians, Egyptians, Chinese, and Turks all historically had things in common with the French, and had developed theories of governance, established formidable cities and states, and contributed to the progress of science, art, and culture. French debates over civilization—whether it was poised for progress or decline—allowed intellectuals and administrators to emphasize certain universal moral characteristics that extended beyond national, religious, or ethnic boundaries. At the same time, however, post-plague wariness of international commerce and its dangers, combined with Louis XV's wars in the mid-century, and the development of new patriotic sensibilities, energized exclusionary and discriminatory utterances suspicious of, and condescending toward, non-French populations. Virtue, in this environment, became increasingly seen as an attribute of the French.

Ultimately, even within France, certain groups lost their grip on the languages of virtue, honor, and patriotism at the end of the Old Regime. We know that after 1789, the nobility's claims to be models of virtue, public spirit, and patriotism disintegrated after the abbé Sieyès denounced them as incapable and uninterested in national belonging. Meanwhile, after the notion of the rights-bearing citizen was introduced with the Declaration of the Rights of Man and Citizen and bolstered by the Constitution of 1791, active citizenship would nevertheless be closed to the majority of Frenchmen and Frenchwomen as the French Revolution ground on. But in the last decades of the Old Regime, the idioms of patriotism, public spirit, virtue, and honor remained relatively inclusive in the context of a modernizing commercial state and society. This study has tried to demonstrate that this was the case in one particular locality, Marseille, where clergymen, nobility, ennobled merchants, and non-noble elite commoners offered various iterations of classical republican thought as they discussed the viability of commercial expansion. But it has also attempted to show that what went on in Marseille reflected larger trends in France as a whole. And while these discussions fostered the intellectual preconditions for the French Revolution, and were part of the long-term conceptual transformations that fractured the Old Regime, they also contributed to prolonging the lifespan of the Bourbon monarchy.

Notes

INTRODUCTION

1. Shovlin, *Political Economy of Virtue*, 18–19.

2. For most recent work on the subject of commerce, virtue, and luxury, see ibid.; Smith, *Nobility Reimagined*; Kessler, *Revolution in Commerce*; Sonenscher, *Before the Deluge*; Venturi, *Virtue, Commerce, History*.

3. For Fénelon vs. Colbert, see Shovlin, *Political Economy of Virtue*, 20–21.

4. Kessler, *Revolution in Commerce*, 17.

5. "Edit pour l'affranchissement du port de Marseille (1732), Archives départementales des Bouches du Rhône (hereafter AdBdR), Fonds Intendance sanitaire de Marseille (hereafter FISM), 200 E 1.

6. Gordon, "Confrontations with the Plague," "The City and the Plague," and *Citizens Without Sovereignty*; Baker, "Enlightenment and the Institution of Society," 95–120.

7. Condorcet, "The Future Progress of the Human Mind," 26–38. Baker, *From Natural Philosophy to Social Mathematics*; Avery, *Progress, Poverty and Population*.

8. I draw away from categorizing this new attitude toward commercial public engagement as "humanistic," because in early modern France, it did not replicate the civic humanist traditions of the Renaissance Italian republics. The commercial civic spirit of seventeenth-century France is not comparable to the intellectual stances vis-à-vis the classical world that Italian civic humanists adopted to disengage from Catholic scholasticism and their support of princes, despots, and elite citizens who patronized the arts and sciences in pursuit of a *vita activa*.

9. Clark, *Compass of Society*, 5–6, and "Commerce, the Virtues and the Public Sphere," 415–40; Shovlin, *Political Economy of Virtue*, 18–19.

10. Baker, "Transformations of Classical Republicanism," 32–53.

11. Fénelon, *Télémaque*, ed. and trans. Riley as *Telemachus*, xvi.

12. Ibid., 195.

13. Ibid., 295–96.

14. For "civic republicanism" in European history, see, e.g., Schilling, "Civic Republicanism in Late Medieval and Early Modern German Cities," and Mijnhardt, "The Dutch Republic as a Town," 345–448.

15. Baron, *Crisis of the Early Italian Renaissance*, and *In Search of Florentine Civic Humanism*; Pocock, *Machiavellian Moment*; Kramnick, *Republicanism and Bourgeois Radicalism*; *Republicanism*, ed. van Gelderen and Skinner; Skinner, *Liberty Before Liberalism*.

16. Such assumptions can be found in Goulemot, "Du républicanisme et de l'idée républicaine," and Venturi, *Utopia and Reform in the Enlightenment*. For other works on classical republicanism, see Baker, "Transformations of Classical Republicanism," 33–34; Bell, *Cult of the Nation in France*; Linton, *Politics of Virtue in Enlightenment France*; Smith, *Nobility Reimagined*; Sonenscher, *Sans-Culottes*; Whatmore, *Republicanism and the French Revolution*; Wright, *Classical Republican in Eighteenth-Century France*.

17. The relationship between Marseillais municipal administrators and the French Crown sheds light on how commercial and political associations could develop between monarchies and republics across Europe (the relationship between France and the Venetian republic being another example), despite dissimilar political structures and traditions. As an analysis of the associative dynamics between municipal politics and state-building, my work provides conceptual models relevant to recent scholarship on the connections between local patriotism and nationalism in Europe, though the framing dates for my study of early modern France are too early for a consideration of French nationalism in any modern sense. My argument can find resonance in recent studies on local, republican, and regional politics and identities in eighteenth- and nineteenth-century central Europe and Germany that show how, as Katherine Aaslestad argues, "within the nation, there is a place for regional and local identity, which can help as well as hinder nation-building." See Aaslestad, *Place and Politics*, 12; Confino, *The Nation as Local Metaphor*; Lindemann, *Patriots and Paupers*.

18. Tocqueville, *Old Regime and the French Revolution*; Beik, *Absolutism and Society in Seventeenth-Century France*, and "Absolutism of Louis XIV." Bien, "Offices, Corps and a System of State Credit"; Bossenga, *Politics of Privilege*; Monahan, *Year of Sorrows*.

19. Beik, *Absolutism and Society*; Bossenga, *Politics of Privilege*; Kwass, *Privilege and the Politics of Taxation*; *Tocqueville and Beyond*, ed. Schwartz and Schneider.

20. I borrow the term "accommodation" from historians of twentieth-century France. Burrin, *France Under the Germans*, introduction.

21. Sonenscher, *Before the Deluge*, 4, 10.

22. Quoted in Baratier, *Histoire de Marseille*, 188–89; and *Recueil d'édits, arrests du conseil, et règlemens*.

23. Busquet, *Histoire de la Provence*, chap. 3.14, pp. 284–89; J.-B. Bertrand, *Historical Relation of the Plague at Marseille*, 30–31; Baratier, *Histoire de Marseille*, 188–89.

24. "Délibérations de la Bureau de la santé," AdBdR, 200 E 37, FISM.

25. Ibid., E 35.

26. Carrière, Courdurié, and Rebuffat, *Marseille ville morte*, 240–41; Lucenet, *Grandes pestes*, 218. For more on culpability, see Panzac, *Quarantaines et lazarets*; Bouyala d'Arnaud, *Evocation du vieux Marseille*.

27. "Editto in materia di sanità," 9 October 1720, 3 December 1721, Archivio di stato di Venezia, Provveditori alla sanità 651.

28. Plague mortality is widely debated. Exaggerated estimations range from 70,000 to 100,000 in Marseille alone. A more plausible figure lies in the vicinity of 50,000, half

the population of Marseille. Daniel Panzac offers the following statistics: 126,000 dead for all Provence, Comtat Venaissin, and Languedoc; eighty-one Provençal communities, their population totaling 293,113 inhabitants, lost 105,417, or 36 percent. Le Comtat and Languedoc lost 8,062 out of 36,641 (22 percent), and 12,597 out of 75,377 (16.7 percent), respectively. Cities with considerable losses included Ollioules (54.8 percent of its 2,500); Marvejols (57.8 percent of its 2,756); Manosque, Brignoles, and Néoules, all with more than half of its inhabitants killed (Panzac, *Quarantaines et lazarets,* 61).

29. *Famine, Disease and Social Order,* ed. Walter and Schofield, 2, 5–6; Appleby, *Famine in Tudor and Stuart England*; Meuvret, "La géographie des prix des cereals et les anciennes economies européens," 63–69; Meuvret, *Le problème des subsistances à l'époque Louis XIV*; for more political approaches, see Kaplan, *Bread, Politics and Political Economy*; Kaplan, *Provisioning Paris.*

30. For social studies on plague, see, e.g., Biraben, *Les hommes et la peste en France*; Benedictow, "Morbidity in Historical Plague Epidemics," 401–31; *Famine, Disease and the Social Order,* ed. Walter and Schofield; Appleby, "Epidemics and Famine in the Little Ice Age," 643–63; Appleby, "Disappearance of the Plague," 161–73.

31. Gordon, "Confrontations with the Plague," 15–16.

32. Jones, "Plague and Its Metaphors in Early Modern France," 97–127; Sontag, *Illness as Metaphor.* I also take into consideration the relationship between the "social" and "language" articulated in Sewell, *Logics of History,* 9, 21.

33. Panzac, *Quarantaines et lazarets.*

34. Smith, *Nobility Reimagined,* 16.

35. Carrière, *Négociants marseillais,* 247.

CHAPTER 1: LOUIS XIV, MARSEILLAIS MERCHANTS, AND THE PROBLEM OF DISCERNING THE PUBLIC GOOD

1. Colbert, *Mémoire,* 1651, in *Lettres, instructions et mémoires de Colbert,* cxxii.

2. Colbert to Rouillé, 21 September 1679, in *Lettres, instructions et mémoires de Colbert,* 2: 706.

3. Baratier, *Histoire de Marseille,* 44.

4. Ibid., 85.

5. Clause from the 1486 treaty, quoted in Bouyala d'Arnaud, *Evocation du vieil Aix-en-Provence,* 16.

6. Busquet, *Histoire de la Provence,* 224.

7. Royal letters patent created the parlement de Provence in 1501 and the Cour des comptes aides et finances in 1555, but the Etats de Provence continued to advise the Crown as a "consultative agency." This structure mirrored that of Languedoc as described by Beik, *Absolutism and Society,* 37. See also Fairchilds, *Poverty and Charity in Aix-en-Provence,* 3–8. The royal intendant served as *premier président* of the parlement of Aix; the archbishop of Aix served ex officio as *procureur-né* and as president of the Assemblée des communautés, a council of representatives from Provence's towns, villages, and cities. As *chef-lieu* of its *viguerie,* Aix had a *sénéchaussée* court and the *maréchaussée.* Around 1,172 administrators, 600 noble heads of households, and 451 lawyers made Aix their home in 1695.

8. Marseillais were not required to participate in the provincial assemblies. The city sent deputies to observe the sessions, but did not take part in them. Zarb, *Histoire d'une autonomie communale*, 134–36.

9. Cubells, "Les pratiques politiques à Marseille au milieu du XVIIe siècle," 71.

10. Zanger, *Scenes from the Marriage of Louis XIV*, 17.

11. Colbert to Mazarin, 7, 10, and 11 July 1658 in *Lettres, instructions et Mémoires de Colbert*, 297, 299, 301–2.

12. Hénin, "L'agrandissement de Marseille," 7.

13. Pérouse de Montclos, *"Les prix de Rome,"* 7–8, 10.

14. Ibid., 19.

15. Emmanuelli, *Vivre à Marseille sous l'Ancien régime*, 22–23.

16. The commission was named by Colbert on 15 June 1666 with an *arrêt du Conseil.*

17. "Articles et conditions accordées à François Roustan," Archives municipales de la ville de Marseille (hereafter AMVM), DD 152.

18. "Requête des échevins en opposition aux Lettres patentes de 1666, relatives à l'agrandissement de Marseille" (1667), AMVM, DD 152. The *échevins* also argued that the expansion would not boost foreign commerce. Foreign residents were already housed in areas suitable for trading; a new area "far from trading routes" would inconvenience them. They added that the old quarters were not susceptible to contagious maladies; citizens owned country houses (*bastides*) where they could take refuge in emergencies.

19. Arnoul, "Lettres et mémoires," 22 January 1667, Archives de la Chambre de commerce de Marseille (hereafter ACCM).

20. "Premier comparant touchant l'agrandissement de Marseille," 22 (1667), AMVM, DD 155, Echevins.

21. Ibid., 23 (1667).

22. Arnoul, "Lettres et mémoires," 2 October 1666.

23. Ibid., 31 August 1666.

24. Ibid., 14 September 1666.

25. Ibid., 18 January 1667.

26. Arnoul, 23 February 1666.

27. Baker, "French Political Thought at the Accession of Louis XVI," 287.

28. Arnoul, "Lettres et mémoires," undated, 1667.

29. Ibid., 16 November 1666.

30. This was particularly the case following Arnoul's departure from Marseille to Toulon in 1673.

31. Unfortunately, Puget's architectural plans are no longer available; all that is left are historical accounts and recent photographs taken of *maisons particuliers* attributed to Puget.

32. Emmanuelli, *Vivre à Marseille sous l'Ancien régime*, 100.

33. "Déliberations du Bureau," 15 October 1687, AMVM DD 94.

34. Hénin, "L'agrandissement de Marseille," 13.

35. Carrière, *Négociants marseillais*, 34. The massive upswing in commercial activity actually began after the first decade of the eighteenth century. "Marseille was becoming—though modestly—an international port" (ibid., 101). The fragmentary evidence blurs the

effects of Louis XIV's policies prior to 1710, but although "the lists of vessels, exception for those from the Levant and Barbary, are not certain prior to 1710," Carrière found 98 Marseillais voyages to the New World in 1699; 90 in 1700; 82 in 1701; 88 in 1702; 22 in 1703; 30 in 1704; 26 in 1705; and 35 in 1706 (ibid., 80–81). The fall in the number of sailings after 1702 was owing to the War of the Spanish Succession.

36. Ibid., 213–15.

37. Ibid., 105.

38. Ibid.; Rambert, *Histoire du commerce de Marseille*; Cole, *Colbert and a Century of French Mercantilism*.

39. *La Chambre de commerce de Marseille à travers ses archives: XVIIe et XVIIIe siècles*, 12–14; Rambert, *Histoire du commerce de Marseille*, 78–87, 300–330; Baratier, 182.

40. Rambert, *Histoire du commerce de Marseille*, 300.

41. Arnoul to Colbert, 25 August 1668, quoted in Rambert, *Histoire du commerce de Marseille*, 207, 300.

42. "Mémoire dressé contre le port franc pour envoyer à Sa Majesté." ACCM, D 23.

43. For full discussion, see Chapter 4.

44. Colbert to Morant, 11 September 1681, in *Lettres, instructions et mémoires de Colbert*, 2: 717n1.

45. Colbert to d'Oppède, 30 May 1669, ibid., 470.

46. "Edit pour l'affranchissement du Port de Marseille" (1732), AdBdR, FISM, 200 E 1.

47. "Edit sur la franchise du port de Marseille," in *Lettres, instructions et mémoires de Colbert*, 2: 796–98.

48. Rambert, *Histoire du commerce de Marseille*, 208.

49. Colbert to d'Oppède, 30 May 1669, in *Lettres, instructions et mémoires de Colbert*, 2: 470–72.

50. Colbert to Rouillé, ibid., 717–18.

51. "Etablissement du droit de 1669: Edits, ordonnances, mémoires et correspondances," ACCM, C 88.

52. Colbert to Rouillé, 26 October 1679, in *Lettres, instructions et mémoires de Colbert*, 2: 709; Colbert to Morant, 17 April 1681, ibid., 717–18.

53. Cole, *Colbert and a Century of French Mercantilism*, 394–95.

54. The French bombarded the Ottoman port of Chios following reports that corsairs from Tripoli had taken French prisoners. The French ambassador promised to pay the sultan 250,000 *livres* to restore Franco-Turkish relations and rebuild the city. Colbert decided that the Marseillais chamber should "borrow this sum" from the Crown to pay the Turks, and then repay the Crown through the *cottimo*. Colbert to Morant, 4 September 1682, in *Lettres, instructions et mémoires de Colbert*, 2: 738.

55. "Extrait des registres du Conseil d'Etat." ACCM, C 88.

56. On piracy in the early modern Mediterranean, see Weiss, "Back from Barbary"; Davis, *Christian Slaves, Muslim Masters*.

57. Cole, *Colbert and a Century of French Mercantilism*, 388.

58. Colbert to Arnoul, 25 May 1669 and 17 October 1670, in *Lettres, instructions et mémoires de Colbert*, 3: 128, 297; Colbert, "Mémoire sur les soldats des vaisseaux de Levant," ibid., 486–88.

59. Colbert to Morant, 27 March 1681, ibid., 2: 716.

60. Colbert to Morant, 17 April 1681, ibid., 717.

61. Colbert to Morant, quoted in Cole, *Colbert and a Century of French Mercantilism,* 389–90.

62. Colbert to Arnoul, 16 August 1669, in *Lettres, instructions et mémoires de Colbert,* 3: 154.

63. Colbert to Morant, 27 March 1681, ibid., 2: 716.

64. Colbert to Rouillé, 3 March 1679, ibid., 695.

65. Colbert, ibid., 698n1.

66. Colbert to Morant, 29 March 1679, ibid., 696.

67. Colbert, ibid., 455n1.

68. Ibid., 403.

69. Kessler, *Revolution in Commerce,* 3, 17, 20.

70. Colbert to French consuls overseas, 15 March 1669, in *Lettres, instructions et mémoires de Colbert,* 2: 453.

71. Colbert to French consuls overseas, 16 March 1669, ibid., 454–55.

72. Colbert to French consuls in the Levant, 10 February 1670, ibid., 517.

73. Colbert also ended abuses committed by the consuls, who farmed out their offices to the highest bidder or used their authority to exact higher taxes on both French and non-French traders. Decrees in 1664, 1669, and 1675 ruled that consulships had to be held in person, excessive duties could not be imposed, and consuls should not abuse executive powers.

74. Colbert to *échevins* and *députés du commerce,* Marseille, 16 February 1670, in *Lettres, instructions et mémoires de Colbert,* 2: 518.

75. Colbert to the marquis de Nointel, ambassador at Constantinople, 1 November 1670, ibid., 575.

76. Ibid., 575n3.

77. Colbert, ibid., 491.

78. Colbert to Louis XIV, 21 September 1669, ibid., 491.

79. Colbert, "Instruction au Sieur de Nointel," ibid., 841.

80. Colbert, "Note sur le commerce et les relations de la France avec le Levant," ibid., 628–29.

81. Louis XIV, *Capitulations renouvellées,* 2.

82. Ibid., 13.

83. Ibid., 8.

84. Chambon quoted in Rambert, *Histoire du commerce de Marseille,* 212.

85. Anonymous quoted in Rambert, *Histoire du commerce de Marseille,* 213–14. Also Archives nationales Marine B 7.488 (1664–1740).

86. For studies on administrative practices after Colbert, see Chapman, *Private Ambition and Political Alliances.*

87. Cole, *Colbert and a Century of French Mercantilism,* 3; for a contrasting viewpoint, see Chapman, *Private Ambition and Political Alliances;* for Marseillais relationships with the Crown post-Colbert, see Rambert, *Histoire du commerce de Marseille;* Masson, *Histoire du commerce français dans le Levant.*

88. See, e.g., Kettering, *Patronage in Sixteenth- and Seventeenth-Century France*; *Patrons, Brokers and Clients in Seventeenth-Century France*; "Brokerage at the Court of Louis XIV"; and "Historical Development of Political Clientelism."

89. Cole, *French Mercantilism, 1683–1700*, 26.

90. Lagny, letter to Pontchartrain, 28 September 1686, ACCM, B 101.

91. Lagny, letter, 15 November 1699, ACCM, B 101.

92. Schaeper, *French Council of Commerce*, 10. Colbert set precedents for such a council with his Council of Commerce in 1664. In 1669, he had also issued an ordinance calling for the creation of assemblies (*assemblées représentatives du commerce*) of municipal officials and *négociants*, who would assemble periodically in their municipalities. Neither of Colbert's plans had panned out: his Council of Commerce was discontinued, and only a handful of cities established *assemblées du commerce*.

93. "Arrest du Conseil d'Estat de Roy portent establissement d'un Conseil de Commerce, du 29 juin 1700," ACCM, A 15.

94. *Commissaires* included Daguesseau, (chair), Controller-General Michel Chamillart, Secretary of State for the Navy Jêrome de Pontchartrain, Michel Jean Amelot de Gournay, and Maîtres des requêtes François Joseph d'Ernothon and Nicolas-Prosper Bauyn d'Angervilliers. Deputies came from Paris, Rouen, Bordeaux, Lyon, Marseille, La Rochelle, Nantes, Saint-Malo, Lille, Bayonne, and Dunkerque.

95. Biography of Fabre from Joseph Fournier, *Chambre de commerce de Marseille et ses représentants*, 42–58; Schaeper, *French Council of Commerce*.

96. Fabre enjoyed a positive reputation at court; he had distinguished himself by serving as Marseille's representative to the Crown to offer formal apologies for Niozelles' seditious activities that set off the conquest of 1660. Furthermore, he had served as Colbert's informant. Following the conquest, Colbert created the office of L'inspection du commerce de Levant. He named *informateurs* to help "execute [the Crown's] decisions, hand over accounts" and inspect commerce, Fabre being the first of these. Rambert, *Histoire du commerce de Marseille*, 285–300.

97. ACCM, A 17.

98. Fabre, letter to the Marseille Chamber of Commerce, 20 January 1701, ACCM, B 153 (all letters from Fabre cited below are to the Marseille Chamber). See Fournier, *Chambre de Commerce de Marseille et ses représentants permanents à Paris*, 47.

99. Schaeper, "Government and Business in Early Eighteenth-Century France," 540.

100. Fabre, 26 April 1701, ACCM, B 153.

101. "Instructions de la Chambre de commerce de Marseille à Monsieur Joseph Fabre" (1700), ACCM, B 152.

102. Fabre, 16 July 1701, ACCM, B 154.

103. Fabre, 8 October, 1701, ACCM, B 154. For more, see ibid., 30 July, 2 August, and 9 August, 1701; also ACCM, B 157, 6 January, 23 January, and 25 January 1703.

104. Fabre, 26 January, 12 and 15 February, 1 March, and 5 April 1701, ACCM, B 1532, and 1 September 1702, ACCM, B 156.

105. Fabre, 23 July 1701, ACCM, B 154.

106. Fabre, 5 February 1701, ACCM, B 153.

107. ACCM, B 153–157.

108. Fabre, 13 September 1701, ACCM, B 154.

109. Fabre, 9 September 1701, ACCM, B 154.

110. Fabre, 21 May 1701, ACCM, B 153.

111. Fabre, 23 and 30 July 1701, ACCM, B 154; 19 and 24 January 1702, ACCM B 155; September 1702, ACCM, B 156.

112. Fabre, letter, 31 January 1701, ACCM, B 153.

113. Schaeper, *French Council of Commerce,* 54.

114. Fabre, 26 April 1701, ACCM, B 153.

115. Fabre, 8 July 1702, ACCM, B 156.

116. Fabre, 7 February 1701, ACCM, B 153.

117. Matthieu Fabre, 9 September 1708.

118. While arguing for three years on behalf of the liberties of "virtuous," "useful" Marseillais merchants who enriched the state, Fabre distributed bribes to win over Chamillart, Pontchartrain, and the *conseillers d'état* who decided his city's fate. "Good politics demand that I encourage those who work for us," Fabre wrote. "It is necessary to have permanent friends, one must manage [people] by giving a pension." Historians have estimated that Fabre's *pots-de-vin* amounted to over 100,000 *livres.* While complaining that such people-managing gave him extreme "arm-aches," Fabre reported that it produced excellent results: "the king told me that he is happy with Marseille." See Fabre, 15 March 1701, ACCM, B 153, and 24 and 30 August 1701, ACCM, B 154;. For more on gifts and bribes, see Schaeper, *French Council of Commerce,* 86; Kettering, "Brokerage at the Court of Louis XIV," 69–87, and "Political Clientelism," 419–47.

119. The delay was caused by *conseiller d'état* Michel Amelot's illness in 1702 and 1703. See 27 March 1703, ACCM, B 157, and letters, 29 July–30 September 1702, ACCM, B 156. "Monsieur Amelot's sickness lasts a bit too long," Fabre wrote the Chamber.

120. Fabre, letter, 27 April 1702, quoted in Fournier, *Chambre de Commerce de Marseille et ses représentants permanents à Paris,* 52.

121. Clark, *Compass of Society,* 34.

122. Kessler, *Revolution in Commerce,* 3.

123. Clark, *Compass of Society,* 5–6.

CHAPTER 2: BETWEEN REPUBLIC AND MONARCHY: DEBATING COMMERCE AND VIRTUE

1. Carrière, *Négociants marseillais,* 247.

2. Kessler, "Question of Name," 50.

3. Clark, *Compass of Society,* 6, and "Commerce, the Virtues, and the Public Sphere," 415–40.

4. Clark, "Commerce, the Virtues, and the Public Sphere," 419.

5. Savary, *Parfait négociant,* Preface to 1st ed. (1675), x.

6. Ibid.

7. Savary, *Parfait négociant,* bk. 1, 1–2.

8. Kessler, "Question of Name," 53.

9. Savary, "Dessein de l'auteur et l'ordre qu'il a venu en son ouvrage," in *Parfait négociant*, 2.

10. Savary, *Parfait négociant*, pt. 1, bk. 1, 27–40.

11. Colonie, *Eclaircissement sur le légitime commerce des intérêts* (1682), 30–32, 60.

12. Kessler, "Question of Name," 50.

13. Lebret, Bibliothèque municipale de Marseille, MS 49002, folio 228.

14. Carrière, *Négociants marseillais*, 259–66.

15. Savary, *Parfait négociant*, pt. 2, bk. 1, 408–9.

16. Savary, "Du commerce en gros et de son excellence," in *Parfait négociant*, 408. The nobility, by definition, were traditionally legally barred from mercantile activity. Also Kessler, "Question in Name," 50–52.

17. Eon, *Commerce honorable*; also Clark, "Commerce, the Virtues, and the Public Sphere," 438.

18. Clark, "Commerce, the Virtues, and the Public Sphere," 439.

19. Savary, *Parfait négociant*, 408.

20. Ibid., 241.

21. Carrière, *Négociants marseillais*, 243–44.

22. *Dictionnaire de l'Académie française*, s.v. "negoce," "négoçiant" 2: 115.

23. Quoted in Carrière, *Négociants marseillais*, 244–45.

24. Panzac, "International and Domestic Maritime Trade in the Ottoman Empire," 193.

25. For more on the Marseillais sword nobility's remonstrances, see Chapter 7.

26. *Encyclopédie, ou dictionnaire raisonné des sciences, des arts et des métiers*, 2.7–12: 799–800, s.v. "Marseille."

27. Koselleck, "Linguistic Change and the History of Events," 649–66. Koselleck describes how languages control events by representing them in "certain ways and not otherwise." Baker expanded on this idea to study the relationship between "memory and political practice" in his analysis of representations of the past by parlementary magistrates in eighteenth-century France. Baker, "Memory and Practice," 134.

28. Mollicone, "Redécouverte," 1: 117, 9.

29. Koselleck, "Linguistic Change," 660.

30. The French monarchy's role in activating civic patriotism remains surprisingly unexplored, but see on this Bell, *Cult of the Nation in France*; Gordon, *Citizens Without Sovereignty*; Bernstein, *Between Crown and Community*. In Marseille, historical research on civic fashioning have been confined to local histories that sacrifice analytical distance and continue to invoke 1660 as the point when the city reclaimed its grandeur. The important question that remains is not whether Marseille reclaimed its greatness in 1660, but rather why the tradition of imagining this resurrection as a republican one emerged.

31. *Dictionnaire de l'Académie française*, s.v. "République."

32. Chasseneuz, *Catalogus gloriae mundi*, quoted in Gojosso, *Concept de république en France*, 79.

33. Gojosso, *Concept de république*, 165.

34. Ibid., 264–70.

35. Cubells, "Vie intellectuelle," 333–38, 339–40, 349. Looking at the inventories of five private library holdings in Provence, Cubells gives a percentage breakdown of different categories of texts for the years 1700 to 1730. The most popular subjects were law and jurisprudence, history, and antiquity.

36. McCabe, *Orientalism in Early Modern France*, 124.

37. Michaud, *Biographie universelle, ancienne et moderne*, 37: 44–45.

38. For the full title, see Bibliography.

39. Ruffi, *Histoire de la ville de Marseille*, Preface. The first edition conserved at the Bibliothèque Méjanes is in delicate condition and no longer accessible to the public. My thanks to the *conservateur* Philip Ferrand, who allowed me use of the text. Because of its fragility, I went through it to note the differences from the second edition; where the chapters were identical, I consulted the latter edition. In sum, the first edition ends its narrative with the defeat of Casaulx and then provides a list of prominent ecclesiastics, bishops, churches, and buildings in Marseille. It ends in the tenth chapter with a discussion of the fertility of the region, its wines, food, and herbs. The 1696 edition adds four chapters. It takes the narrative up to the birth of Louis XIV, and then discusses the bishops, churches, buildings, and artifacts of the city, as in the first edition, with the addition of images of artifacts and coins found. The latter edition also includes chapters on the royal galleys and French naval and commercial power after 1660, as well as a list of famous Marseillais from ancient and modern times.

40. Ibid., 13, 16–17.

41. Ibid., 12, 205, 13–14. Massilia's women allegedly shunned alcohol and were as virtuous as its men. Ruffi says that "comedians and actors were not allowed entry into the city for fear that the youth would accustom themselves to adultery and other falsities."

42. Ibid., 364–381. This institution taught grammar, rhetoric, poetry, philosophy, medicine, jurisprudence, theology, mathematics, and astrology.

43. Ibid., 20, 23, 208, 236.

44. Ibid., 417, 425–28.

45. "Franciscus Patricius Senensis, Episcopus Caietanus libro tertio titulo 3. de institute. reipubl.," in Ruffi, *Le Règlement du sort*, Preface. Bibliothèque Méjanes, M FP Anc. F. 0103. My short summary of the ruling bodies is gleaned from Pocock, *Machiavellian Moment*, 278–82.

46. Ruffi, *Règlement du sort*, Preface.

47. "Extrait des Délibérations du Conseil," 4 January 1654, in Ruffi, *Règlement du sort*.

48. "Extrait des Délibérations de l'Hostel de Ville de Marseille," 28 October 1652, in Ruffi, *Règlement du sort*.

49. *Règlement du sort*, articles 1–11.

50. Ibid., articles 1–5.

51. Ibid. Members of the council convened to vote on the Sunday before the Feast of Saints Simon and Jude: "without distinction of quality . . . they would be called upon by the secretary in alphabetical order, to write their names on an equal piece of paper, which would be folded . . . in a ball." The balls were tossed into "the Vase of Destiny," and a young boy drew names at random.

52. Ibid., article 10.

53. Ibid., article 25.

54. Ibid., "Des privilèges de Marseille," 122.

55. Ruffi, *Histoire de la Ville de Marseille*, "Epître."

56. Ruffi, *Histoire de la Ville de Marseille*, 2nd ed., bk. 1, 4.

57. Ibid., bk. 14, 295–97, 346–64.

58. Ibid., 277.

59. For more, see list of local works in Guys, *Marseille ancienne et moderne*, 149–50.

60. Gaufridi, *Histoire de Provence*, 4, 7, 838.

61. Pliny quoted in Busquet, *Histoire de la Provence*, 81.

62. Ruffi, *Histoire de Marseille*, bk. 13, 312.

63. Gautier, *Histoire de la ville de Nismes*, introduction.

64. On Louis XIV and the Arles obelisk, see Mollicone, "Redécouverte," 1:120–24.

65. Archaeological studies suggest that the remains in Rome's western provinces date to early imperial Rome, and Augustan settlement in particular. Provençal ruins dated to the Hellenic period have been found at the sites of ancient Massilia, Glanum, Saint-Rémy, and Narbonensis in the Bouches-du-Rhône. When Hellenic settlements gave way to romanization, imperial Roman architecture dominated. See Ward-Perkins, "From Republic to Empire," 1–19.

66. Smith, *Nobility Reimagined*, 26, 30–33.

67. Van Kley, *Religious Origins of the French Revolution*, 55.

68. Fénelon, *Télémaque*, ed. and trans. Riley as *Telemachus*, 36–37.

69. Ibid., 49, 52, 152.

70. Riley, Introduction, Fénelon, *Telemachus*, xvii, xxi.

71. This combination of republicanism and religion was not limited to Fénelon. His adversaries the Jansenists also used republican motifs in their discussions of Church governance and reform. For a discussion of the convergence of republicanism, civic spirit, and religion in Marseille, see Chapter 6.

72. Riley, Introduction, Fénelon, *Telemachus*, xxii.

73. Fénelon, *Education of a Daughter*, 24, 57.

74. Van Kley, *Religious Origins of the French Revolution*, 56–57; Riley, Introduction, Fénelon, *Telemachus*, xiv–xv.

75. Shovlin, *Political Economy of Virtue*, 21.

76. Smith, *Nobility Reimagined*, 44.

77. Ibid., 28; Kaiser, "Evil Empire?"; Richter, "Despotism," in *Dictionary of the History of Ideas*; McCabe, *Orientalism in Early Modern France*.

CHAPTER 3: FRANCE AND THE LEVANTINE MERCHANT

1. Guys, *Marseille ancienne et moderne*, 29.

2. As Thomas Kaiser has shown, "running through these narratives was the steady theme of a society operating on the inversion of natural law" (Kaiser, "Evil Empire?" 8).

3. I use several works as my springboard: Adamovsy, *Euro-Orientalism*; Kaiser, "Evil Empire?"; Wolff, *Inventing Eastern Europe*.

4. McCabe, *Orientalism in Early Modern France*.

5. A similar argument, that discussions about "race" informed and were informed by individuals and groups struggling to position themselves in the metropole, has been made in studies of imperial Britain in the nineteenth century. See Cannadine, *Ornamentalism.*

6. Through this chapter, I use the terms, "Mohammad," "Mahomet," "Mahometan," depending on the terminology used by French and British authors.

7. Colbert, "Edit sur la franchise du port de Marseille," in *Lettres, instructions et mémoires de Colbert,* 2: 796–98.

8. Colbert in *Lettres, instructions et mémoires de Colbert,* 2: clxxiii.

9. Jensen, "Ottoman Turks in Sixteenth-Century French Diplomacy," 451–470.

10. Panzac, *Commerce et navigation dans l'empire Ottoman,* 198.

11. McCabe, *Orientalism in Early Modern France,* chaps. 6–9. See also Castelluccio, *Carrousels.*

12. Fontenelle, "Eloge," in Tournefort, *Relation d'un voyage du Levant.*

13. Tournefort, *Relation d'un voyage du Levant,* introduction.

14. Ibid., 8–9.

15. Poullet, *Nouvelles relations du Levant,* 35.

16. Ibid., 305–6.

17. Fermanel, *Voyage d'Italie et du Levant,* 111–12.

18. Poullet, *Nouvelles relations du Levant,* 314.

19. Ibid., 22, 51, 72.

20. Ibid., 280.

21. Fermanel, *Voyage d'Italie et du Levant,* 113 -4.

22. Poullet, *Nouvelles relations du Levant,* 329.

23. Ibid., 31.

24. Fermanel, *Voyage d'Italie et du Levant,* 109, 332 -33.

25. Ibid., 460.

26. I refer to Istanbul as Constantinople here as my sources all use the latter name.

27. Avril, *Voyages en divers états,* 113.

28. Ibid., 50–51.

29. Fermanel, *Voyage d'Italie et du Levant,* 42, 23–24, 18.

30. Avril, *Voyages en divers états,* 342.

31. Poullet, *Nouvelles relations du Levant,* 35.

32. Herbelot de Molainville, *Bibliothèque orientale,* preface.

33. Cousin, "Eloge de Monsieur d'Herbelot," in Herbelot de Molainville, *Bibliothèque orientale.*

34. Herbelot de Molainville, *Bibliothèque orientale,* s.v., "Turc."

35. Ibid., preface.

36. Ibid., s.v., "Mohammed."

37. *Histoire de l'islam et des musulmans en France,* ed. Arkoun, 452.

38. Thévenot, *Relation d'un voyage fait au Levant;* Chardin, *Journal de voyage du chevalier Chardin;* Tavernier, *Six voyages.*

39. *Histoire de l'islam et des musulmans en France,* ed. Arkoun, 448, 450.

40. Ibid., 452.

41. Ibid.

42. The 1752 English translation of Boulainvilliers' *Histoire* and *Vie de Mahomet* begins with a translator's preface that notes: "the idea of Mahomet, which the Count of Boulainvilliers here presents us with, is so new and surprising, so different, and even contrary to all that we have hitherto been taught." It warns that this text, which paints Islam and its founder as exemplary models, would seem offensive to Christians. The translator qualifies Boulainvilliers' criticisms of Christianity, however, reminding the reader that the author had "lived in a country, where civil and ecclesiastic tyranny was combined in the glorious design of suppressing reason, truth and freedom." Boulainvilliers' arguments were not criticisms of Christianity, but rather justified condemnation of "the pollutions of Popery." "Translator's Preface," in Boulainvilliers, *Life of Mahomed*, i–iv.

43. Boulainvilliers, *Life of Mahomed*, 1–3.

44. Ibid., 20, 21, 22, 25, 26.

45. Ibid., 26, 28–30, 34.

46. Ibid., 12–13.

47. Ibid., 118–19, 131, 145–46, 147, 150

48. Ibid., 156–57, 160, 163.

49. Eon, *Commerce honorable.*

50. Eon, *Commerce honorable,* "Epître."

51. Ibid., 19, 20–22, 25. Eon described how for every ten to twelve French ships in active duty, there were fifty to sixty foreign ones; forty years back, the Dutch had only had four to five hundred vessels, but they now had over ten thousand.

52. Ibid., 49, 45–46.

53. Ibid., 50.

54. Ibid., 56, 57.

55. Ibid., 57, 59.

56. Ibid., 84, 95.

57. Ibid., 61, 97.

58. Sahlins, *Unnaturally French*, 72–74.

59. Ibid., 102–3, 9, 106, 180–84.

60. Ibid., 31–56.

61. The Crown did not single out aliens as the targets of such practices; the withdrawal and reinstitution of naturalized status in exchange for payment can be compared to the practices of Louis XIV's successors in regards to the selling of venality. See Bien, "Offices, Corps and a System of State Credit," 89–114.

62. Echinard and Temime, *Histoire des migrations à Marseille*, 51, 28.

63. The Corsican diaspora was such a large part of the Marseillais immigrant population in the sixteenth century that Braudel calls the city "demi corse." Echinard and Temime, *Histoire des migrations à Marseille,* vol. 1, chap. 2.

64. Charles VIII, letter, 10 May 1485, quoted in Echinard and Temime, *Histoire des migrations à Marseille,* 1: 33.

65. "Instructions données par le Conseil municipal de Marseille à ses envoyés auprès du Conseil royal de Provence," quoted in Echinard and Temime, *Histoire des migrations à Marseille.*

66. Ferrier, ambassador to Venice, letter to Charles IX, 18 April 1572, in Echinard and Temime, *Histoire des migrations à Marseille,* 1: 44.

67. Ibid., 45.

68. Rambert, *Histoire du commerce de Marseille,* 507–9.

69. Echinard and Temime, *Histoire des migrations à Marseille,* 1: 27. Historians have not been able to calculate the percentage of foreigners given the large number of *petites gens* and temporary guest workers who escaped documentation.

70. Colbert, "Edit sur la franchise du port de Marseille," in *Lettres, instructions et mémoires de Colbert,* 2: 796–98.

71. Collection A. Fiorentino, Musée de la Marine, Marseille.

72. Echinard and Temime, *Histoire des migrations à Marseille,* 1: 51.

73. McCabe, *Orientalism in Early Modern France,* 149.

74. Richelieu, "Edit du 24 juin 1635 organizant le commerce des arméniens," in Echinard and Temime, *Histoire des migrations à Marseille,* 1: 45.

75. Echinard and Temime, *Histoire des migrations à Marseille,* 1: 54.

76. Colbert to Oppède, 16 October 1671, quoted in *Lettres, instructions et mémoires de Colbert,* 2: clxxii.

77. Rambert, *Histoire du commerce de Marseille,* 498–504.

78. Anonymous *mémoire,* ACCM, G5.

79. Colbert to Rouillé, 8 September 1673, in *Lettres, instructions et mémoires de Colbert,* 2: 679.

80. Colbert to Morant, 20 November 1681, ibid., 722.

81. "Mémoire contre les Juifs residans à Marseille et de l'ordonnance du Roy qui ordre qu'ils sortirons de ladite ville" (2 May 1682), ACCM, G5, "Juifs à Marseille."

82. Seignelay scribbled a letter to his uncle Charles Colbert de Croissy, secretary of state for foreign affairs, calling on him to "expel the Jews from Marseille" (*Lettres, instructions et mémoires de Colbert,* 6: 159n4).

83. "Mémoire à Monseigneur le marquis de Seignelay ministre et secretaire d'Etat," ACCM, G5, "Juifs à Marseille."

84. Thomas-Alexandre Morant, letter, ACCM, G5.

85. "Extrait des registres du Conseil d'Etat" (Versailles, 15 February 1710), ACCM, G5.

86. "Declaration du Roy concernant le commerce des Soyes de Levant du 21 octobre 1687" (Paris, 1687), ACCM, J 1585.

87. Pontchartrain, quoted in Echinard and Temime, *Histoire des migrations à Marseille,* 1: 54.

88. "Chambre de Commerce à Monsigneur l'Intendant" (n.d.). ACCM, J 1585.

89. Rambert, *Histoire du commerce de Marseille,* 508.

90. "Declaration du Roy qui revoque et annulle les lettres de naturalité accordées aux étrangers" (5 February 1720) and "Declaration du Roy qui revoque et annulle les lettres de naturalité accordées aux Genois" (21 August 1718), ACCM, F 35.

91. "Ordonnance du Roy du juin 1726; aoust 1681, avril 1689, aoust 1725," ACCM, F 35.

92. Governor Alphonse de Fortia Forville de Pilles, letter to François Agneau et al., ACCM, G 6, "Religion prétendue réformée et Musulmans, 1685–1775."

93. "Ordonnance du Roy portent defenses à ses sujets nouveaux convertis, de passer dans les pays étrangers et aux refugiez de venire en France sans Sa permission" (Marseille, 1713), ACCM, G 6.

94. Seignelay, letter to Morant, 27 October 1685, quoted in Rambert, *Histoire du commerce de Marseille,* 502n3.

95. Colbert, letter to Intendant of the Galleys Brodart, 14 April 1680, in *Lettres, instructions et mémoires de Colbert,* 6: 130. The king would send "an ecclesiastic capable of instructing those who would like to place themselves in a state of knowing their own errors" to Marseille, Colbert wrote.

CHAPTER 4: PLAGUE, COMMERCE, AND CENTRALIZED DISEASE CONTROL IN EARLY MODERN FRANCE

1. Pestalozzi, *Avis de précaution contre la peste,* 40.

2. Tournefort, *Relation d'un voyage du Levant,* 470–71.

3. Gaudereau, *Relation des differentes espèces de peste,* 129–30, 133.

4. Paris, "Mémoire sur la peste," 10, bound in *Recueil de pièces relatifs à la peste qui sévit en Provence,* vol. 2.

5. G.-A. Olivier, *Voyage dans l'Empire Othoman, l'Egypte et la Perse.*

6. Stephen Tobriner, "Safety and Reconstruction of Noto after the Sicilian Earthquake of 1693," in *Dreadful Visitations,* ed. Johns, 51.

7. G. A. Starr, "Defoe and Disasters," in *Dreadful Visitations,* ed. Johns, 38.

8. Carla Hesse, in *Dreadful Visitations,* ed. Johns, 183.

9. Gordon, "Confrontations with the Plague," and "The City and the Plague"; Jones, "Plague and Its Metaphors," 97–127.

10. Nineteenth-century scientists determined how rats native to the Trans-Caucasian and Balkan steppes, Mongolia, and Kurdistan spread plague as far as the Arctic Circle and America. Accidental encounters between man and rat—not rodent migration—transmitted plague; travelers inadvertently carried rats and fleas from one location to another. Upon the rodents' deaths, fleas could survive a month within merchandise until they landed on human hosts. Plague decimated the human population through bubonic, pneumonic, or septicemic transmission. The most common, bubonic plague spread through the fleabite, attacking the body's lymphatic system. When fleas hibernated, plague could persist in pneumonic form; coughing transmitted bacilli from person to person. Septicaemic transmission involved fleabites that injected bacilli into the bloodstream. Without antibiotics, the fatality rate for victims of plague ran from 60 to 90 percent. Hudson, *Disease and Its Control,* 33.

11. Chicoyneau, "Relation succinte touchant les accidens de la Peste," in *Pièces historiques sur la peste de Marseille,* ed. Jauffret, 178.

12. Pestalozzi, *Avis de précaution contre la peste,* 40.

13. Harrison, *Disease and the Modern World,* 41.

14. Panzac, *Quarantaines et lazarets,* 58–59.

15. Panzac, *La peste dans l'empire Ottoman,* 192, 198, 360–61.

16. Panzac, *Quarantaines et lazarets,* 11.

17. Ibid.

18. Dols, *Black Death*, 88. The works of Arabic scholars were made available to Europeans by Gerard of Cremona (1114–87), among other translators, and Gentile di Foligno's fourteenth-century treatise on the plague explicitly drew upon works Avicenna and other Muslim writers. See Hamarneh, "Islamic Medicine and Its Impact," in id., *Health Sciences in Early Islam*, 169–87.

19. P.-J. Fabre, *Remèdes, curatifs et préservatifs*, 6–7.

20. Hamarneh, "A Brief Survey of Islamic Medicine," in id., *Health Sciences in Early Islam*, 40.

21. Vallant, *Consultation sur la maladie de Provence faite le vingt-uniéme novembre 1720*, 37–38.

22. Thucydides, *History of the Peloponnesian War*, 98–101.

23. Chicoyneau, *Notice sur les principales pestes*, 1, 2–4.

24. Bertrand, *Relation historique*, 5, 9.

25. Ibid., 298.

26. Pitton, *Histoire de la ville d'Aix*, 499.

27. *Dictionnaire de l'Académie française* (1694), s.v. "Peste."

28. Féraud, *Dictionnaire critique de la langue française*, 4.

29. Ibid., 1–2.

30. Though no complete inventory has been compiled in France, Colin Jones's research in the Bibliothèque nationale's *Catalogue des sciences médicales* and Jean-Noël Biraben's *Les hommes et la peste* reveal an extensive collection of early modern plague treatises. Jones traced 264 French and Latin texts written between 1500 and 1770. Two-thirds of these were published in the provinces.

31. Jones, "Plague and Its Metaphors," 104, 115.

32. Pestalozzi, *Dissertation sur les causes et la nature de la peste*.

33. Ibid.

34. Pestalozzi, *Avis de precaution contre la peste*, 34.

35. *Dictionnaire de l'Académie française* (1762), s.v. "Economie."

36. Pestalozzi, *Avis de precaution contre la peste*, 2–3.

37. Ibid., 5–7.

38. Chicoyneau, "Notice sur les principales pestes," in *Pièces historiques sur la peste de Marseille*, ed. Jauffret, 1,4.

39. Ibid., 2–4.

40. Chicoyneau, *Discours prononcé le 26 octobre de l'année 1722*, 59. Quoted in Gordon, "Confrontations with the Plague," 22.

41. Gordon, "Confrontations with the Plague," 22.

42. Chicoyneau, "Notice sur les principales pestes," 185, 188.

43. "Mémoire du Bureau de la santé de Marseille," ii, AdBdR, 200 E 7 FISM.

44. Panzac, *Quarantaines et lazarets*, 91–92.

45. Foucault, *Discipline and Punish*, 198–200.

46. Panzac, *Quarantaines et lazarets*, 33.

47. Letter in "Rapport sur les terrains du Lazaret, Marseille, le 18 juillet 1849," AMVM, DD 47.

48. "De par le Roy Comte de Provence," Vincennes, 25 August 1666. AMVM, DD 47.

49. Porter, *Blood and Guts*, 136.

50. Hildesheimer, *Bureau de la santé de Marseille*, 43.

51. Ibid., 37.

52. Panzac, *Quarantaines et lazarets*, 35.

53. Ibid., 173.

54. Howard, *Histoire des principaux lazarets*, 3.

55. Ibid., 6.

56. J.-B. Bertrand, *Historical Relation*, 30.

57. *Encyclopédie, ou dictionnaire raisonné*, s.v. "Lazaret."

58. *The Confessions of Jean Jacques Rousseau*, bk. 7, www.gutenberg.org/files/3913/3913.txt (accessed 2 July 2010).

59. Marchebeus, *Voyage de Paris à Constantinople par bateau à vapeur*, 217–20.

60. Hildesheimer, *Bureau de la santé*, 213.

61. "Mémoire sur les infirmeries" in Chicoyneau, *Traité des causes*, 177–78; Panzac, *Quarantaines et lazarets*, 41.

62. "Instruction pour les intendants de la santé" in Panzac, *Quarantaines et lazarets*, 134.

63. *Mémoire instructif sur ce qui doit être observé dans les villes*, 4.

64. Bertrand, *Historical Relation*, 31–33.

65. Mémoire sur les infirmeries" in Chicoyneau, *Traité des causes*, 175–76.

66. "Mémoire sur le Bureau de la santé de Marseille et sur les règles qu'on y observe" (1730), AdBdR, 200 E 7 FISM.

67. Guys, *Marseille ancienne et moderne*, 90–91.

68. Panzac, *Quarantaines et lazarets*, 33.

69. "A monseigneur l'intendant de justice" and the intendant's reply, 22 June 1688, AdBdR, 200 E 1 FISM.

70. "De par le Roy, Comte de Provence," 6 August 1689, AdBdR, 200 E 1 FISM.

71. Lebret, "Ordonnance," 22 March 1690, AdBdR, 200 E 1 FISM.

72. "De par le Roy," 31 July 1709, AdBdR, 200 E 1 FISM.

73. "Ordonnance du Roi portent defenses aux batimens qui ne sont pas en quarantaine d'entrer dans la reserve du Bureau de la santé," 9 January 1718, AdBdR, 200 E 1 FISM.

74. Memorandum of October 1721 quoted in Hildesheimer, *Bureau de la santé de Marseille*, 156–57. See also AdBdR, 200 E 166 FISM.

75. "Arrêt du Conseil du 7 octobre, 1694," AdBdR, 200 E 1 FISM.

76. Hildesheimer, *Bureau de la santé*, 164, 157. See also AdBdR, 200 E 287 FISM.

77. Hildesheimer, *Bureau de la santé*, 156–58.

78. Letter, 12 November 1770, AdBdR, 200 E 290 FISM and Hildesheimer, *Bureau de la santé*, 156–58.

79. "Mémoire pour le Bureau de la santé" (1721), bound in "Registres: Correspondence générale. Copies de lettres addressées aux ministres et à divers, 1713–1726," AdBdR, 200 E 166.

80. Lucenet, *Grandes pestes en France*, 226, 228.

81. Croissante, *Journal abregé*, 5.

82. Bertrand, *Historical Relation*, 63–64.

83. Bureau de la santé, Marseille, letter to health authorities, République de Genève, 19 March 1721, Archivio di stato di Venezia, Provveditori alla sanità, 651.

84. Ibid.

85. The Archivio di stato di Venezia, Provveditori alla sanità, 650–51, preserves series of letters sent from the Toulon and Marseillais health bureaux to Geneva, Milan, Venice, and Genoa. Particularly complete are the weekly letters from Marseille to Geneva. The series also contains letters sent by Italian consuls in Marseille to their home offices in Milan, Venice, and Genoa.

86. Pouliquen, *Oculiste*, 55.

87. Sturgill, *Claude Le Blanc*, 161, 163. Half of Le Blanc's correspondence from August 1720 to March 1723 dealt with his war against plague.

88. "Arrêt du Conseil d'Etat du Roi, au sujet de la maladie contagieuse de la ville de Marseille," 14 September 1720, in *Pièces historiques sur la peste de Marseille*, ed. Jauffret, 147–57.

89. "Décisions du Conseil de la santé," in Chicoyneau, *Traité des causes*, 32.

90. "Instruction générale pour exécuter les premieres décisions du Conseil de santé," in Chicoyneau, *Traité des causes*, 117–19.

91. "Décisions du Conseil de la santé," in Chicoyneau, *Traité des causes*, 95.

92. Sturgill, *Claude Le Blanc*, 162.

93. "Instruction générale pour exécuter les premieres décisions du Conseil de santé," in Chicoyneau, *Traité des causes*, 69, 75.

94. Ibid., 72–73.

95. Ibid., 75.

96. Ibid., 89.

97. Lucenet, *Grandes pestes en France*, 226, 228.

CHAPTER 5: VIRTUE WITHOUT COMMERCE

1. Bertrand, *Historical Relation*, 3, 85.

2. Gordon, "The City and the Plague," 84.

3. Bertrand, *Historical Relation*, 5.

4. Boccaccio, *Decameron*, "Introduction."

5. Boccaccio, quoted in Hudson, *Disease and Its Control*, 37.

6. Defoe, *Journal of the Plague Year*, 12–13.

7. Gabriel, *Proselite charitable*, in Jones, "Plague and Its Metaphors," 126.

8. "Ordres à observer pour empêcher que la peste ne se communique."

9. Ibid., 10.

10. Ibid., 13–14, 15, 11.

11. "Règlements de police et remèdes contre la peste," bound in *Recueil de pieces relatives à la peste qui sévit en Provence*, 13–14, 16–17.

12. "Ordres à observer pour empêcher que la peste ne se communique," 16.

13. Ranchin, *Traité politique et médical de la peste*, 6, 60.

14. Maurice de Toulon, *Capucin charitable,* preface. Maurice provided service in southern France and northern Italy in the plagues of 1650, 1657, and 1665. His first publication, *Trattato politico da pratticarsi nei tempi de peste* was dedicated to the Genoese Senate. The *Capucin charitable* was published in 1662, 1668, and 1720. Dubois, *Homme de peste.*

15. Maurice de Toulon, *Capucin charitable,* 38, 66–76.

16. Ibid., 31.

17. Valeriolle, *Ordre politique,* 214, 217.

18. Ranchin, *Traité nouveau,* 77.

19. Gabriel, *Proselite charitable,* in Jones, "Plague and Its Metaphors," 115.

20. Ibid., 169.

21. Villiers, *Peste de 1720–1721,* 19.

22. "Remonstrance du parlement de Provence sur les désordres", 3.

23. "Ordres donnez par Messieurs les consuls gouverneurs de Marseille," in *Arrêt et règlement général fait . . . pour la conservation de la santé publique,* 1–8.

24. *Arrêt et réglement général fait . . . pour la conservation de la santé publique,* 3, 4, 6, 16, 35–40 (articles 110–34).

25. "Extrait des registres de parlement tenant la chambre des vacations, du septième août 1720," AdBdR, C 908.

26. "Extrait des registres . . . , du huitième août 1720," AdBdR, C 908.

27. "Note des divers arrêts et réglemens rendus et publiés par le parlement," 29, ACM, BB1.

28. Croissante, *Journal abregé,* 10–12.

29. "Mémoire sur quelques abus qui se commettent," in Chicoyneau, *Traité des causes,* 204.

30. Croissante, *Journal abregé,* 10, 22.

31. "Declaration du Roy, gouvernant les procés criminals, qu'il s'agira d'instruire dans les villes et lieux infectés du mal contagieux (1720), AMVM, GG 426.

32. Ibid.

33. "Declaration du Roy . . . du 11 novembre 1721," 3, ACM, GG 426.

34. Croissante, *Journal abregé,* 42.

35. Valeriolle, *Ordre politique,* 3–6.

36. Croissante, *Journal abregé,* 42–43.

37. Ibid., 21, 66, 43.

38. Bertrand, *Historical Relation,* 176.

39. *Poëme héroïque sur la peste.*

40. Troy, *La peste dans la ville de Marseille en 1720* (1723), AMVM, 11 Fi 12.

41. Autran, *Eloge historique du chevalier Roze.*

42. *Poëme héroïque sur la peste.*

43. Ordinance, *De par le Roy,* 20 January 1721, no. 148, AMVM, FF.

44. Bertrand, *Historical Relation,* 240–43.

45. The Regent called for the presence of three lawyers in these procedures, but none of the dossiers show signs of any such presence.

46. "Dossier Limoge, Fidelle, Rabeau et Boulle–vol nocturne," AMVM, FF.

47. "Dossier Laurens Audrie–armes prohibées,"AMVM, FF.

48. Bertrand, *Historical Relation*, 240–43.

49. Ordinance of 22 March 1721, AMVM, FF 324.

50. Langeron, Ordinance, *De par le Roy*, 1 May 1721, no. 163, AMVM, FF.

51. Bertrand, *Historical Relation*, 240–45.

52. "Deliberation du Bureau de la Maison du refuge," AMVM, FF 238.

53. "Police locale, prostitution et débauche: dénonces et jugements, 1721–1724," AMVM FF 239.

54. Belsunce, "Mandement de Mgr d'évêque de Marseille pour l'ouverture des églises," in *Pièces historiques sur la peste de Marseille*, ed. Jauffret, 327–35.

55. "Lettres . . . pour la punition des femmes et filles d'une débauche publique," 4 May 1691, AMVM, FF 238.

56. Ibid., 7.

57. AMVM, FF 239.

58. "A Monsieur le commandant et messieurs les échevins, commissaires du Roy, lieutenants généraux de police" (1721), AMVM, FF 239.

59. "Conclusions diffinitives de M. du Procureur du Roy," 26 March 1721, AMVM, FF 239.

60. Croissante, *Journal abregé*, 33.

61. Terran, *Discours*, 7, 27–28.

62. Ibid., 38.

63. Because many of the trial documents from the plague are damaged by fire or inaccessible, I was unable to count the number of rape trials. The majority of the cases I found are from November 1720 on. There are no dossiers for rape in the first three months of plague.

64. "Dossier Honoré Taneron," summary (1721), AMVM, GG 428.

65."Extrait des registres du greffe de la police," 2 July 1721, AMVM, GG 428.

66. "Interrogations . . . de Honoré Taneron," 19 July 1721, AMVM, GG 428.

67. "Nous ordonnons . . . conclusions diffinitives," 14 July 1721, ACM, GG 428.

68. Langeron, "Mémoire au sujet d'une disinfection," in Chicoyneau, *Traité des causes*, 208.

69. "Mémoire dressé par Messieurs les échevins, et députés de la Chambre du Commerce," in Chicoyneau, *Traité des causes*, 220–22.

70. Ibid., 225–27.

71. Quoted in Carrière, Courdurié, and Rebuffat, *Marseille ville morte*, 251.

72. Ibid., 255.

73. Croissante, *Journal abregé*, 50.

74. On 21 May 1720, the same week that plague arrived in Marseille, Law reduced the value of government banknotes by 20 percent, making them "legally worth less than their stated value in *livres*." Hamilton, "Prices and Wages at Paris Under John Law's System," 42–70; Kaiser, "Money, Despotism and Public Opinion."

75. Echevins de Marseille, letter, "A Mgr Law conseiller d'Etat du 3 novembre 1720," AMVM, BB 268.

76. "Mémoire au sujet d'une disinfection générale," in Chicoyneau, *Traité des causes*, 208–09.

77. "Mémoire sur les infirmaries," in Chicoyneau, *Traité des causes*, 181.

78. Ibid., 187, 181.

79. Ibid., 200–201; 192–93.

80. "Mémoire sur quelques abus qui se commettent," in Chicoyneau, *Traité des causes*, 204–5.

81. France, Gouvernement de Marseille, *Acte déclaratif de l'état présent de la santé de la ville de Marseille et de la désinfection générale que y a été faite par ordre du Roi.*

82. *De par le Roy. Le Bailly de Langeron, lieutenant général des armées du Roy, Chef d'escadre de ses galères, commandant pour sa majesté dans la ville de Marseille, et Mrs. Les Echevins, Lieutenants généraux de police de Ladite ville . . . 17 août 1723.*

83. "Remonstrance du parlement de Provence sur les desordres . . ." 11, 3, 9, ACM, BB1.

84. Ibid., 2–5.

85. Ibid., 16, 18, 13.

86. Ibid., 9, 12–14.

87. Ibid.,13–4. Langeron did, on 8 November 1720, impose rates on goods without the knowledge or participation of the parlement.

88. Michel Foucault analyzed the draconian measures taken in plague contexts within broader studies on the development of repressive mechanisms of power in the modern period. See Chapter 4 and Foucault, *Discipline and Punish*, 195–200.

89. Harrison, *Disease and the Modern World*, 47; Paul Slack, "The Response to Plague in Early Modern England: Public Policies and Their Consequences," in *Famine, Disease and Social Order*, ed. Walter and Schofield, 167–87.

90. Baehrel, "Epidémie et terreur," 137.

CHAPTER 6: CIVIC RELIGIOSITY AND RELIGIOUS CITIZENSHIP IN PLAGUE-STRICKEN MARSEILLE

1. Belsunce, "Mandement de Mgr l'évêque de Marseille, sur la desolation," in *Pièces historiques sur la peste de Marseille*, ed. Jauffret, 169.

2. Jacques de Forbin de Janson, "Mandement de Mr. l'Archevêque d'Arles," in *Pièces historiques sur la peste de Marseille*, ed. Jauffret, 158–62.

3. Belsunce, letter to the abbé de Gay, 4 August 1720," in *Correspondences*, 146–47.

4. Belsunce, "Ordonnance de Mr. l'évêque de Marseille, sur la desolation," in *Pièces historiques sur la peste de Marseille*, ed. Jauffret, 135. Also archbishop of Arles, letter to Mgr Languet, 26 September 1720, in Ardoin, *Jansénisme en Basse-Provence*, 186.

5. For the religious interpretation of disease beyond France, see Greenspan, "Religious Contagion in Mid-Seventeenth Century England," in *Imagining Contagion*, ed. Carlin, 212–27.

6. *Dictionnaire de l'Académie française*, eds. 4, 5, 6, and 8 (1762, 1798, 1832–35, and 1932–35 respectively), s.v. "Contagion." Only in the 8th ed. (1932–35) was "plague" dropped as a definition of "contagion."

7. Van Kley, *Religious Origins of the French Revolution*, 34.

8. Raymond Jonas traces the history of the cult, and shows how the Sacred Heart became "a Christian patriotic alternative to the idealized Republic" after the Old Regime. Jonas, *France and the Cult of the Sacred Heart*, 3.

9. Habermas's analysis of a bourgeois public sphere, a collection of private individuals come together as a public, has served as a springboard for historians studying the political culture of the eighteenth century. See Habermas, *Structural Transformation of the Public Sphere*; Baker, *Inventing the French Revolution*; *Habermas and the Public Sphere*, ed. Calhoun. For more on "public," see Chartier, *Cultural Origins of the French Revolution*; Goodman, *Republic of Letters*; Haine, *World of the Paris Café*; Eisenstein, *Printing Press*; Melton, *Rise of the Public*.

10. "French politics broke out of the absolutist mold" through the 1750s debates over the refusal of sacraments, the 1760s discussions over grain trade, and the Maupeou coup, Keith Michael Baker argues. See Baker, *Inventing the French Revolution*, 170.

11. As Thomas Kaiser has shown, writers became aware of the power of "public opinion," and "public judgment" as early as the late seventeenth century; they imagined the "Public" as the ideal tribunal that "rarely judged incorrectly in the political sphere when making assessments of . . . generals, magistrates, or government ministers." See Kaiser, "Rhetoric in the Service of the King," 191, and "Abbé de Saint-Pierre," 618–43.

12. See, e.g., Horrox, *Black Death*; Aberth, *Black Death*.

13. Biraben attributes this hysteria to the fact that Jews in the Dauphiné and Provence were suspected of having easy access to poisons because many worked as retail merchants, apothecaries, and grocers. Biraben, *Les hommes et la peste*, 58–59.

14. Moote and Moote, *Great Plague*.

15. Naphy, *Plagues, Poisons and Potions*; Closson, "The Devil's Curses," in Carlin, ed. *Imagining Contagion*, 63–77.

16. "Note des divers Arrêts et Règlements rendus et publiés par le Parlement de Provence, relativement à la Peste en 1720," in *Pièces historiques sur la peste de Marseille*, ed. Jauffret, 23–38.

17. Burns and Izbicki, *Conciliarism and Papalism*, viii.

18. Van Kley, *Religious Origins of the French Revolution*, 34.

19. Quoted in ibid., 37.

20. Burns and Isbicki, *Conciliarism and Papalism*, x.

21. Cornette, *Histoire de la France*, 40.

22. Quesnel, *Réflexions sur les cent et une propositions*, 45.

23. Languet de Gergy, bishop of Soissons, in Van Kley, *Religious Origins of the French Revolution*, 84–85.

24. Cornette, *Histoire de la France*, 39.

25. Le Gros, *Abrégé chronologique*, 34.

26. Clement XI, *Constitution Unigenitus*, prop. 79, p. 28; prop. 92, p. 33.

27. Le Gros, *Abrégé chronologique*, 33, 35.

28. These included the declaration of 1672 against parlementary remonstrance, the Gallican declaration of 1682, the edict of 1695 that extended episcopal authority over priests, the edict of Fontainebleau, and *Unigenitus* in 1713. See further, Van Kley, *Religious Origins of the French Revolution*.

29. Ardoin, *Jansenisme en Basse-Provence*, 130; Busquet, *Histoire de la Provence*, 302.

30. *La politique des Jésuites demasquée*, 7, 9, 33–34.

31. Ibid., 146.

32. Ibid., 77, 145.

33. *Lettre à Monseigneur l'évêque de Marseille*, 5, 17.

34. Born in Toulouse in 1680, La Borde entered the Oratory in 1699 and became chair of philosophy at Vendôme and director of the seminary at St. Magloire. His works include *Lettre au cardinal de Noailles touchant les artifices et intrigues du P. Tellier et quelques autres jésuites contre Son Eminence* (1711); *Examen de la constitution Unigenitus selon la méthode des géomètres* (1714); *Du témoignage de la verité dans l'Eglise* (1714); and the posthumously published *Principes sur l'essence, la distinction et les limites des deux puissances, spirituelle et temporelle* (1753). During the plague, he criticized Belsunce for denouncing the Oratory and organized conferences attended by "persons of all ranks," urging Catholics to serve in a "tribunal" to cleanse the Church of error. Michaud, *Biographie universelle*, 22: 284–86.

35. La Borde, *Principes sur l'essence*, 86.

36. La Borde, *Témoignage*, 2: 16.

37. Van Kley, *Religious Origins of the French Revolution*, 78.

38. La Borde, *Témoignage*, 2: 20–21.

39. Ibid., 1: 79, 25.

40. Ibid., 2: 91–92, 25, 74.

41. Ibid., 129–31, 31.

42. *Justification des PP. de l'Oratoire*, 7.

43. Ardoin, *Jansénisme en Basse-Provence*, 142.

44. Clement XI, *Constitution Unigenitus*, 1–3.

45. Then the youngest bishop in France, La Tour expressed his hatred for Jansenists violently. He condemned a large number to the galleys, and "he took his fist to the throat of Monsieur the archbishop of Narbonne claiming that he was led by the hand of Cardinal de Noailles." "Avertissement sur le lettre de Monsieur l'évêque d'Apt," in Foresta, *Lettre de Monsieur l'évêque d'Apt*, 46.

46. Belsunce, letter to Pope Clement XI, in *Correspondences*, 38–39.

47. Belsunce, "Requête en cassation," in *Correspondences*, 104.

48. "Lettre pastorale de Monseigneur l'évêque d'Apt supprimée par Arrêt du Parlement d'Aix, du 15 Juin 1716," in Foresta, *Lettre de Monsieur l'évêque d'Apt*, 46–47.

49. On 25 October 1717, the parlement in Aix registered the declaration to reestablish religious tranquility as law (Ardoin, *Jansénisme en Basse-Provence*, 142). They deemed ultramontane arguments "pernicious to the repose of the Church and the tranquility of the state." The parlement issued numerous *arrêts* against Foresta and Belsunce; in 1718, it sentenced de Foresta and Belsunces's mandates against the Jansenists to be "lacerated and burned" (*Arrest de la Cour de Parlement de Provence . . . du 20 decembre 1718 dans la Grand Chambre*,159, 170).

50. Revenues from the 17, 18, 19, 21 and 22 of January 1719. See *Arrest de la Cour de Parlement de Provence . . . du 20 decembre 1718 dans la Grand Chambre*, 159–70.

51. Belsunce, "Requête en cassation," in *Correspondences*, 103–18.

52. Belsunce, letter to Mgr Alamanno Salviati, 24 May 1716, in *Correspondences*, 59–60.

53. Belsunce, "Requête en cassation," in *Correspondences*, 113.

54. Belsunce, letter to Salviati cited n. 52 above.

55. Pope Clement XI, letter to Belsunce, December 1717, in Belsunce, *Correspondences,* 470.

56. Parlement de Provence, *Arrest du Parlement de Provence, 21 Octobre 1718.* Also Ardoin, *Jansénisme en Basse-Provence,* chap. 5, 153–84.

57. Belsunce, *Statuts synodaux,* 5.

58. Ibid., 3, 15, 146, 7–9, 146.

59. Ibid., 30, 10–11,13.

60. Belsunce, "Ordonnance de Mgr l'évêque de Marseille sur les immodesties," in *Statuts synodaux,* 147.

61. Ibid., 143–50. Belsunce also appealed to the Crown to help curb sexual excess. He cited as a precedent Henri II's order punishing "women who have conceived children through dishonest means . . . disguised their pregnancies . . . and delivered their children without the sacrament of Baptism." In 1708, following the bishop's wish, Louis XIV reactivated this edict. See France, Acte Royal, *Déclaration . . . qui ordonne que l'édit du Roy Henri II . . . de février 1556 contre les femmes.* This declaration deemed that if children born in secret died without baptism, the mothers would be presumed guilty of murder.

62. Ibid., 73–74.

63. Jonas, *France and the Cult of the Sacred Heart,* 1–7.

64. Martin, *Jesuit Mind,* 74–75; Rose Marie San Juan, "Corruptible Bodies and Contaminating Technologies," in *Imagining Contagion,* ed. Carlin, 107–23.

65. Martin, *Jesuit Mind,* 199. Ignatius Loyola, the father of the Society of Jesus, had written in his "Guidelines for Discernment of Spirits" appended to his *Spiritual Exercises* that the devil was comparable to women.

66. Belsunce, "Mandement de Mgr l'évêque de Marseille pour l'ouverture des églises," in *Pièces historiques sur la peste de Marseille,* ed. Jauffret, 327–335.

67. Carrière, Courdurié, and Rebuffat, *Marseille ville morte,* 199.

68. Belsunce, "Mandement de Mgr l'évêque de Marseille, sur la desolation," in *Pièces historiques sur la peste de Marseille,* ed. Jauffret, 168–69.

69. Belsunce, letter to the abbé de Gay, in *Correspondences,* 155.

70. Belsunce, *Mandement, 28 octobre 1720.*

71. Jonas, *France and the Cult of the Sacred Heart,* 16–17, 14.

72. The Sacred Heart, Alacoque asserted, "wants to reign in his palace, to be painted on his standards, and engraved on his arms, in order to render them victorious over their enemies" (ibid., 25).

73. Ardoin, *Jansénisme en Basse-Provence,* 212.

74. *Vie de la très honorée soeur Anne Magdelaine Rémuzat,* 15.

75. Rémuzet reported "the same pain one feels when fire touches the body, with this difference—the pain was accompanied by sweet feelings I cannot describe" (Jonas, *France and the Cult of the Sacred Heart,* 37).

76. Rémuzat's daily routine involved fifteen minutes of "cruelty against herself"; she cut the letters J-E-S-U-S on her chest and wore bracelets and belts studded with metal thorns (ibid., 37–39).

77. *Vie de la très honorée soeur Anne Magdelaine Rémuzat,* 131–33.

78. Ibid., 139.

79. Belsunce, "Mandement de Mgr l'évêque de Marseille, sur la desolation," in *Pièces historiques sur la peste de Marseille*, ed. Jauffret, 170–71.

80. Belsunce, letter to Mgr Languet, in *Correspondences*, 317–21.

81. Gordon, "The City and the Plague," 83–84.

82. Ardoin, *Jansénisme en Basse-Provence*, 228–29.

83. Van Kley, *Religious Origins of the French Revolution*, 51.

84. Forrestal, *Fathers, Pastors and Kings*, 182–84, 186.

85. Goujon, *Journal du sieur Goujon, maître d'hôtel de Mgr de Belsunce*, 7; Belsunce, Mandement de Mgr l'évêque de Marseille pour l'ouverture des églises, in *Pièces historiques sur la peste de Marseille*, ed. Jauffret, 334–35.

86. Abbé de Gay, letter to the cardinal–secretary of state, in Belsunce, *Correspondences*, 152.

87. Ibid., 26, 36.

88. These included "42 Capuchins, 21 Jesuits, 32 Observationalists, 29 Recolets, more than 10 Carmelites, 22 reformed Augustinians, the Trinitarians, the Religious of Mercy, the Dominicans, the Grand Augustinians." Croissante, *Journal abregé*, 20–21, 36.

89. Belsunce, letter to the abbé de Gay, in *Correspondences*, 154–56.

90. "Each day since the arrival of the plague, I have repeatedly passed in front of the door of the Fathers of the Oratory, which I have always seen well shut," Belsunce wrote. "I have never seen a single person . . . priests, secondaries, confessors, in the city or the neighborhoods." "Langeron also found the House of the Oratory abandoned," he continued, "and you know that Monsieur de Langeron is a man of honor." Belsunce, "Réponse de Mgr de Belsunce à Madame de XXX," in *Correspondences*, 207–8, 210–11.

91. Ibid., 218.

92. Decormis and Saurin, *Ancien barreau*, 156.

93. In Ciotat, the Superior of the Oratory argued that Belsunce's persecution of the Jansenists, "ambitious zeal, falsehood and self-interest" had invited God's fury in the form of plague. Ibid., 30, 34–35, 44–45, 68–69. Also Belsunce, letter to the abbé de Gay, in *Correspondences*, 156.

94. Montesquieu, *Lettres persanes*, 1.

95. *Justification des PP. de l'Oratoire*, 3–4.

96. Ibid., 3–4.

97. Ibid., 6.

98. Ibid., 13, 7.

99. Ibid., 13–14.

100. Ibid., 25, 141, 12.

101. La Borde, *Lettre d'un gentilhomme*, 66, 143.

102. Ibid., 18.

103. Echevins Dieude and Audimar in *Justification des PP. de l'Oratoire*, 30.

CHAPTER 7: POSTMORTEM

1. Eldem, *French Trade in Istanbul*, 14–15.

2. Panzac, *Commerce et navigation dans l'empire Ottoman*, 200–201.

3. Eldem, *French Trade in Istanbul*, 23–24. Ottoman trade with Marseille slowly declined in the nineteenth century.

4. Daniel Roche, Martin Fitzpatrick, and Maxine Berg, among others, have demonstrated how French commercial expansion in the Enlightenment transformed cityscapes, gardens, and the living spaces of the urban elite. See Roche, *France in the Enlightenment*; Berg, *Consumers and Luxury*; *Luxury in the Eighteenth-Century*, ed. Berg; Fitzpatrick, *Enlightenment World*.

5. Giraud in Carrière, *Négociant marseillais*, 201–3, 205. Some like Bishop Belsunce, were critical of immigration, claiming that Protestants and heretic immigrants threatened the city: "Since the plague," he complained, "the Huguenots have flooded Marseille. . . . They take over all commerce here." The idea that the majority of immigrants were Protestant was a miscalculation. As Carrière corrects, Languedocians formed only a small minority of immigrants, and few of them were Protestant.

6. Discussion of establishing an academy in Marseille began in 1715, but the plague postponed plans. After the epidemic, the governor of Provence, the maréchal de Villars, was named "protector" of the Marseille Académie in 1726. Boudin, *Histoire de Marseille*, 473.

7. Roche, *Siècle des lumières en province*, 40, 242.

8. Letter from royal delegate to Crown, 12 January 1726, Archive de l'académie, Marseille, portefeuille I.

9. Scott, *Terror and Repression*, 6.

10. *Après le discours de Mr. le directeur*, in *Recueil de plusiers pièces de poesies*, 10.

11. Olivier, "Dissertation historique," in *Recueil de plusiers pièces de poesies présentées à l'académie de Marseille*, 57, 59–60.

12. Romieu, *Discours*, 104; also *Académie de Marseille*, 21.

13. Michaud, *Biographie universelle*, 20: 293.

14. Guys, *Marseille ancienne et moderne*, 1–2, 5–6, 8, 10–11.

15. Ibid. 28–30, 44–45.

16. Ibid., 195–96.

17. Ibid., 207, 215–16, 222–23, 204.

18. Ibid., 230, 204, 200, 225.

19. Liquier, *Discours qui a remporté le prix de l'Académie de Marseille*, 5–6, 19, 23–27.

20."Mémoire présenté au nom de la noblesse de Marseille, qui demande d'être réintegrée dans l'administration municipale de cette ville" (Paris, 1759), 15, AdBdR, C3651.

21. "Requette presentée au Roy par la noblesse de Marseille de Mars 1716," 34–40, AdBdR, C3651.

22. "Mémoire pour la ville de Marseille," AN, Paris, H 1239, in Carrière, *Négociants marseillais*, 214–15.

23. Ibid., 2.

24. "Mémoire" cited n. 20 above, 12–13 15.

25. "Mémoire . . . au sujet du rétablissement de la noblesse dans la premiere place de l'Administration municipale" (Paris, 1759), 8, 10, AdBdR, C3651.

26. Ibid., 42, 12.

27. Ibid.

28. Ibid.,13.
29. Ibid., 6.
30. Ibid., 11.
31. Ibid., 17, 46.
32. Ibid., 24.
33. *Observations des négociants de Marseille*, 4, 8–12, 18, 19, 33.
34. Carrière, *Négociants marseillais*, 214–215.
35. Ramsay, *New Cyropaedia*, 3–4, 12.
36. Ibid., 56, 70, 73, 75.
37. Ibid., 94, 99, 111, 113–23.
38. Ibid., 115, 117.
39. Ibid., 6–10.
40. Boureau-Deslandes, *Essay on Maritime Power and Commerce*, ix, 2, 3, 5–10.
41. Ibid., 10–15, 23, 24–26.
42. Ibid., 34–35.
43. Ibid., 151–61, 10–15.
44. Ibid., 48–50, 58, 62, 74, 93, 75, 83–84.
45. Ibid., 100, 101, 122, 126, 145–49.
46. Ibid., 97–99.
47. Boureau-Deslandes, *Lettre sur le luxe*, Avertissement, 1.
48. Boureau-Deslandes cited historical examples to show how luxury destroyed strong republics. Unlike the argument he presented in his *Essai*, what emerges here is a darker interpretation of Greek and Roman history, where virtues expired as a result of luxury. He described how Greece became wealthier but fell into utter disarray after the death of Alexander the Great. Republics were "disfigured," laws deteriorated, and universities fell into intellectual decay. Ibid., 1–12, 16, 18–20, 25. See also Boureau-Deslandes, *Lettre sur le luxe, "Fragmens d'un auteur grec . . ."* 56–67.
49. Jay Smith, *Nobility Reimagined*, 6, 8.

Bibliography

ARCHIVAL SOURCES

Archives de la Chambre de commerce de Marseille (ACCM)

SÉRIE A

1 Actes constitutifs de la Chambre de commerce de Marseille

15 Conseil de commerce et Bureau du commerce à Paris, 1664–1790

17 Conseil de commerce, Dossier Joseph Fabre

SÉRIE B

152 Instructions données à M. Fabre nommé en 1700 député du commerce

153 Lettres de Joseph Fabre, député au Conseil de commerce, janvier–juin 1701

154 Lettres de Joseph Fabre, député au Conseil de commerce, juillet–dec. 1701

155 Lettres de Joseph Fabre, député au Conseil de commerce, janvier–juin 1702

156 Lettres de Joseph Fabre, député au Conseil de commerce, juillet–dec. 1702

157 Lettres de Joseph Fabre, député au Conseil de commerce, janvier–nov. 1703

1487 Histoire du Massacre des Turcs à Marseille en 1620

SÉRIE C

88 Droit du cottimo, 1669–1727

SÉRIE D

23 Port du Marseille: Franchise de la ville et du port, 1664–1792

SÉRIE F

35 Lettres de naturalité, 1696–1758

SÉRIE G

5 Affaires religieuses: Juifs à Marseille et à Aix, et Protection des Juifs en Levant, 1672–1773

5 Affaires religieuses: Protestants et Musulmans, 1685–1775

6 Instruction publique, 1666–1792

SÉRIE H

6 Commerce de Marseille: Généralités, 1659–1791

8 Commerce des étrangers à Marseille, 1613–1791

SÉRIE J

46 Enfants de langue, ou Jeunes de langue: Institution, affaires générales, 1669–1789

47 Enfants de langue, ou Jeunes de langue: Avis, 1673–1717

55 Enfants de langue, ou Jeunes de langue: Contestation avec les Capucins de Constantinople au sujet des comptes de la pension des enfants de langue, 1669–91

1585 Commerce des étrangers, 1622–1724

1586 Commerce des Juifs, 1719–93

Archives Départementales des Bouches Du Rhône, Marseille (AdBdr)

SÉRIE 200E FONDS INTENDANCE SANITAIRE DE MARSEILLE (FISM)

1 Lois, ordonnances, arrêts, décrets, édits

7 Mémoires sur l'organisation du Bureau de la santé et réglements de l'Intendance sanitaire de Marseille

8 Liste des intendants de la santé

27 Délibérations et actes notables

35–36 Délibérations, 1720–23

166 Registres: Correspondence générale: copies de lettres addressées aux ministres et à divers, 1713–26

290 Lettres

479 Déclarations faites par les capitaines de bâtiments à leur arrivée

SÉRIE C

908 Extrait des registres

3651 Mémoires de la noblesse de Marseille

Archives municipales de la ville De Marseille (AMVM)

SÉRIE BB CORRESPONDENCE GÉNÉRALE DES OFFICIERS MUNICIPAUX

1 Ordinances

251D CORRESPONDENCE DES ÉCHEVINS, 1660–69

268 Correspondence des échevins

SÉRIE DD TRAVAUX PUBLICS

47 Lazaret de Marseille

94 Agrandissement de Marseille

152 Agrandissement de Marseille, arrêts, lettres patentes, mémoires

153 Agrandissement de Marseille, arrêts, lettres patentes, mémoires

155 Grand registre de l'agrandissement

156 Déliberations du Bureau de l'agrandissement

SÉRIE FF POLICE ET JUSTICE

225 Police locale, Prostitution et débauche, réglements, 1682–1776

227 Police locale, Prostitution et débauche, dénonces et jugements 1671–86

228 Police locale, Prostitution et débauche, dénonces et jugements 1688

238 Police locale, Prostitution et débauche, dénonces et jugements 1713–20

239 Police locale, Prostitution et dbauche, dénonces et jugements 1721–24

324 Procédures, 1720

325 Procédures, 1721

SÈRIE GG

313 Lettres patentes portent pouvoir aux consuls de Marseille d'exercer la justice souveraine pendant et durant la contagion

426 Procédures

428 Procédures de rapt et viol

SÉRIE 11FI, COLLECTION DES ESTAMPES

Archivio di Stato di Venezia

Provveditori alla sanità, 650–51, Editto in materia di sanità

PRINTED PRIMARY SOURCES

Advis au roy contenans les principales causes de la ruine du commerce de Marseille avec les moyens d'y remédier. 1664.

Aillaud, M. l'abbé. *De l'ancienneté de Marseille: Dissertation lue dans l'assemblée publique de l'Académie des Belles Lettres de Marseille.* Marseille: Brebion, 1764.

Avril, Philippe, Père. *Voyages en divers états d'Afrique et d'Asie, entrepris pour découvrir un chemin à la Chine.* Paris: Claude Barbin, Jean Boudot, George & Louis Josse, 1692.

Beaufort, Jehan de. *Traité et préservation de peste à la ville d'Aix.* Aix-en-Provence: Thomas & Guillaume Maillou, 1580.

Belsunce, Henri-François-Xavier de. *Correspondences, composées de lettres et documents en partie inédits.* Edited by Louis-Antoine Porrentruy. Marseille: J. & X. Aschero, 1911.

———. *Mandement, 28 octobre 1720.* Marseille: Brebion, 1720.

———. "Mandement de Mgr l'évêque de Marseille pour l'ouverture des églises de la ville." In *Pièces historiques sur la peste de Marseille . . . ,* ed. Louis-François Jauffret, 327–35. Marseille: Chez les principaux libraires, 1820.

———. "Mandement de Mgr l'évêque de Marseille, sur la desolation qu'a causé la peste à Marseille, et sur l'établissement de la Fête du Sacré Coeur de Jésus, 22 octobre 1720." In *Pièces historiques sur la peste de Marseille . . . ,* ed. Louis-François Jauffret, 164–73. Marseille: Chez les principaux libraires, 1820.

———. *Mandement de Monseigneur l'illustrissime et révérendissime évêque de Marseille.* Avignon: Frères Delorme, 1720.

———. "Ordonnance de Mr. l'évêque de Marseille, lors des premiers bruits de l'invasion du mal contagieux." In *Pièces historiques sur la peste de Marseille . . . ,* ed. Louis-François Jauffret, 134–36. Marseille: Chez les principaux libraires, 1820.

———. "Ordonnance de Mgr l'évêque de Marseille sur les immodesties et les profanations qui se commettent dans les églises." In id., *Statuts synodaux,* 143–50. Marseille: Brebion, 1775.

———. *Requête en cassation de Mre Henri-François-Xavier de Belsunce de Castelmoron, évêque de Marseille, contre deux arrêts du parlement d'Aix. . . . Et Arrêt du Conseil d'Etat du roi, rendu en conséquence . . . (22 juillet 1719).* In id., *Correspondences,* 103–18. Marseille: J. & X. Aschero, 1911.

———. *Statuts synodaux du diocese de Marseille, lûs et publiés dans le synode tenu dans le Palais Episcopal, le 18 avril, 1712.* Marseille: Brebion, 1775.

Bertrand, Jean-Baptiste. *A Historical Relation of the Plague at Marseille in the Year 1720.* Translated by Anne Plumptre. London: Gregg International, 1973.

———. *Observations sur la maladie contagieuse de Marseille.* In *Pièces historiques sur la peste de Marseille . . .*, ed. Louis-François Jauffret, 201–21. Marseille: Chez les principaux libraires, 1820.

———. *Relation historique de la peste de Marseille en 1720.* Cologne, 1721.

———. *Relation historique de tout ce qui s'est passé à Marseille pendant la dernière peste.* Cologne: P. Marteau, 1723.

Boccaccio, Giovanni. *Decameron: A New Translation.* Edited by Peter Bondanella and Mark Musa. New York: Norton, 1977.

Boulainvilliers, Henri de. *Essai sur la noblesse de France.* Amsterdam, 1732.

———. *Histoire de l'ancien gouvernement de la France.* Amsterdam, 1727.

———. *La vie de Mahomed.* London: Humbert, 1730. Translated as *The Life of Mahomed.* London: W. Hinchliffe, 1731.

Boureau-Deslandes, André-François. *Essay sur la marine et sur le commerce.* N.p., 1743. Translated as *An Essay on Maritime Power and Commerce, Particularly Those of France* (London: Paul Vaillant, 1743).

———. *Lettre sur le luxe. Suivi de "Fragmens d'un auteur grec . . ." et de "Dialogue: Pourquoi il est si difficile aux personnes d'un certain merite de s'avancer dans le monde."* Paris: Joseph-André Vanebben, 1745.

Les capitulations renouvellées entre Louis XIV empereur de France et Mehmet IV empereur des Turcs. 1673.

Catelin, Camille de. *Le chevalier Roze et la peste de Marseille de 1720: Documents inédits.* Villedieu-Vaison: Grande imprimerie provençale, 1907.

Chaillan, Marius. *Documents inédits concernant les relations de Marseille avec le Maroc.* Paris: A. Picard, 1906.

Chalvet, Marc Antoine. *Eloge du Roy Louis XIV ou Discours sur la proposition d'ériger une Statue équestre à sa Majesté dans Marseille, prononcé dans la salle de l'Hôtel de Ville par Monsieur Marc Antoine Chalvet, avocat au Parlement, de l'Académie Royale d'Arles, et Assesseur de Marseille.* Marseille: Pierre Mesnier, 1685.

Chardin, Pierre Teilhard de. *Journal du voyage du chevalier Chardin en Perse et aux Indes orientales.* London, 1686.

Chicoyneau, François de. *Discours prononcé . . . le 26 octobre de l'année 1722.* Montpellier, 1723.

———. "Notice sur les principales pestes qui ont ravagé le monde," in *Pièces historiques sur la peste de Marseille . . .*, ed. Louis-François Jauffret, 1–32. Marseille: Chez les principaux libraires, 1820.

———. "Relation succinte, touchant les accidens de la peste de Marseille, son prognostic et sa curation," in *Pièces historiques sur la peste de Marseille . . .*, ed. Louis-François Jauffret, 177–78. Marseille: Chez les principaux libraires, 1820.

———. *Traité des causes, des accidens et de la cure de la peste.* Paris: P.-J. Mariette, 1744.

Chicoyneau, Francçis de, and François Verny. *Observations touchant la nature, les evenemens et le traitement de la peste de Marseille et d'Aix.* Lyon, 1721.

Clément XI, Pope. *La constitution Unigenitus, avec des remarques et des notes, augmentée du systême des Jesuites opposé à la doctrine des propositions du Pere Quesnel, & d'un parallele de ce systême avec celui des Pelagiens.* Paris, 1733.

Colbert, Jean-Baptiste. *Lettres, instructions et mémoires de Colbert publiés d'après les ordres de l'empereur.* Paris: Imprimerie impériale, 1861–82. 8 vols. in 10. Nendeln, Liechtenstein: Kraus Reprint, 1979.

Colonie, André de. *Eclaircissement sur le légitime commerce des intérêts.* 1675. Marseille, 1682.

Condorcet, Nicolas de. "The Future Progress of the Human Mind." In Isaac Kramnick, *The Portable Enlightenment Reader.* New York: Penguin Books, 1995.

Conseil de Marseille. "Décisions du Conseil sur le commerce." In François Chicoyneau, *Traité des causes, des accidens et de la cure de la peste.* Paris: P.-J. Mariette, 1744.

Conseil de la santé de France. *Instruction générale pour exécuter les premières décisions du Conseil de santé sur la manière de secourir la Provence.* In François Chicoyneau, *Traité des causes, des accidens et de la cure de la peste.* Paris, 1744.

Conseil de la santé de Marseille. *Decisions du Conseil de la santé sur les secours que demandoient les pays menaces de la contagion, ou ceux qui en étoient infectés.* In François Chicoyneau, *Traité des causes, des accidens et de la cure de la peste.* Paris: P.-J. Mariette, 1744.

Conseil d'Estat. *Arrest du Conseil d'Estat du Roy, qui ordonne que les habitans de la ville de Marseille, & les marchands & négocians, tant sujets de sa Majesté qu'estrangers, & autres personnes de toutes nations & qualites, jouïront dans l'étendue de la ville, port & territoire de Marseille, des exemptions, privileges & franchises accordes en faveur du commerce, et portes par l'édit du mois de mars 1669. Déclaration de Sa Majesté, arrests & reglemens rendus en consequence. Du 10 juillet 1703.* Marseille: Vve de Jean-Baptiste Boy & Pierre Boy, 1703.

Coyer, Gabriel-François. *Développement et défense du systéme de la noblesse commerçante.* Paris: Duchesne, 1757.

Croissante, Pichatty de. *Journal abregé de ce qui s'est passé en la ville de Marseille, depuis qu'elle est affligée de la contagion; tiré du Mémorial de la Chambre du Conseil de l'Hôtel de Ville; tenu par le Sieur Pichatty de Croissainte.* Marseille: Jean-Baptiste Boy, 1720.

———. *Journal veritable de ce qui c'est passé en la ville de Marseille depuis qu'elle est affligée.* Marseille: Jean Baptiste Boy, 1720.

Decormis, François, and Charles de Saurin, *L'ancien barreau du parlement de Provence, ou Extraits d'une correspondance inédite échangée pendant la peste de 1720 entre François Decormis et Pierre Saurin.* Marseille: Vve. M. Olive, 1861.

Defoe, Daniel. *A Journal of the Plague Year.* 1722. New York: Modern Library, 2001.

Deidier, Antoine. *Discours académique . . . sur la contagion de la peste de Marseille prononcé pour l'ouverture solemnelle des écoles de médecine de Montpellier le 22 octobre 1725.* 1725.

Dictionnaire de l'Académie française. 1st ed. 1694. Chicago: University of Chicago ARTFL Project, 1998.

Dissertation sur la peste qui a désolé la ville de Marseille pendant les années 1720 et 1721. Avignon, 1721.

Edit du Roi Henri II contre les femmes qui célent leur grossesse. In Belsunce, *Statuts Synodaux,* 160–63. Marseille: Brebion, 1775.

Encyclopédie, ou dictionnaire raisonné des sciences, des arts et des métiers. Paris, 1755–65.

Eon, Jean, Mathias de Saint-Jean. *Le Commerce honorable, ou Considérations politiques, contenant les motifs de nécessité, d'honneur et de profit, qui se treuvent à former des compagnies de personnes de toutes conditions pour l'entretien du négoce de mer en France, composé par un habitant de la ville de Nantes*. Nantes: Guillaume Le Monnier, 1646.

Fabre, Pierre-Jean. *Remèdes, curatifs et préservatifs de la peste, donnez au public en 1652, par M. Pierre-Jean Fabre*. Avignon: François-Sebastien Offray, 1720.

Fénelon, François de. *Les Avantures de Télémaque*. Paris: Vve de C. Barbin, 1699. Edited and translated by Patrick Riley as *Telemachus, Son of Ulysses*. Cambridge: Cambridge University Press, 1994.

———. *Education of a Daughter*. Carlisle, MA: Applewood, 1996.

Féraud, Jean-François. *Dictionnaire critique de la langue française*. Marseille: Mossy, 1787–88.

Fermanel, Gilles. *Le voyage d'Italie et du Levant de MM. Fermanel, . . . Fauvel, . . . Baudouin de Launay et de Stochove, sieur de Ste-Catherine*. . . . Rouen: Jacques Hérault, 1664.

La fête séculaire de la peste de 1720, ou Eloge de Belsunce. Marseille: Rouchon, 1821, 1830.

Foresta, Joseph-Ignace de. *Lettre de M. l'évêque d'Apt* [Foresta de Colongue] *à Mgr le Régent, et son mandement contre la Sorbonne, ou plutôt nouveau tocsins adoptez par ce prélat*. Apt: n.p., 1717.

France. Acte royal. *Déclaration . . . qui ordonne que l'édit du Roy Henri II . . . de février 1556 contre les femmes qui auroient celé leur grossesse et leur accouchement etc. sera publié de trois mois en trois mois par tous les curez ou leurs vicaires aux prônes des messes paroissiales*. Paris: de Vaileyre [*sic*], n.d. [1708].

France. Gouvernement de Marseille. *Acte déclaratif de l'état présent de la santé de la ville de Marseille et de la désinfection générale qui y a été faite par ordre du Roi*. Marseille: J.-B. Boy & J.-A. Mallard, 1722.

Gabriel, Pierre. *Le prosélite charitable, ou petit discours de la peste*. Tübingen: J. H. Reis, 1666.

Gaudereau, Martin, Abbé. *Relation des différentes espèces de Peste que reconnoissent les Orientaux, des précautions et des Remedes qu'ils prennent pour en empêcher la communication et le progrès, et de ce que nous devons faire à leur exemple pour nous en preserver, et nous en guerir*. Paris: Estienne Ganeau, 1721.

Gaufridi, Jean-François de. *Histoire de Provence*. Aix-en-Provence: Charles David, 1694.

Gautier, H. *L'histoire de la ville de Nismes et de ses antiquitez*. Nismes: A. A. Belle, 1720.

Goujon. *Journal du sieur Goujon, maître d'hôtel de Mgr de Belsunce durant la peste de Marseille, 1720–1722*. Edited by Théophile Bérengier. Paris: V. Palmé, 1878.

Guybert, Philibert. *Le médecin charitable, enseignant la manière de faire et preparer en la maison les remèdes propres à toutes les maladies, suivi d'un traité de la peste*. Lyon, 1635.

Guys, Pierre-Augustin. *Marseille ancienne et moderne*. Paris: Vve Duchesne, 1786.

Herbelot de Molainville, Barthélemy d'. *Bibliothèque orientale, ou Dictionnaire universel contenant généralement tout ce qui regarde la connaissance des peuples de l'Orient*. Paris: Compagnie des libraires, 1697.

Howard, John. *Histoire des principaux lazarets de l'Europe, accompagnée de différens mémoires relatifs à la peste, et suivie d'observations sur quelques prisons et hôpitaux, ainsi que de remarques sur l'état présent de ceux de la Grande-Bretagne et de l'Irlande*. Paris: Henri Agasse, an 7 (1798). A translation of *An Account of the Principal Lazarettos in Europe, with Various Papers Relative to the Plague, Together with Some Further Observations on Some Foreign Prisons and Hospitals, and Additional Remarks on the Present State of Those in Great Britain and Ireland* (London, 1789).

Les illusions, les calomnies et les erreurs de Monsigneur l'évêque de Marseille, démonstrées, ou Justifications des differens arrêts du parlement de Provence, rendus contre ce prélat, et en particulier de celui qui a ordonné la saisie de son temporal, pour servir de réponse à un écrit intitulé Requète en cassation de Monseigneur Henri François Xavier de Belsunce de Castelmoron, évêque de Marseille, contre deux arrêts du Parlement d'Aix. Paris, 1720.

Jauffret, Louis-François, ed. *Pièces historiques sur la peste de Marseille et d'une partie de la Provence en 1720, 1721 et 1722, trouvées dans les archives de l'Hôtel de ville, dans celles de la préfecture, au bureau de l'administration sanitaire, et dans le cabinet des manuscrits de la bibliothèque de Marseille, publiées en 1820 à l'occasion de l'année séculaire de la peste; avec le portr. de Mr de Belsunce*. Vols. 1 and 2. Marseille: Chez les principaux libraires, 1820.

Justification des PP. de l'Oratoire de Marseille, contre les accusations de l'évêque de cette ville. Marseille: n.p., 1721.

La Borde, Vivien de. *Du témoignage de la verité dans l'Eglise: Dissertation théologique, où l'on examine quell est ce témoignage, tant en général qu'en particulier, au regard de la derniere Constitution..* 1714. New rev. ed. N.p., 1754.

———. *Lettre d'un gentilhomme de Provence à M. L. M. D. au sujet des lettres de M. de Marseille contre les Pères de l'Oratoire. le 26 janvier 1721*. N.p., 1721.

———. *Principes sur l'essence, la distinction et les limites des deux puissances, spirituelle et temporelle, ouvrage posthume du Père de La Borde de l'Oratoire*. Paris: Le Clère, 1753.

Langeron, Charles, Bailli de. *De par le Roy. Le Bailly de Langeron, lieutenant general des armées du Roy, Chef d'escadre de ses galères, commandant pour sa majesté dans la ville de Marseille, et Mrs. Les Echevins, Lieutenants generaux de police de Ladite ville . . .* Marseille: n.p.,1723.

———. *Mémoire au sujet d'une désinfection générale*. In François Chicoyneau, *Traité des causes, des accidens et de la cure de la peste*. Paris: P.-J. Mariette, 1744.

Le Gros, Nicolas. *Abrégé chronologique des principaux evénémens qui ont précédé la Constitution Unigenitus, qui y ont donné lieu, ou qui en sont les suites*. Utrecht: Corneille Guil. Le Febvre, 1730.

Lettre à Monseigneur l'évêque de Marseille. Paris: 1720.

Lettres patentes portent etablissement d'une académie de belles lettres à Marseille. Marseille: J. B. Boy, 1727.

Liquier, André. *Discours qui a remporté le prix de l'Académie de Marseille, en 1777, sur cette question: "Quelle a été dans tous les temps l'influence du commerce sur l'esprit et les moeurs des peuples?"* Paris: Demonville, 1777.

Louis XIV, King. *Les capitulations renouvellées entre Louis XIV, empereur de France et Mehemet IV, empereur des Turcs par l'entremise de M. Charles François Olier, marquis de Nointel, conseiller du Roy . . . et son ambassadeur au Levant, fait à Andrinople le cinquième juin 1673*. Fr. Leondard, 1689.

Marchebeus. *Voyage de Paris à Constantinople par bateau à vapeur.* Paris: A. Bertrand, 1839.

Le marriage de dom Japhet d'Arménie et de l'infante Ahihva-Mascarade. Aix: J. B. & E. Roize, 1669.

Maurice de Toulon, Père. *Le Capucin charitable, enseignant la méthode pour remédier aux grandes misères que la peste a coûtume de causer parmi des Peuples, et des Remedes propres à cette Maladie, dedié à Messieurs les Magistrats et Intendans de la Police des Villes de France.* 1662. Lyon: Bruyset, 1721.

———. *Règlements de police et remèdes contre la peste.* Avignon: Delorme, 1720.

Melon, Jean-François. *Essai politique sur le commerce.* Bordeaux: n.p., 1736.

Mémoire instructif sur ce qui doit être observé dans les villes et dans chaque famille en temps de contagion, par l'expérience arrivée à Marseille et autres villes de Provence. Lyon: Frères Bruyset, 1721.

"Mémoire sur les infirmeries." In François Chicoyneau, *Traité des causes, des accidens et de la cure de la peste,* 175–76. Paris: P.-J. Mariette, 1744.

"Mémoire sur quelques abus qui se commettent dans les villes de Marseille et Toulon à l'égard des quarantaines et de la santé." In François Chicoyneau, *Traité des causes, des accidens et de la cure de la peste.* Paris: P.-J. Mariette, 1744.

Montesquieu, Charles-Louis de Secondat, baron de La Brède et de. *Lettres persanes.* Edited by Paul Vernière. Paris: Bordas, 1992.

Observations des négociants de Marseille sur le dernier Mémoire de la noblesse, qui a pour titre: "Mémoire de la noblesse de Marseille contre les négociants de la même ville, au sujet du rétablissement de la noblesse dans la première place de l'administration municipale." Marseille: n.p.,1760.

Olivier, Guillaume-Antoine. *Voyage dans l'Empire Othoman, l'Egypte et la Perse, fait par ordre du gouvernement, pendant les six premières années de la République.* Paris: H. Agasse, an IX–XII (1800–1803).

Olivier, M. *Dissertation historique sur l'ancienne académie de Marseille par Mr. Olivier, Avocat, un des Académiciens.* Marseille: J. B. Boy, 1727.

"Ordres à observer pour empêcher que la peste ne se communique hors les lieux infectez." In *Recueil de pièces relatives à la peste qui sévit en Provence.* 1720–25.

Papon, Jean-Pierre. *De la peste, ou Epoques mémorables de ce fléau et les moyens de s'en preserver.* Paris: Lavillette, an VIII (1799).

Paris, Jean-François. *Mémoire sur la peste.* Marseille: Jean Mossy, 1778.

Parlement de Provence. *Arrêt du parlement de Provence, au sujet de l'Edit donné à Versailles au mois de mars 1762, concernant les ci-devant se disants jésuites. Du 18 janvier 1763.* Aix-en-Provence: Veuve de J. David & Esprit David, 1763.

———. *Arrest de la Cour de parlement de Provence . . . du 20 Decembre 1718 dans la Grand Chambre.* Aix-en-Provence, 1718.

———. *Arrest du parlement de Provence, 21 Octobre 1718.* Aix-en-Provence, 1718.

———. *Arrêt et règlement général fait par la chambre ordonnée en temps de vacations du parlement de Provence pour la conservation de la santé publique.* Aix-en-Provence, 1629.

———. *Extrait des Registres du parlement d'Aix du 24 Janvier 1718 dans la Grand Chambre.* Aix-en-Provence, 1718.

———. *Remonstrance du parlement de Provence sur les désordres arrivés dans cette province pendant la durée de la contagion, presentées au mois de Septembre 1722, et renouvellées au mois de Décembre, 1723.* Aix-en-Provence, 1723.

Peilhe, F. *Poème à la gloire d'un arc de triomphe et un mausolée antique des romains que l'on voit à Saint Rémy, ville de Provence.* Provence, 1725.

Pestalozzi, Jérôme-Jean. *Avis de précaution contre la maladie contagieuse de Marseille qui contient une idée complete de la peste.* Lyon: Bruyset, 1721.

———. *Avis de précaution contre la peste, que contiennent une idée de cette maladie et de ses accidens, avec des moyens préservatifs et curatifs, des formulas choisies, un catalog général de remèdes tant simples que composez.* Lyon, 1723.

———. *Dissertation sur les causes et la nature de la peste.* Bordeaux, 1722.

Pitton, Jean-Scholastique. *Histoire de la ville d'Aix, capitale de la Provence, contenant tout ce qui c'y est passé de plus memorable dans son état politique, dépuis sa fondation jusques en l'année 1665.* Aix-en-Provence, 1665.

Plantet, Eugène. *Correspondance des Deys d'Alger avec la Cour de France (1579–1833) et (1700–1833) recueillie dans les dépôts d'archives des Affaires étrangères, de la Marine, des Colonies et de la Chambre de Commerce de Marseille.* Paris: Félix Alcan, 1889.

Poëme heroique sur la peste qui a regné en divers endroits en l'année 1720 et 1721. Avignon: Charles Giraud, 1722.

La politique des Jésuites démasquée et l'appel justifié par les principes des libertés de l'Eglise gallicane dans l'examen des mandements de M. l'évêque d'Apt des 30 avril et 20 décembre 1717. Extrait des registres du parlement d'Aix du 24 janvier 1718. Arrêt de la cour de Parlement de Provence. N.p., 1719.

Poullet, Sieur. *Nouvelles relations du Levant. . . .* Paris: Louis Billaine, 1668.

Quesnel, Pasquier. *Le Nouveau Testament en francois, avec des reflexions morales sur chaque verset, pour en rendre la lecture plus utile, & la meditation plus aisée.* Amsterdam: Joseph Nicolai, 1727.

———. *Plainte et protestation du Père Quesnel contre la condemnation des cent-une propositions.* Brussels, 1715.

———. *Réflexions sur les cent et une propositions tirées du livre intitulé Le Nouveau Testament en françois avec des réflexions.* Paris: L. Seneuze, 1715.

Ramsay, Andrew Michael, Chevalier. *Les Voyages de Cyrus, avec un discours sur la mythologie.* Paris, 1727. Translated as *A New Cyropaedia, or the Travels of Cyrus, with a Discourse on the Theology and Mythology of the Ancients* (London: T. Wilcox, 1760).

Ranchin, François. *Traité politique et médical de la peste; et histoire de la peste qui ravagea Montpellier en 1629 et 1630.* Liège, 1721.

———. *Traité nouveau politique et médical de la peste, et histoire de la peste qui ravagea Montpellier en 1629 et 1630.* Liège, 1721.

Recueil d'édits arrests du conseil, et règlemens pour la municipalité de la ville de Marseille. Marseille: Sibié, 1772.

Recueil des mandemens, ordonnances . . . faits pendant le tems que Marseille a été affligée de la peste. Marseille: J. P. Breton, 1721.

Recueil de pièces relatifs à la peste qui sévit en Provence. N.p.,1725.

Recueil de plusiers pièces de poesies présentées à l'académie de Marseille pour le prix de l'année 1727. Marseille: J. B. Boy, 1727.

"Règlements de police et remèdes contre la peste." In *Recueil de pièces relatives à la peste qui sévit en Provence*. N.p., 1725.

Relation de ce qui s'est passé en la reception de Louis XIV dans la ville d'Arles le 13 janvier 1660. Arles: F. Mesnier, 1660.

Romieu, Chevalier de. *Discours prononcé par Monsieur le Chevalier de Romieu, associé de l'Acadèmie*. Marseille: J. B. Boy, 1727.

Rousseau, Jean Jacques. *Lettres écrites de la montagne*. Neuvième lettre. www.ac-grenoble.fr/PhiloSophie/file/rousseau_lettres_de_la_montagne.pdf (accessed 8 July 2010).

———. *Social Contract and Discourses*. London: Everyman, 1973.

Ruffi, Antoine de. *Histoire des comtes de Provence*. Aix, 1655.

———. *Histoire de la ville de Marseille contentant tout qui est passé de plus mémorable depuis sa fondation, durant le tems qu'elle a été République et sous la domination des Romains, Bourgoignans, Visigots, Ostrogots, Rois de Bourgoigne, Vicomtes de Marseille, Comtes de Provence et de nos Rois trés-Chrêtiens*. Marseille: Garcin, 1642.

———. *Le Règlement du sort, contenant la forme et la manière de procéder à l'élection des officiers de la ville de Marseille*. Marseille: Garcin, 1654.

Ruffi, Louis Antoine de. *Histoire de la ville de Marseille contenant tout qui est passé de plus mémorable depuis sa fondation, durant le tems qu'elle a été République et sous la domination des Romains, Bourgoignans, Visigots, Ostrogots, Rois de Bourgoigne, Vicomtes de Marseille, Comtes de Provence et de nos Rois trés-Chrêtiens*, Marseille: Henri Martel, 1696.

Savary, Jacques. *Le parfait négociant, ou Instruction générale pour ce qui regarde le commerce de toutes sortes de marchandises tant de France que des pays étrangers*. 1675. New ed. Paris: Frères Estienne, 1712.

Saint-Simon, Louis de Rouvroy, duc de. *Mémoires*. Paris, 1879–1928.

———. *Tableau de la folie sur le Système de Law, dessins curieux et burlesques*. Amsterdam, 1720.

Spon, Jacob. *Voyage d'Italie, de Dalmatie, de Grèce et du Levant, fait en 1675 et 1676*. Paris, 1724.

Tavernier, Jean-Baptiste. *Les six voyages de M. Jean-Baptiste Tavernier*. Rouen: P. Ribou, 1713.

Terran, M. *Discours sur ce qui s'est passé à Marseille pendant la Contagion compose par monsieur Terran beneficie à l'Eglise cathedrale de la Major de cette ville de Marseille l'an 1720 au mois d'août*. Marseille: Jean Antoine Mallard, 1734.

Thévenot, Jean. *Relation d'un voyage fait au Levant*. Paris: Billaine, 1664.

Thucydides, *The History of the Peloponnesian War*. Translated by Richard Crawley. London: Dent, 1961.

Tournefort, Joseph Pitton de. *Relation d'un voyage du Levant fait par ordre du Roy*. . . . 2 vols. Paris: Imp. royale, 1717.

Travessac, Antoine Valette de. *Sonnets sur les antiquités de la ville de Nimes, avec des remarques historiques*. Nîmes: A. A. Belle, 1748.

Valeriolle, Nicolas de. *L'ordre politique tenue en la ville d'Arles, en temps de la peste, année 1629*. Avignon: J. Bramereau, 1632.

Vallant, C. *Consultation sur la maladie de Provence faite le vingt-uniéme Novembre 1720.* Lyon: P. Valfray, 1720.

Veron de Forbonnais, François. *Questions sur le commerce des François au Levant.* Marseille: Carapatria, 1755.

La vie de la très honorée soeur Anne Magdelaine Remuzat, religieuse de la Visitation Sainte-Marie, morte en odeur de sainteté dans le premier monastère de Marseille. Marseille: Brebion, 1760.

SECONDARY SOURCES

Aaslestad, Katherine. *Place and Politics: Local Identity, Civic Culture, and German Nationalism in North Germany During the Revolutionary Era.* Boston: Brill, 2005.

Aberth, John. *The Black Death: The Great Mortality of 1348–1350. A Brief History with Documents.* Boston: St. Martin's Press, 2005.

Académie de Marseille. Marseille: Académie de Marseille, 2003.

Adamovsky, Ezequiel. *Euro-Orientalism: Liberal Ideology and the Image of Russia in France (c. 1740–1880).* New York: Peter Lang, 2006.

Ames, Glenn J. *Colbert, Mercantilism and the French Quest for Asian Trade.* Dekalb: Northern Illinois University Press, 1996.

Appleby, Andrew B. "The Disappearance of the Plague: A Continuing Puzzle." *Economic History Review* 33, no. 2 (1980):161–73.

———. "Epidemics and Famine in the Little Ice Age." *Journal of Interdisciplinary History* 10, no. 4 (Spring 1980): 643–63.

———. *Famine in Tudor and Stuart England.* Stanford: Stanford University Press, 1978.

Ardoin, Paul. *Le Jansénisme en Basse-Provence au XVIIIe siècle: La bulle Unigenitus dans les diocèses d'Aix, d'Arles, de Marseille, de Fréjus et de Toulon, 1713–1789.* Vol. 1. Marseille: St. Lazare, 1936.

Arkoun, Mohammed, ed. *Histoire de l'islam et des musulmans en France: Du Moyen âge à nos jours.* Paris: A. Michel, 2006.

Artaud, Antonin. *Collected Works.* Translated by Victor Corti. London: Calder & Boyars, 1974.

Autran, Paul. *Eloge historique du chevalier Roze.* Marseille: A. Ricard, 1821.

Avery, John. *Progress, Poverty and Population: Re-reading Condorcet, Godwin and Malthus.* London: Frank Cass, 1997.

Baehrel, René. "Epidémie et terreur: Histoire et sociologie." *Annales historiques de la Révolution française* 23 (1951): 113–46.

Baker, Keith Michael. "Enlightenment and the Institution of Society: Notes for a Conceptual History." In *Main Trends in Cultural History,* ed. Willem Meching and Wyger Velema, 95–120. Amsterdam: Rodopi, 1994.

———. "French Political Thought at the Accession of Louis XVI." *Journal of Modern History,* 50, no. 2 (June 1978): 279–303.

———. *From Natural Philosophy to Social Mathematics.* Chicago: Chicago University Press, 1975.

———. *Inventing the French Revolution.* Cambridge: Cambridge University Press, 1990.

———. "Memory and Practice: Politics and the Representation of the Past in Eighteenth-Century France." *Representations*, no. 11 (Summer 1985): 134–64.

———. "Transformations of Classical Republicanism in Eighteenth-Century France." *Journal of Modern History* 73, no. 1 (March 2001): 32–53.

———, ed. *The Old Regime and the French Revolution.* Chicago: University of Chicago Press, 1986.

Baratier, Edouard. *Histoire de Marseille.* Toulouse: Privat, 1973.

Baron, Hans. *The Crisis of the Early Italian Renaissance: Civic Humanism and Republican Liberty in an Age of Classicism and Tyranny.* Princeton, NJ: Princeton University Press, 1955.

———. *In Search of Florentine Civic Humanism: Essays on the Transition from Medieval to Modern Thought.* Princeton, NJ: Princeton University Press, 1988.

Barrielle, Chantal. *Les livres des voyages dans les pays d'Europe et du Levant aux XVIe et XVIIe siècles: Livres imprimés et conservés à la bibliothèque Méjanes.* Aix-en-Provence: Université de Provence, Aix-Marseille I, 1999.

Barry, Jonathan, and Colin Jones, eds. *Medicine and Charity before the Welfare State.* London: Routledge, 1991.

Beik, William. *Absolutism and Society in Seventeenth-Century France: State Power and Provincial Aristocracy in Languedoc.* Cambridge: Cambridge University Press, 1985.

———. "The Absolutism of Louis XIV as Social Collaboration," *Past and Present*, no. 188 (2005): 195–224.

Bell, David A. *The Cult of the Nation in France: Inventing Nationalism, 1680–1800.* Cambridge, MA: Harvard University Press, 2001.

———. "The Unbearable Lightness of Being French: Law, Republicanism, and National Identity at the End of the Old Regime." *American Historical Review* 106, no. 4 (October 2001): 1215–35.

Belmonte, Lydie. *De la petite Arménie au boulevard des Grand pins: Evolution de l'espace communautaire arménien d'un quartier de Marseille, des origins à nos jours.* Marseille: Tacussel, 1999.

Benedictow, O. J. "Morbidity in Historical Plague Epidemics." *Population Studies* 41, no. 3 (November 1987): 401–31.

Berg, Maxine. *Consumers and Luxury: Consumer Culture in Europe, 1650–1850.* Manchester: Manchester University Press, 1999.

———, ed. *Luxury in the Eighteenth Century: Debates, Desires and Delectable Goods.* New York: Palgrave Macmillan, 2003.

Berger, Robert W. *A Royal Passion: Louis XIV as Patron of Architecture.* Cambridge: Cambridge University Press, 1994.

Bernstein, Hilary J. *Between Crown and Community: Politics and Civic Culture in Sixteenth-Century Poitiers.* Ithaca, NY: Cornell University Press, 2004.

Bertrand, Regis. "De la toponymie à la statuare: Les formes de Christianisation du paysage marseillais depuis le XVIIIe siècle." *Annales du Midi* 98, no. 173 (January–March 1986): 95–115.

Bien, David. "Offices, Corps and a System of State Credit: The Uses of Privilege Under the Old Regime." In *The French Revolution and the Creation of Modern Political Culture*, ed. Keith Michael Baker, 1: 89–114. Oxford: Oxford University Press, 1987.

Biraben, Jean-Noël. *Les hommes et la peste en France et dans les pays européens et méditerranéens.* Paris: Mouton et Ecole des hautes études en sciences sociales, 1975.

Blet, Pierre. *Le clergé de France: Louis XIV et le Saint Siège de 1695 à 1715.* Vatican City: Archivio vaticano, 1989.

Boehler, Jean-Michel, Christine Lebrau, and Bernard Vogler, eds. *Les élites régionales, XVIIe–XXe siècle: Construction de soi-même et service de l'autre.* Strasbourg: Presses universitaires de Strasbourg, 2002.

Bossenga, Gail. *The Politics of Privilege: Old Regime and Revolution in Lille.* Cambridge: Cambridge University Press, 1991.

Bouches-du-Rhône. Archives départementales. *L'Intendence sanitaire de Marseille: Répertoire numérique de la sous-série 200E / Archives de la région Provence–Alpes–Côte-d'Azur et du département des Bouches-du-Rhône.* Marseille: Archives départementales, 1979.

Boudin, Amédée. *Histoire de Marseille.* Marseille: Terris, 1852.

Bouville, Maïthé, and Isabelle Bonnet-Rambaud, eds. *Les criées de Marseille: Inventaire des affiches, 1565–1789: 1 BB1–3360 / Archives de la Ville de Marseille.* Marseille: Archives de la ville de Marseille, 1992.

Bouyala d'Arnaud, André. *Evocation du vieil Aix-en-Provence.* Paris: Minuit, 1964.

———. *Evocation du vieux Marseille.* Paris: Minuit, 1959.

Boyer, Jean. *Le patrimoine architectural d'Aix-en-Provence, XVIe–XVIIe–XVIIIe siècles.* Aix-en-Provence: Service des affaires culturelles de la ville, 1985.

Brenier, Henri. *Neuf siècles de France au Levant.* Marseille: Chambre de commerce, 1919.

Brockliss, Laurence, and Colin Jones. *The Medical World of Early Modern France.* Oxford: Clarendon Press, 1997.

Burns, J. H., and Thomas M. Izbicki. *Conciliarism and Papalism.* Cambridge: Cambridge University Press, 1997.

Burrin, Philippe. *France Under the Germans: Collaboration and Compromise.* New York: New Press, 1998.

Busquet, Raoul. *Histoire de la Provence des origins à la révolution française.* Monaco: Imprimerie nationale de Monaco, 1954.

Calhoun, Craig, ed. *Habermas and the Public Sphere.* Boston: MIT Press, 1992.

Calvi, Giulia. *Histories of a Plague Year: The Social and the Imaginary in Baroque Florence.* Translated by Dario Biocca and Bryant T. Ragan Jr. Berkeley: University of California Press, 1989.

———. "A Metaphor for Social Exchange: The Florentine Plague of 1630." *Representations*, no. 13 (Winter 1986): 139–63.

Camus, Albert. *The Plague.* Translated by Stuart Gilbert. London: Penguin Books, 1960.

Cannadine, David. *Ornamentalism: How the British Saw their Empire.* Oxford: Oxford University Press, 2002.

Carlin, Claire, ed. *Imagining Contagion in Early Modern Europe.* Basingstoke, UK: Palgrave Macmillan , 2005.

Carmichael, Ann G. "Contagion Theory and Contagion Practice in Fifteenth-Century Milan." *Renaissance Quarterly* 44, no. 2 (Summer 1991): 213–56.

Carnoy, Dominique. *Représentations de l'Islam dans la France du XVIIe siècle*. Paris: l'Harmattan, 1998.

Carrière, Charles. *Négociants marseillais au XVIIIe siècle: Contribution à l'étude des economies maritimes*. Marseille: Institut historique de Provence, 1973.

———. *Le port mondial au XVIIIe siècle: Richesse du passé marseillais*. Marseille: Chambre de commerce et d'industrie, 1979.

Carrière, Charles, Marcel Courdurié, and Ferréol Rebuffat. *Marseille ville morte: La peste de 1720*. Marseille: Robert, 1968.

Castelluccio, Stéphane. *Les carrousels en France du XVIe au XVIIIe siècle*. Paris: L'amateur, 2002.

Cattelona, Georg'ann. "Control and Collaboration: The Role of Women in Regulating Female Sexual Behavior in Early Modern Marseille." *French Historical Studies* 18, no. 1 (Spring 1993): 13–33.

La Chambre de commerce de Marseille à travers ses archives: XVIIe et XVIIIe siècles. Marseille: A. Robert & Chambre de commerce de Marseille, 1976.

Chapman, Sara. *Private Ambition and Political Alliances: The Phelypeaux de Pontchartrain Family and Louis XIV's Government, 1650–1760*. Rochester, NY: University of Rochester Press, 2004.

Chartier, Roger. *Cultural Origins of the French Revolution*. Durham, NC: Duke University Press, 1991.

Chéruel, Adolphe. *De l'administration de Louis XIV (1661–1672) d'après les mémoires inédits d'Olivier d'Ormesson*. Paris: Joubert, 1850.

Cipolla, Carlo M. *Faith, Reason and the Plague in Seventeenth-Century Tuscany*. Translated by Muriel Kittel. New York: Harvester Press, 1979.

Clark, Henry C. "Commerce, the Virtues, and the Public Sphere in Early-Seventeenth-Century France." *French Historical Studies* 21, no. 3 (Summer 1998): 415–40.

———. *Compass of Society: Commerce and Absolutism in Old Regime France*. Lanham, MD: Lexington Books, 2007.

Cole, Charles Woolsey. *Colbert and a Century of French Mercantilism*. Hamden, CT: Archon Books, 1964.

———. *French Mercantilism, 1683–1700*. New York: Octagon Press, 1971.

Colyar, H. A. de. "Jean-Baptiste Colbert and the Codifying Ordinances of Louis XIV." *Journal of the Society of Comparative Legislation* 13, no. 1 (1912): 56–86.

Confino, Alon. *The Nation as Local Metaphor: Wurttemberg, Imperial Germany, and National Memory, 1871–1918*. Chapel Hill: University of North Carolina Press, 1997.

Cornette, Joël. *Histoire de la France: Absolutisme et lumières, 1652–1783*. Paris: Hachette, 2000.

Cubells, Monique. *La noblesse provençale du milieu du XVIIe siècle à la Révolution*. Aix-en-Provence: Université de Provence, 2002.

———. *La Provence des lumières: Les parlementaires d'Aix au 18me siècle*. Paris: Maloine, 1984.

Culot, Maurice, and Daniel Drocourt. *Marseille, la passion des contrasts*. Paris: Mardaga, 1991.

Daston, Lorraine. "Marvelous Facts and Miraculous Evidence in Early Modern Europe." *Critical Inquiry* 18, no. 1 (Autumn 1991): 93–124.

Davis, Robert. *Christian Slaves, Muslim Masters: White Slavery in the Mediterranean, the Barbary Coast, and Italy, 1500–1800*. New York: Palgrave Macmillan, 2003.

Dols, Michael. *The Black Death in the Middle East*. Princeton, NJ: Princeton University Press, 1977.

Dubois, Pierre. *Un homme de peste: Maurice Tassi de Toulon, Capucin, 1610–1666*. Toulon: P. Dubois, 1970.

Duchène, Roger. *Et la Provence devint française*. Paris: Mazarine, 1982.

Dumoulin, Jacqueline. *Le coût de la santé à Aix-en-Provence du XVIe au XVIIIe siècle: Le financement de la lutte contre la peste*. Marseille: Presses universitaires Aix-Marseille (PUAM), 2003.

Dursteller, Eric. *Venetians in Constantinople: Nation, Identity and Coexistence in the Early Modern Mediterranean*. Baltimore: Johns Hopkins University Press, 2006.

Echenberg, Myron J. *Black Death, White Medicine: Bubonic Plague and the Politics of Public Health in Colonial Senegal*. Portsmouth, NH: Heinemann, 2001.

Echinard, Pierre. *Grecs et philhellènes à Marseille de la Révolution française à l'indépendance de la Grèce*. Marseille: A. Robert, 1973.

Echinard, Pierre, and Emile Temime. *Histoire des migrations à Marseille, 1482–1830*. Vol. 1. *La préhistoire de la migration*. Aix-en-Provence: Edisud, 1989.

Eisenstein, Elizabeth L. *The Printing Press as an Agent of Social Change: Communications and Cultural Transformations in Early-Modern Europe*. 2 vols. Cambridge: Cambridge University Press, 1979.

Eldem, Edhem. *French Trade in Istanbul in the Eighteenth Century*. Leiden: Brill, 1999.

Emmanuelli, François-Xavier. *Vivre à Marseille sous l'Ancien régime*. Saint-Amand-Montrond: Perrin, 1999.

Emmanuelli, François-Xavier, Marie-Hélène Froeschle-Chopard and Martine Lapied, eds. *La Provence moderne (1481 à 1800)*. Rennes: Editions Ouest-France, 1991.

Euzennat, Maurice. "Ancient Marseille in the Light of Recent Excavations." *American Journal of Archaeology* 84, no. 2 (April 1980): 133–40.

Fairchilds, Cissie. *Poverty and Charity in Aix-en-Provence, 1640–1789*. Baltimore: Johns Hopkins University Press, 1976.

Farber, Jules B. *Les Juifs du pape en Provence*. Arles: Actes Sud, 2003.

Faure, Edgar. *La banqueroute de Law, 17 juillet 1720*. Paris, 1977.

Féraud-Giraud, Louis-Joseph-Delphin. *De la jurisdiction française dans les Echelles du Levant et de Barbarie: Etude sur la condition légale des étrangers dans les pays hors chrétienté*. Paris: A. Durand, 1866.

Ferrier-Caverivière, Nicole. *L'image de Louis XIV dans la littérature française de 1660 à 1715*. Paris: Presses universitaires de France, 1981.

Figarella, Jean. *Jacques Daviel: Maître Chirurgien de Marseille, Oculiste du Roi, 1693–1762*. Marseille: Robert, 1979.

———. "La Provence et la peste de 1720." *Revue Marseille*, no. 112 (1978): 16.

Fitzpatrick, Martin. *The Enlightenment World*. New York: Routledge, 2004.

Ford, Caroline. *Creating the Nation in Provincial France: Religion and Political Identity in Brittany*. Princeton, NJ: Princeton University Press, 1993.

Forrestal, Alison. *Fathers, Pastors and Kings: Visions of Episcopacy in Seventeenth-Century France*. Manchester: Manchester University Press, 2004.

Foucault, Michel. *The Archaeology of Knowledge*. New York: Routledge, 1972.

———. *The Birth of the Clinic: An Archaeology of Medical Perception*. Translated by A. M. Sheridan Smith. New York: Vintage Books, 1994.

———. *The Order of Things: An Archaeology of the Human Sciences*. New York: Vintage Books, 1970.

———. *Surveiller et punir: Naissance de la prison*. Paris: Gallimard, 1975. Translated by Alan Sheridan as *Discipline and Punish: The Birth of the Prison* (1977; New York: Vintage Books, 1995).

Fournier, Joseph. *La Chambre de commerce de Marseille d'après des archives historiques*. Marseille: Barlatier, 1910.

———. *La Chambre de commerce de Marseille et ses représentants permanents à Paris (1599–1875)*. Marseille: Barlatier, 1920.

———. *Inventaire des archives de la Chambre de commerce de Marseille*. Marseille: Chambre de commerce, 1940.

Fukasawa, Katsumi. *Toilerie et commerce du Levant: d'Alep à Marseille*. Paris: CNRS, 1987.

Furet, François. *Interpreting the French Revolution*. Translated by Elborg Forster. Cambridge: Cambridge University Press, 1981.

———. *Revolutionary France, 1770–1880*. Translated by Antonia Nevill. Cambridge: Blackwell, 1992.

Gaffarel, Paul, and Marquis de Duranty. *La peste de 1720 à Marseille et en France*. Paris: Perrin, 1911.

Gauchet, Marcel. *The Disenchantment of the World: A Political History of Religion*. Translated by Oscar Burge. Princeton, NJ: Princeton University Press, 1997.

Gerson, Stephane. "Parisian Litterateurs, Provincial Journeys and the Construction of National Unity in Post-Revolutionary France." *Past and Present*, no. 151 (May 1996): 141–73.

Göçek, Fatma Müge. *East Encounters West: France and the Ottoman Empire in the Eighteenth Century*. Oxford: Oxford University Press, 1987.

Gojosso, Eric. *Le concept de république en France, XVI–XVIII siècle*. Aix-en-Provence: Presses universitaires d'Aix-Marseille, 1998.

Golub, Edward S. *The Limits of Medicine: How Science Shapes Our Hope for the Cure*. New York: Random House, 1994.

Goodman, Dena. *The Republic of Letters: A Cultural History of the French Enlightenment*. Ithaca, NY: Cornell University Press, 1994.

Gordon, Daniel. *Citizens Without Sovereignty: Equality and Sociability in French Thought, 1670–1789*. Princeton, NJ: Princeton University Press, 1994.

———. "The City and the Plague in the Age of Enlightenment." *Yale French Studies* 92 (1997): 67–87.

———. "Confrontations with the Plague in Eighteenth-Century France." In *Dreadful Visitations: Confronting Natural Catastrophe in the Age of Enlightenment*, ed. Alessa Johns, 67–87. New York: Routledge, 1999.

Goulemot, Jean-Marie. "Du républicanisme et de l'idée républicaine au XVIIIe siècle." In *Le siècle de l'avènement républicain*, ed. François Furet and Mona Ozouf, 25–56. Paris: Gallimard, 1993.

Guilhaumou, Jacques. *Marseille républicaine, 1791–1793*. Paris: Presse de la Fondation nationale des sciences politiques, 1992.

Guiral, Pierre. *Tournefort et son voyage au Levant*. Paris, 1957.

Gunn, J. A. W. *Queen of the World: Opinion in the Public Life of France from the Renaissance to the Revolution*. Oxford: Oxford University Press, 1995.

Habermas, Jürgen. *The Structural Transformation of the Public Sphere: An Inquiry into a Category of Bourgeois Society*. Translated by Thomas Burger. Boston: MIT Press, 1989.

Haine, Scott. *The World of the Paris Café: Sociability Among the French Working Class, 1789–1914*. Baltimore: Johns Hopkins University Press, 1996.

Hamarneh, Sami K. *Health Sciences in Early Islam: Collected Papers*. San Antonio, TX: Noor Health Foundation and Zahra Publications, 1983.

Hamilton, Earl J. "Prices and Wages at Paris under John Law's System." *Quarterly Journal of Economics* 51, no. 1 (November 1936): 42–70.

Harrison, Mark. *Disease and the Modern World: 1500 to the Present Day*. Cambridge: Polity Press, 2004.

Headley, John M., and John B. Tomaro. eds. *San Carlo Borromeo: Catholic Reform and Ecclesiastical Politics in the Second Half of the Sixteenth Century*. Washington, DC: Folger Shakespeare Library, 1988.

Henin, Béatrice. "L'Aggrandissement de Marseille (1666–1690): Un compromise entre les aspirations monarchiques et les habitudes locales." *Annales du Midi* 98, no. 173 (January–March 1986): 7–20.

Hildesheimer, Françoise. *Le Bureau de la santé de Marseille sous l'Ancien régime: Le renfermement de la contagion*. Marseille: Fédération historique de Provence, 1980.

———. *La terreur et la pitié: L'Ancien régime a l'épreuve de la peste*. Paris: Publisud, 1990.

Horrox, Rosemary. *The Black Death*. Manchester: Manchester University Press, 1994.

Hudson, Robert. *Disease and Its Control: The Shaping of Modern Thought*. Westport: Greenwood Press, 1983.

Hunt, Lynn. *The Family Romance of the French Revolution*. Berkeley: University of California Press, 1992.

Jensen, De Lamar. "The Ottoman Turks in Sixteenth-Century French Diplomacy." *Sixteenth Century Journal* 16, no. 4 (1985): 451–70.

Johns, Alessa, ed. *Dreadful Visitations: Confronting Natural Catastrophe in the Age of Enlightenment*. New York: Routledge, 1999.

Jonas, Raymond. "Anxiety, Identity and the Displacement of Violence during the Année Terrible: The Sacred Heart and the Diocese of Nantes, 1870–1871." *French Historical Studies* 21, no. 1 (Winter 1998): 55–75.

———. *France and the Cult of the Sacred Heart: An Epic Tale for Modern Times*. Berkeley: University of California Press, 2000.

Jones, Colin. *The Charitable Imperative: Hospitals and Nursing in Ancien Régime and Revolutionary France*. New York: Routledge, 1989.

———. "The Great Chain of Buying: Medical Advertisement, the Bourgeois Public Sphere, and the Origins of the French Revolution." *American Historical Review* 101 (February 1996): 13–40.

———. *The Great Nation: France from Louis XV to Napoleon*. New York: Allen Lane, 2002.

———. "Plague and Its Metaphors in Early Modern France." *Representations* 53 (Winter 1996): 97–127.

Jones, Colin, and Roy Porter. *Reassessing Foucault: Power, Medicine and the Body*. London: Routledge, 1994.

Kaiser, Thomas. "The Abbé de Saint-Pierre, Public Opinion, and the Reconstitution of the French Monarchy." *Journal of Modern History* 55, no. 4 (December 1983): 618–43.

———. "The Evil Empire? The Debate on Turkish Despotism in Eighteenth-Century French Political Culture." *Journal of Modern History* 72, no. 1 (March 2000): 6–34.

———. "Money, Despotism and Public Opinion in Early Eighteenth-Century France: John Law and the Debate on Royal Credit." *Journal of Modern History* 63, no. 1 (March 1991): 1–28.

———. "Rhetoric in the Service of the King: The Abbé Dubos and the Concept of Public Judgment." *Eighteenth-Century Studies* 23, no. 2 (Winter: 1989–90): 182–99.

Kaplan, Steven. *Bread, Politics and Political Economy in the Reign of Louis XV*. Leiden: Martinus Nijhoff, 1976.

______. *Provisioning Paris: Merchants and Millers in the Grain and Flour Trade During the Eighteenth Century*. Ithaca, NY: Cornell University Press, 1984.

Kessler, Amalia. "A 'Question of Name': Merchant-Court Jurisdiction and the Origins of the *Noblesse Commerçante*." In *A Vast and Useful Art: The Gustave Gimon Collection on French Political Economy*, ed. Mary Jane Parrine, 49–65. Stanford, CA: Stanford University Libraries, 2004.

———. *A Revolution in Commerce: The Parisian Merchant Court and the Rise of Commercial Society in Eighteenth-Century France*. New Haven, CT: Yale University Press, 2007.

Kettering, Sharon. "Brokerage at the Court of Louis XIV." *Historical Journal* 36, no. 1 (March 1993): 69–87.

———. "The Historical Development of Political Clientelism." *Journal of Interdisciplinary History* 18, no. 3 (Winter 1988): 419–47.

———. *Patronage in Sixteenth- and Seventeenth-Century France*. Aldershot, UK: Ashgate, 2002.

———. *Patrons, Brokers and Clients in Seventeenth-Century France*. New York: Oxford University Press, 1986.

Kévorkian, Raymond. *Catalogue des "incunables" arméniens (1511–1695): Ou Chronique de l'imprimerie arménienne*. Geneva: Patrick Cramer, 1986.

Klaits, Joseph. *Printed Propaganda Under Louis XIV: Absolute Monarchy and Public Opinion*. Princeton, NJ: Princeton University Press, 1976.

Koselleck, Reinhart. "Linguistic Change and the History of Events." *Journal of Modern History* 61, no. 4 (December 1989): 649–66.

Kramnick, Isaac. *Republicanism and Bourgeois Radicalism: Political Ideology in Late Eighteenth-Century England and America*. Ithaca, NY: Cornell University Press, 1990.

Kreiser, B. Robert. *Miracles, Convulsions, and Ecclesiastical Politics in Early Eighteenth-Century Paris.* Princeton, NJ: Princeton University Press, 1978.

Kwass, Michael. *Privilege and the Politics of Taxation in Eighteenth-Century France: Liberté, égalité, fiscalité.* Cambridge: Cambridge University Press, 2000.

Lindemann, Mary. *Patriots and Paupers: Hamburg, 1712–1830.* New York: Oxford University Press, 1990.

Linton, Marisa. *The Politics of Virtue in Enlightenment France.* Basingstoke, UK: Palgrave Macmillan, 2001.

Lopez, Renée, and Emile Temime. *Histoire des migrations à Marseille.* Vol. 2. Aix-en-Provence: Edisud, 1990.

Loseby, S. T. "Marseille: A Late Antique Success Story?" *Journal of Roman Studies* 82 (1992): 165–85.

Lucenet, Monique. *Les grandes pestes en France.* Aubier: Aubier Montaigne, 1985.

MacMullen, Ramsey. "Roman Imperial Building in the Provinces." *Harvard Studies in Classical Philology* 64 (1959): 207–35.

Martin, Lynn A. *The Jesuit Mind: The Mentality of an Elite in Early Modern France.* Ithaca, NY: Cornell University Press, 1988.

———. *Plague? Jesuit Accounts of Epidemic Disease in the 16th Century.* Kirksville, MO: Sixteenth Century Journal Publishers, 1996.

Masson, Paul. *Histoire du commerce français dans le Levant au XVIIe siècle.* Paris: Hachette, 1896.

———, ed. *Les Bouches-du-Rhône Encyclopédie départementale.* Marseille: Conseil général avec le concours de la Ville de Marseille et de la Chambre de commerce, 1924.

Maza, Sarah. *Private Lives and Public Affairs: The Causes Célèbres of Prerevolutionary France.* Berkeley: University of California Press, 1993.

McCabe, Ina Baghdiantz. *Orientalism in Early Modern France: Eurasian Trade, Exoticism and the Ancien Régime.* Oxford: Berg, 2008.

Melton, James Van Horn. *The Rise of the Public in Enlightenment Europe.* Cambridge: Cambridge University Press, 2001.

Mermann, Alan C. *Some Chose to Stay: Faith and Ethics in a Time of Plague.* Atlantic Highlands, NJ: Humanities Press, 1997.

Meuvret, Jean. *Le problème des subsistances à l'époque Louis XIV.* 3 vols. Paris: Ecole des hautes études en sciences sociales, 1977–88.

Michaud, Louis-Gabriel. *Biographie universelle ancienne et moderne.* 45 vols. Paris: Desplaces, 1843–65.

Mijnhardt, Wijnand W. "The Dutch Republic as a Town." *Eighteenth-Century Studies* 31, no 3 (Spring 1998): 345–48.

Mollicone, Sarah. "La redécouverte de l'Antiquité à Arles, 1517–1676." Vols. 1 and 2. Ph.D. diss., Université de Provence, 2004.

Monahan, W. Gregory. *Year of Sorrows: The Great Famine of 1709 in Lyon.* Columbus: Ohio State University Press, 1993.

Moote, A. Lloyd, and Dorothy Moote. *The Great Plague: The Story of London's Most Deadly Year.* Baltimore: Johns Hopkins University Press, 2004.

Mortreuil, Anselme. *Institutions marseillaises au moyen âge: Consulats marseillais dans le Levant, consuls étrangers dans Marseille.* Marseille: Veuve Marius Olive, 1859.

Naphy, William. *Plagues, Poisons and Potions: Plague-Spreading Conspiracies in the Western Alps, 1530–1640.* Manchester: Manchester University Press, 2002.

Omnes, Christine. "La peste de Marseille de 1720 dans la littérature du XXe siècle." *Provence historique* 52 (March 2003): 99–111.

Ozouf, Mona. "Space and Time in the Festivals of the French Revolution." *Comparative Studies in Society and History* 17, no. 3 (July, 1975): 372–84.

Naphy, William. *Plagues, Poisons and Potions: Plague-Spreading Conspiracies in the Western Alps, 1530–1640.* Manchester: Manchester University Press, 2002.

Noiriel, Gerard. "Immigration: Amnesia and Memory." *French Historical Studies* 19, no. 2 (Autumn 1995): 367–80.

Panzac, Daniel. *La caravane maritime: Marins européens et marchands ottomans en Méditerranée (1680–1830).* Paris: CNRS, 2004.

———. *Commerce et navigation dans l'empire Ottoman au XVIIIe siècle.* Istanbul: Isis, 1996.

———. "International and Domestic Maritime Trade in the Ottoman Empire during the 18th Century." *International Journal of Middle East Studies* 24, no. 2 (May 1992): 189–206.

———. *La Peste dans l'empire Ottoman, 1700–1850.* Leuven: Peeters, 1985.

———. *Quarantaines et lazarets: L'Europe et la peste d'Orient.* Aix-en-Provence: Edisud, 1986.

Parrine, Mary Jane, ed. *A Vast and Useful Art: The Gustave Gimon Collection on French Political Economy.* Stanford, CA: Stanford University Libraries, 2004.

Peabody, Sue, and Tyler Stovall, eds. *The Color of Liberty: Histories of Race in France.* Durham, NC: Duke University Press, 2003.

Pérouse de Montclos, Jean-Marie. *"Les prix de Rome": Concours de l'Académie royale d'architecture au XVIIe siècle; inventaire général des monuments et richesses artistiques de la France.* Paris: Berger-Levrault, Ecole nationale supérieure des Beaux-Arts, 1984.

Pocock, J. G. A. *The Machiavellian Moment: Florentine Political Thought and the Atlantic Republican Tradition.* Princeton, NJ: Princeton University Press, 1975.

Porter, Roy. *Blood and Guts: A Short History of Medicine.* London: Penguin Books, 2002.

Pouliquen, Yves. *Un oculiste au siècle des lumières: Jacques Daviel, 1693–1762.* Paris: Odile Jacob, 1999.

Rambert, Gaston, ed. *Histoire du commerce de Marseille: de 1599 à 1789.* Vol. 4. Paris: Plon, 1954.

———. *Nicolas Arnoul, intendant des galères à Marseille, 1665–1674.* Marseille: Provincia, 1931.

Rapley, Elizabeth. "Women and the Religious Vocation in Seventeenth-Century France." *French Historical Studies* 18, no. 3 (1994): 613–31.

Rebuffat, Ferréol. *Chambre de commerce et d'industrie de Marseille: Répertoire numérique des archives.* Marseille: Robert, 1965.

Reynaud, Jean. *Chambre de commerce de Marseille: Répertoire numérique des archives . . . archives antérieures à 1801, fonds particulier de la Chambre.* Marseille: F. Robert, 1947.

Richter, Melvin. "Despotism." In *Dictionary of the History of Ideas: Studies of Selected Pivotal Ideas,* vol. 2, ed. Philip P. Weiner. New York: Charles Scribner's Sons, 1973.

Riskin, Jessica. *Science in the Age of Sensibility: The Sentimental Empiricists of the French Enlightenment.* Chicago: University of Chicago Press, 2002.

Robert, Potet L. *Nicolas Roze, chevalier de Saint-Lazare de Jérusalem, 1675–1733: Essai de biographie critique.* Marseille: Institut historique de Provence, 1938.

Roche, Daniel. *France in the Enlightenment.* Translated by Arthur Goldhammer. Cambridge, MA: Harvard University Press, 1998.

———. *Le siècle des lumiéres en province: Académies et académiciens provinciaux, 1680–1789.* Paris: Ecole des hautes études en sciences sociales, 1978.

Roosen, William J. "The Functioning of Ambassadors under Louis XIV." *French Historical Studies* 6, no. 3 (Spring 1970): 311–32.

Rosenberg, Charles. "Cholera in Nineteenth-Century Europe: A Tool for Social and Economic Analysis." *Comparative Studies in Society and History* 8, no. 4 (July 1966): 452–63.

———. *Explaining Epidemics and Other Studies in the History of Medicine.* Cambridge: Cambridge University Press, 1992.

———. "Science in American Society: A Generation of Historical Debate." *Isis* 74, no. 3 (September 1983): 356–67.

Rosenberg, Charles, and Janet Golden, eds. *Framing Disease: Studies in Cultural History.* New Brunswick, NJ: Rutgers University Press, 1992.

Rosenblum, Robert. *Transformations in Late Eighteenth Century Art.* Princeton, NJ: Princeton University Press, 1966.'

Sahlins, Peter. *Unnaturally French: Foreign Citizens in the Old Regime and After.* Ithaca, NY: Cornell University Press, 2004.

Schaeper, Thomas J. *The French Council of Commerce, 1700–1715: A Study of Mercantilism After Colbert.* Columbus: Ohio State University Press, 1983.

———. "Government and Business in Early Eighteenth-Century France: The Case of Marseilles." *Journal of European Economic History* 17, no. 3 (Winter 1988): 531–57.

Schilling, Heinz. "Civic Republicanism in Late Medieval and Early Modern German Cities." In id., *Religion, Political Culture and the Emergence of Early Modern Society: Essays in German and Dutch History.* Leiden: Brill, 1992.

Schwartz, Robert, and Robert Schneider, eds. *Tocqueville and Beyond: Essays in Honor of David D. Bien.* Newark, NJ: University of Delaware Press, 2003.

Scott, Joan. *Only Paradoxes to Offer: French Feminists and the Rights of Man.* Cambridge, MA: Harvard University Press, 1996.

Scott, William. *Terror and Repression in Revolutionary Marseilles.* London: Macmillan, 1973.

Searle, J. R., ed. *The Philosophy of Language: Oxford Readings in Philosophy.* Oxford: Oxford University Press, 1971.

Sewell, William H., Jr. "Historical Events as Transformations of Structures: Inventing Revolution at the Bastille." *Theory and Society* 25, no. 6 (December 1996): 841–81.

———. *Logics of History: Social Theory and Social Transformation.* Chicago: University of Chicago Press, 2005.

Shank, John Bennett. "Before Voltaire: Newtonianism and the Origins of the Enlightenment in France, 1687–1734." Ph.D. diss., Stanford University, 2000.

Shovlin, John. "The Cultural Politics of Luxury in Eighteenth-Century France." *French Historical Studies* 23, no. 4 (2000): 577–606.

———. *The Political Economy of Virtue: Luxury, Patriotism and the Origins of the French Revolution.* Ithaca, NY: Cornell University Press, 2006.

Skinner, Quentin. *Liberty Before Liberalism.* Cambridge: Cambridge University Press, 1998.

Smith, Jay. *Nobility Reimagined: The Patriotic Nation in Eighteenth-Century France.* Ithaca, NY: Cornell University Press, 2005.

Soboul, Albert, "De l'Ancien Regime à la Revolution: Problème régional et réalités sociales." In *Régions et régionalisme en France du XVIIIe siècle à nos jours,* ed. Christian Gras and Georges Livet. Strasbourg: Presses universitaires de France, 1977.

Sonenscher, Michael, *Before the Deluge: Public Debt, Inequality and the Intellectual Origins of the French Revolution.* Princeton, NJ: Princeton University Press, 2007.

———. *Sans-Culottes: An Eighteenth-Century Emblem in the French Revolution.* Princeton, NJ: Princeton University Press, 2008.

Sontag, Susan. *Illness as Metaphor.* New York: Farrar, Straus & Giroux, 1977.

Sturgill, Claude C. *Claude Le Blanc: Civil Servant to the King.* Gainesville: University Press of Florida, 1975.

Talamante, Laura Emerson. "Les Marseillaises: Women and Political Change During the French Revolution, 1789–1794." Ph.D. diss., UCLA, 2003.

Tavernier, Félix. *La vie quotidienne à Marseille, de Louis XIV à Louis-Philippe.* Paris: Hachette, 1973.

Tocqueville, Alexis de. *The Old Regime and the French Revolution.* Translated by Alan S. Kahan. Chicago: University of Chicago Press, 1998.

Touré, Papa Aboucabar. "Périclès vu par l'abbé J.-J. Barthélemy." *Provence historique* 52 (March 2003): 35–46.

Van Gelderen, Martin, and Quentin Skinner, eds. *Republicanism: A Shared European Heritage.* Cambridge: Cambridge University Press, 2002.

Van Kley, Dale. *The Religious Origins of the French Revolution: From Calvin to the Civil Constitution, 1560–1791.* New Haven, CT: Yale University Press, 1996.

Vanderveken, Daniel. *Meaning and Speech Acts.* Cambridge: Cambridge University Press, 1990.

Venturi, Franco. *The End of the Old Regime in Europe, 1776–1789.* Translated by R. Burr Litchfield. Princeton, NJ: Princeton University Press, 1991.

———. "Oriental Despotism." *Journal of the History of Ideas* 24, no. 1 (1963): 133–42.

———. *Utopia and Reform in the Enlightenment.* Cambridge: Cambridge University Press, 1971.

Villiers, Mareva. "La peste de 1720–1721 à Aix-en-Provence." Ph.D. diss., Université de Provence, Aix-Marseille I, 1995.

Vovelle, Michel. *Piété baroque et déchristianisation en Provence au XVIIIe siècle: Les attitudes devant la mort d'après des clauses des testaments.* Paris: Plon, 1973.

Walter, John, and Roger Schofield, eds. *Famine, Disease and the Social Order in Early Modern Society.* Cambridge: Cambridge University Press, 1989.

Walton, Guy. "Pierre Puget in Rome: 1662." *Burlington Magazine* 111, no. 799 (October 1969): 582–87.

Ward-Perkins, J. B. "From Republic to Empire: Reflections on the Early Provincial Architecture of the Roman West." *Journal of Roman Studies* 60 (1970): 1–19.

Wehl, Jonas. *Les juifs protégés français aux échelles du Levant et en Barbarie sous les règnes de Louis XIV et Louis XV d'après des documents inédits tirés des archives de la Chambre de commerce de Marseille.* Paris: Durlacher, 1886.

Weiss, Gillian. "Back from Barbary: Captivity, Redemption, and French Identity in the Seventeenth- and Eighteenth-Century Mediterranean." PhD diss., Stanford University, 2002.

Whatmore, Richard. *Republicanism and the French Revolution: An Intellectual History of Jean-Baptiste Say's Political Economy.* New York: Oxford University Press, 2001.

Wolff, Larry. *Inventing Eastern Europe: The Map of Civilisation on the Mind of the Enlightenment.* Stanford, CA: Stanford University Press, 1996.

———. *Venice and the Slavs: The Discovery of Dalmatia in the Age of Enlightenment.* Stanford, CA: Stanford University Press, 2002.

Wright, Johnston Kent. *A Classical Republican in Eighteenth-Century France: The Political Thought of Mably.* Stanford: Stanford University Press, 1997.

Zanger, Abby E. *Scenes from the Marriage of Louis XIV: Nuptial Fictions and the Making of Absolute Power.* Stanford, CA: Stanford University Press, 1997.

Zarb, Mireille. *Histoire d'une autonomie communale: Les privilèges de la ville de Marseille du Xe siècle à la Revolution.* Paris: A. & J. Picard, 1961.

Zysberg, André. *Marseille au temps des galères, 1660–1748.* Marseille: A. Robert, 1983.

Index